THE CAMPAIGN OF 1815

THE
CAMPAIGN OF 1815

CHIEFLY IN FLANDERS

BY

LIEUT.-COLONEL W. H. JAMES, P.S.C.

R.E. (RETIRED)

AUTHOR OF 'MODERN STRATEGY';
EDITOR OF "THE WOLSELEY SERIES"

The Naval & Military Press Ltd

published in association with

FIREPOWER
The Royal Artillery Museum
Woolwich

Published by
The Naval & Military Press Ltd
Unit 10 Ridgewood Industrial Park,
Uckfield, East Sussex,
TN22 5QE England
Tel: +44 (0) 1825 749494
Fax: +44 (0) 1825 765701
www.naval-military-press.com

in association with

FIREPOWER
The Royal Artillery Museum, Woolwich
www.firepower.org.uk

In reprinting in facsimile from the original, any imperfections are inevitably reproduced and the quality may fall short of modern type and cartographic standards.

"*For a battle, there is not perhaps in Europe an army equal to the British.* . . .

"*The British soldier is vigorous, well fed, by nature brave and intrepid, trained to the most vigorous discipline, and admirably well armed. The infantry resist the attacks of cavalry with great confidence, and, when taken in the flank or rear, British troops are less disconcerted than any other European army.*

"*These circumstances in their favour will explain how this army, since the Duke of Wellington conducted it, has never yet been defeated in the open field.*"—MÜFFLING.

"*The English infantry is the best in the world; happily there is but little of it.*"—BUGEAUD.

"*Their infantry is firm under fire, well-trained, and fires perfectly; their officers are the bravest and most patriotic in Europe.*"—FOY.

"*In my opinion the principal cause of our reverses, although not mentioned by any of the soldiers who have written on the wars of Spain and Portugal, was the immense superiority in accuracy of fire of the English infantry—a superiority which comes from the very constant target practice and a good deal also from the formation in two ranks.*"—MARBOT.

PREFACE.

THE Campaign of 1815 will always be a subject of interest to Englishmen. It was the culminating point in the career of one of the greatest commanders the country has ever produced, and its successful issue was due largely to that great quality of our infantry, the capacity for suffering loss unflinchingly, which has always formed one of the most important factors of success in English military operations.

The literature of the Waterloo period would fill a library, and much of it might properly be placed on the shelves usually reserved for fiction. But of late years many works have been published of great value. Newer historical methods have prevailed, and recourse has been had to original records rather than to the author's imagination for the statements put forward. Far above all the French books hitherto published is that of Henri Houssaye, whose '1815' forms a most reliable account of the campaign. Lieutenant-Colonel A. Grouard, so well known as "A. G.", has published an excellent account of the campaign, called 'La Critique de la Campagne de 1815,' devoted chiefly to dealing with certain statements of M. Houssaye.

Impartial and penetrating in his criticism, his work can be strongly recommended to all students, as also his pamphlet entitled 'Réponse à M. Houssaye.'

Of German contributors to Waterloo literature Pflugk - Hartung stands at the top. His 'Vor Geschichte der Schlacht bei Belle Alliance' is written without the slightest tinge of unfairness to the British side, and is based on an exhaustive examination of actual documents.[1] Besides this he has furnished many articles to the German press, notably one published in August and September 1905 in the 'Jahrbucher für die deutsche Armee und Marine' dealing with the question of the part played by Zieten's corps at Waterloo.

Colonel de Bas of the Dutch Staff has produced an important work, valuable not only for the author's opinions but also for the collection of documents which he has published with it: it is entitled 'Prins Frederik der Nederlanden en zijn Tijd.' While it is impossible to admit of all his arguments, his book must always form one of the most reliable contributions to Waterloo literature.[2]

For some years past a number of German authors have devoted their attention to depreciating the part taken by the British troops, and in some cases have gone so far as to accuse the Duke of Wellington of deliberately deceiving Blucher. To investigate these charges and to determine certain other questions, such as the reasons for the delay in issuing the

---

[1] An old German book, but still a very good one, is Hofmann's 'Zur Geschichte des Feldzuges von 1815,' &c. Second edition, 1851.

[2] His last work, 'La Campagne de 1815 aux Pays-Bas,' was only published when these pages were in the press.

PREFACE

orders for the concentration of the Anglo-Allied army, the instructions given by Napoleon to Ney on the 15th June, the cause of the Prussian hesitation on the 18th, and the formation of the Imperial Guard in its last attack, is the object of the following pages.

WALTER H. JAMES.

BUSHMEAD HALL,
   BEDFORD.

CONTENTS.

CHAP.		PAGE
	PREFACE	v
I.	NAPOLEON'S ESCAPE FROM ELBA—THE SITUATION IN FRANCE	1
II.	PREPARATIONS FOR WAR—RENEWAL OF THE TREATY OF CHAUMONT—THE MILITARY SITUATION IN FRANCE—THE ARMIES OF NAPOLEON AND THE ALLIES—THE COMMANDERS—THE PLAN OF CAMPAIGN .	10
III.	THE SITUATION AT THE COMMENCEMENT OF THE CAMPAIGN—THE EVENTS OF THE 15TH JUNE .	52
IV.	THE EVENTS OF THE 16TH JUNE—BATTLE OF LIGNY—BATTLE OF QUATRE BRAS	105
V.	THE WANDERING OF D'ERLON—WELLINGTON'S "DISPOSITION"	151
VI.	THE EVENTS OF THE 17TH JUNE—THE RETREAT TO WATERLOO—THE FRENCH ADVANCE TO GEMBLOUX—THE PRUSSIANS UNITE AT WAVRE . .	168
VII.	THE EVENTS OF THE 18TH—THE BATTLE OF WATERLOO—THE ACTION OF WAVRE	192
VIII.	COMMENTS ON THE BATTLE OF WATERLOO—GENERAL COMMENTS ON THE WAR UP TO THE 18TH JUNE .	276

CONTENTS

IX. GROUCHY'S ADVANCE TO WAVRE—GROUCHY'S RETREAT FROM WAVRE TO NAMUR—THE INVASION OF FRANCE—THE CAPTURE OF PARIS AND END OF THE WAR . 301

APPENDIX—

    WELLINGTON'S DESPATCH TO THE EARL BATHURST   311

    STRENGTH OF ANGLO-ALLIED, PRUSSIAN, AND FRENCH FORCES 319

INDEX 333

LIST OF MAPS AND SKETCHES.

		PAGE
I. GENERAL MAP, CAMPAIGN OF 1815		*at end of book*
II. THE BATTLEFIELDS OF LIGNY AND QUATRE BRAS	*facing p.*	150
III. SKETCH NO. 1, HOUGOMONT		211
IV. SKETCH NO. 2, LA HAYE SAINTE		213
V. SKETCH NO. 3, FORMATION OF THE 3RD DIVISION		219
VI. SKETCH NO. 4, ATTACK OF THE IMPERIAL GUARD		260
VII. THE BATTLEFIELD OF WATERLOO	*facing p.*	300
VIII. MAP FOR OPERATIONS AFTER 18TH JUNE	*facing p.*	310

The Campaign of 1815,
Chiefly in Flanders.

CHAPTER I.

NAPOLEON'S ESCAPE FROM ELBA—THE SITUATION IN FRANCE.

AFTER his abdication in April 1814 Napoleon had, in accordance with the arrangements made by the Allied Sovereigns, been placed on the island of Elba. Situated as it was at so short a distance from both Italy and France, he was able to obtain constant information from both countries, while his agents in Vienna kept him well posted with the proceedings at the Congress. Judging from the reports he received that the state of affairs was favourable to him, he determined to make an attempt to recover the supreme power in France. On the 26th February 1815, therefore, he embarked at Port Ferrajo with the small force he had been allowed to retain at his disposal, and landed near Cannes on the 1st March.

It is beyond the scope of this work to deal in detail with the general history of the period concerned, but it is not possible to understand rightly either the action of the Emperor or the conduct of his opponents without sketching briefly the events which brought about the political situation, which in its turn influenced so largely the subsequent military operations.

Why did Napoleon leave Elba?

Why did the Allies refuse all intercourse with him, and decline to let him hold the throne he had reascended with the cordial assent of a considerable portion of the French people, and thus compel him to appeal to arms?

The reasons for the Emperor's return to France were many. In the first place, it is scarcely doubtful that he never meant to remain in Elba unless compelled to do so. In giving up the throne for himself and his heirs he only yielded to the pressure of the moment. "I abdicate and I yield nothing," said he to Bausset just before he left Fontainebleau, and in this phrase lies the key to his subsequent conduct.[1]

It was scarcely to be expected that he whose aspirations for world-wide dominions had kept Europe in a state of ferment for fourteen years would remain quietly in the humble exile in which his enemies had placed him. Especially was this the case when the state of affairs was such as to offer him a favourable opportunity to regain the throne from which he had been driven in the previous year.

When Louis XVIII. returned to France a great opportunity was open to him: a little prudence and tact would have calmed the fears of those who dreaded injury to their interests from a kingly ruler, and

[1] Bausset, 'Cour de Napoleon.' Bausset was Prefect of the Palace.

NAPOLEON RETURNS TO FRANCE

would have consolidated his position. An easy-going man himself, he might have succeeded in the difficult task imposed on him had he governed in accordance with his own views. But his immediate advisers, to whom he yielded, were blind and foolish, too ignorant and stupid to know the limits of their powers, and too obstinate to appreciate the disrepute into which their preposterous acts would bring the monarchy.

Ten months of Bourbon rule thus sufficed to render France thoroughly discontented with the Government which had been imposed on her. The holders of national property, though guaranteed in the possession of their lands by the Charter, yet feared they would be compelled to restore them. For the language of the clergy in the pulpit, and of their supporters in the press, left no doubt as to the aims of those whose influence was now paramount. France, if not exactly irreligious, was certainly not enthusiastic in the cause of the Catholic faith, and the attempt of the Director-General of Police, in agreement with the Court, to dragoon the people into the rigorous observance of Sundays and Holy days by vexatious and minute orders forbidding all work, coupled with the closing of the cafés, restaurants, and public-houses during the hours of divine service, produced the worst effect, and indicated clearly the direction in which the dominant party would go if the priests had their way. This decree was issued five weeks after the King reached his capital, and the hostile sentiment which it roused was increased by the expiatory services held in all the cathedrals of France in memory of Louis XVI. and Marie Antoinette. The priests, in accordance with the habitual custom of their kind when they feel themselves dominant, no matter what their faith, made their sermons into political addresses, and denounced all alike who had taken any part in the Revolution. The utterances from the pulpit were echoed in the press, and as the censure had been re-established plainly these diatribes voiced the opinion of the Government.

But the religious rancour of the returned exiles carried them even further. Masses were said on behalf of Moreau, Pichegru, and Georges Cadaudal. In the case of the last, a mere political conspirator against the Government of his day, the King himself bore the expenses! During the Empire, the priesthood had been kept in its proper place. The barefaced attempts now made to regain its former power, the reiterated claims for the old possessions of the Church, the unmeasured denunciations of all who held the opinions current in France for the past twenty years, aroused on every side suspicions as to what length the foolish King and his vindictive satellites might go, and thus led to a contrast being drawn between the Imperial and Royal Governments, greatly to the disadvantage of the latter.

The debt left by the Empire, and the impoverished state of the country, rendered it necessary to construct the budget with the greatest economy. The army was larger than required, and had therefore to be diminished. But its reduction was carried out without the slightest regard to the feelings of those who formed it. The men were dismissed, clothed in ragged and worn-out uniforms; the officers placed on half-pay, and given a pittance which, in the case of the junior ranks, was so small as to be barely sufficient to keep body and soul together.[1] Yet these measures had at least the excuse of necessity. Not so the renumbering of the regiments and the abolition of the tricolour—ungracious attempts to break the record of the soldiers' glories; nor, worst of all, the re-institution of the Maison du Roi, a small and highly privileged army of 6000 men, which had formerly existed under the King's predecessors. Thus at a time when officers who had fought and bled for their country were being cast wholesale on the world, this opera-bouffe force was constituted at an annual cost of over twenty million francs, while with the exception of the 200 Horse Grenadiers and the company of the Swiss Hundred, every man in its ranks was given the grade of sub-lieutenant![2]

But insult was added to the injury thus created. The Imperial Guard, at any rate so far as the Old Guard was concerned, consisted of the heroic survivors of many campaigns; the Maison du Roi, which now replaced it, was formed for the most part from former bodyguards of Louis XVI., from those who had served against their country, or from noble youths possessed of no qualification but their birth. By a decree of the 12th May 1814 one-third of the vacant positions in the army were to be filled by nomination by the King, who gave them to the old *emigrés* or

---

[1] While Frenchmen were thus sent about their business, the several foreign regiments in the service were maintained, and an eighth added to them!

[2] The privates in these had the rank of non-commissioned officers.

striplings of this new creation, and the number of the latter class thus posted as sub-lieutenants cut off all hope of promotion from the non-commissioned grades, and became another grievance to the rank and file of the army.

The people at large dreaded the restitution of the feudal rights and forced labour; the army was actively hostile to the King, whom they looked on as a usurper, while he failed to gain over to him either the middle classes, the men of politics, or the old nobility. To please the latter, indeed, it would have been necessary to re-establish the absolute monarchy as it existed before 1789. So far as the greater portion of the civilian population was concerned, the Bourbon rule was regarded with indifference or dislike, and it was acquiesced in solely because no other government was available. Opposed to it was a seething mass of military discontent, ready at any moment to aid in the restoration of the Empire. Thus Napoleon succeeded in regaining the throne because the soldiery being actively on his side there was no effective means of opposing him. But when the Army was defeated, the nation turned at once against the Emperor. For his return had once more led to war, abhorrence of which was the one point on which the whole of France was united.

Louis XVIII. came back to France, to find her shorn of the territory which had been added to the Bourbon kingdom during the years of his exile, knowing that he was the nominee of those who had done the shearing, accompanied by a host of men who, even if they had not served actively against their country, had for years approved the policy of her foes, and who now owed their return to her defeat and humiliation. Common-sense, nay, common decency, should have dictated to all of them, from the King downwards, a modest attitude and the desire to conciliate those who had at least remained in France and shared her fortunes. But both qualities were somewhat lacking in the monarch and entirely in his advisers. Instead of modesty there was insolence; instead of trying to live on terms of amity with their fellow-citizens, the King's supporters lost no opportunity of wounding their feelings and threatening the rights solemnly guaranteed them by the monarch on three occasions. Small wonder that Napoleon came back from Elba. King, ministers, and priests together, by their fatuous conduct, brought about his return, and on them must lie the responsibility for the fresh sufferings thereby inflicted on their unhappy country.[1]

The progress of events at the Vienna Congress also aided Napoleon's plans. The Czar wished to retain Western Poland, and made a bargain with the Prussian king, who consented to the proposal provided he was given the whole of Saxony, the Saxon monarch being compensated by obtaining fresh territories on the Rhine. England, France, and Austria bound themselves to oppose this arrangement, even if it were necessary to appeal to arms; and thus the French people saw themselves, as they thought, on the brink

[1] In his proclamation, issued at Cambray on the 28th June, the King said: "My Government was liable to commit errors; perhaps it did commit them." That it most certainly had done, and the history of France from 1815 till the expulsion of Charles X. shows most conclusively that the Bourbons were always willing to commit them.

of war, and this time for an object in which they had but little interest. This did not tend to improve the position of Louis XVIII. Italy, too, was in a ferment. Once more her aspirations for unity, which had been gratified to a large extent by Napoleon, were dashed to the ground, and she was again divided up among her former rulers. There was, consequently, some fear at Vienna that Napoleon might be tempted to take advantage of this state of affairs and land in Italy, but it was scarcely expected he would return to France.

In the early spring of 1815, therefore, the political position in both countries was such as to invite Napoleon's intervention. The mistakes of the Bourbon Government, the disputes between the Allies, were all well known to him, and gave him the chance he longed for. This his own words show:

"J'ai vu de l'Ile d'Elbe les fautes que l'on commettait et j'ai resolu d'en profiter. . . . Il n'était pas douteux que les soldats, les paysans, les classes moyennes elles-mêmes, après tout ce que l'on avait fait pour les blesser, m'accueilleraient avec transport." . . .

And he added that in five - and - twenty years the Bourbons,

"N'avaient rien appris, rien oublié."[1]

---

[1] See Thiers' 'Histoire du Consulat et de l'Empire,' vol. xiv. p. 200. Marmont expressed practically the same sentiment a few years later, when he said of the Bourbons: "Ils sont perdus. Ils ne connaissant ni le pays ni le temps. Ils vivent en dehors du monde et du siècle. Partout ils portent leur atmosphère avec eux on ne peut les éclairer, ni même le tenter; c'est sans ressource." The same was true of them at Coblentz, in England, and when they returned to France.

On the 8th March it became known at Vienna that the Emperor had landed in France, thus choosing the country he had ruled for the past fourteen years for the scene of his further efforts for power. The news served to quiet for a time the dissensions which had arisen between the various Powers, and, putting aside their differences, they united once more against their common enemy. However peaceful might be his protestations, they had no reliance on them. His promises were made, only to be broken when it suited him; he entered into negotiations merely to give time for further preparations. This they had learned on many occasions when his power was at its full height and even when on the wane, during the armistice in the summer of 1813, and at the Congress of Châtillon. So long as he ruled in France European peace was a mere armed truce. Experience had shown he was not to be trusted. It is useless to say that he might have acted differently in the future, for there is no reason to believe that his disposition was one whit altered, or that his ambitions would not have revived if he had subsequently seen a favourable opportunity for gratifying them. To allow him, therefore, to remain on the throne of France was a standing menace to the tranquillity of Europe—and tranquillity Europe was determined to have, after twenty years of war, no matter what the cost might be to Napoleon or to the nation which had supported him in his ambitious schemes of conquest.

CHAPTER II.

PREPARATIONS FOR WAR—RENEWAL OF THE TREATY OF CHAUMONT—THE MILITARY SITUATION IN FRANCE—THE ARMIES OF NAPOLEON AND THE ALLIES—THE COMMANDERS—THE PLAN OF CAMPAIGN.

It is unnecessary to trace the events which marked Napoleon's progress from the coast to the capital. It was one continued triumph, and on the evening of the 20th March he entered Paris without firing a shot, the King having left on the previous day.

Immediately after the Allies became aware of Napoleon's escape from Elba they issued a proclamation (dated the 13th March) which declared Napoleon "an enemy and disturber of the tranquillity of the world," and abandoned him to public justice. They declined to enter into any negotiations with him, and on the 25th March England, Austria, Prussia, and Russia bound themselves by treaty to furnish each 150,000 men to carry on the war against the Emperor until he was placed in a position which would render it impossible for him again to seize the supreme power in France.

England, as usual, deficient in the number of her troops, made up for the deficiency by providing the

Allies with money, of which they were in sore need, being reduced to the verge of bankruptcy by the previous wars, and further engaged to contribute the sum of £30 annually for every horse soldier, and £20 for every foot soldier below the promised quota.

The dissensions which had arisen among the Allies in the Congress at Vienna had led them to keep their forces practically on a war footing. France alone had somewhat reduced her army.[1] The Emperor's first efforts therefore were directed to raising his troops to the numbers he thought necessary to contend on a footing of equality with united Europe; the required strength he estimated at 800,000 men.[2]

As he found it, the army was composed of—

> 107 regiments of infantry,
> 61 regiments of cavalry,
> 12 regiments of artillery,

besides engineers and train, forming a total of about 200,000 men. He began by giving back the regiments their old numbers, thus renewing their association with their former glories, and proceeded to add three additional battalions to each, besides reconstituting the Old Guard and raising four regiments of the Middle Guard and sixteen regiments of the Young Guard.[3] To each regiment of cavalry two squadrons were added; the artillery and train were

---

[1] England, in accordance with her usual practice, had proceeded, immediately peace was proclaimed in 1814, to reduce her army—a course which largely affected the forces she was able to put in the field in 1815.

[2] 'Commentaires de Napoléon Ier,' vol. v. p. 84.

[3] The Young Guard had been entirely suppressed by Louis XVIII., and only one regiment of Grenadiers and one of Chasseurs of the Old Guard retained to form the Royal Guard.

considerably augmented; the men of the navy were taken for shore duty; the National Guard was called out, and from them a hundred selected battalions were to be made available for field duty. Further, all the old soldiers and those on furlough were recalled to the colours, as well as the conscripts of 1815.

There was not time for these various measures to have their full effect before hostilities broke out, but early in June the active army amounted to 291,000 men, while behind it were troops of secondary value consisting of National Guards, pensioners, sailors, gendarmes, armed custom-house officers, volunteers, &c., numbering 220,000. A month later the force would have been increased by another 280,000, thus practically reaching the total aimed at by the Emperor.[1]

The army suffered to some extent from the fact that it was a newly raised one; but the greater part of the first line was composed of men who had served, and the officers were throughout good and experienced men.

It is true that many of the well-known marshals were absent, but there was not a man in charge of any important unit who had not had wide experience of military operations and shown himself capable in war. Ney was a very able tactician and a man of resolute will on the battlefield; D'Erlon, Reille, Vandamme, Gérard, Lobau, Pajol, Exelmans, Kellermann, and Milhaud had all distinguished themselves in the wars of the Republic and the Empire. Grouchy is generally considered to have proved a failure. But Napoleon had previously employed him in important positions—*e.g.*, in 1807, in command of

---

[1] Henry Houssaye, '1815: Waterloo,' p. 33 *et seq.* Details of the three armies will be found in the Appendix.

the cavalry at the battle of Friedland, and he had a good reputation acquired over thirty-five years of service, during the last fifteen years of which he had occupied high positions with success. He appears, however, to have been inclined to an excess of caution and to a somewhat rigid adherence to orders.

The rank and file of the army were very enthusiastic in the cause of their Emperor. But there existed among them considerable distrust of their superior officers, of whom they believed many were quite willing to follow the example of Marmont and Augereau in the previous year. Yet, on the whole, the army was a good one, containing as it did large numbers of veteran soldiers.[1] It was not perhaps the best the Emperor had ever commanded, but was better on the whole than the Prussian, and certainly superior to the miscellaneous collection of troops under Wellington.

On the other hand, the equipment available was insufficient for the whole force. There was a lack of the necessary uniforms, of muskets, ammunition, provisions, and horses. But although some of the troops raised by the Emperor were not completely furnished, the Army of the North, as it was called, which he assembled for the invasion of Belgium, received all that was necessary to enable it to take the field. It numbered at the outset of the campaign 124,000 men, of whom 23,000 were cavalry, with 370 field-guns.

[1] In his address to the army, dated the 14th June, he refers to this: "Let those among you who have been prisoners of the English tell the history of their hulks, and the terrible afflictions they suffered on them." Seventy thousand had returned from England in 1814, over 130,000 from Germany and Russia, and a large number of these trained soldiers were in the ranks.

The Emperor, however, laboured under one great disadvantage in the Waterloo campaign—he no longer had Marshal Berthier as his Chief of the Staff. Now the Prince of Wagram, though not a great general, understood Napoleon's methods, knew how to elaborate his instructions, and could be trusted to see that the business of the General Staff was properly carried out. Soult, who took his brother-marshal's place, had had no previous experience of the duties, and he does not appear to have been the man for the post, as, to give one instance, the letter to Ney, sent by Napoleon on the 16th June, fairly shows.[1] Moreover, the register of documents sent out by the Chief of the Staff is known to be very incomplete, thus showing that he was not up to the business requirements of his office. It would not, however, be just to put forward the administrative deficiencies of the Duke Dalmatia as in any way accounting for the loss of the campaign. A number of small faults may be admitted, but none of capital importance have been proved against him.

The Army of the North was situated as follows at the beginning of June:—

1st Corps,	D'Erlon	20,731	Lille.
2nd "	Reille	25,179	Valenciennes.
3rd "	Vandamme	18,105	Mézières.
4th "	Gérard	15,404	Thionville.
6th "	Lobau	10,821	Soissons.
Imperial Guard		20,755	Near Paris.
Reserve Cavalry,	Grouchy	13,144	Between the Aisne and the Sambre.
		124,139, with 370 guns.	

---

[1] See *post*, p. 111.

THE ANGLO-ALLIED ARMY

Two other army corps and four corps of observation were also formed and placed as follows: The 5th Corps (Army of the Rhine) under General Rapp, the Emperor's well-known aide-de-camp, occupied the lines of the Lauter. It consisted of about 20,000 soldiers, with a reserve of 3000 National Guards.

Le Courbe, with a corps of observation some 8000 strong, the greater portion being National Guards, watched the passes of the Jura.

Marshal Suchet, with the Army of the Alps, numbering about 23,000 men, of whom three-fifths were National Guards badly armed and equipped, was observing the Swiss frontier; while a detachment under Marshal Brune, some 6000 strong, guarded the line of the Var.

The 7th Corps, divided into two portions under General Decaen and General Clausel, the total not exceeding 14,000, watched the line of the Pyrenees; General Lamarque, with 10,000 men, was occupied with royalist risings in the west of France.

The Anglo-Allied army, under the Duke of Wellington, comprised the soldiers of many nations—Englishmen, Hanoverians, Germans from Nassau, Dutch, and Belgians, were all represented in it.[1] It was not a really efficient fighting force, and its commander held it to be the worst he had ever led to war, although he also expressed his admiration for the way it fought

[1] I have used the term Anglo-Allied in preference to the one usually employed for the force—viz., Anglo-Dutch—because it is more accurate and expresses the fact that it included other nationalities besides the English and Dutch-Belgians. The German race, indeed, formed far the largest part of it.

at Waterloo.¹ Nor were the two views incompatible. Speaking to the Earl of Ellesmere, the Duke stated of the English and German infantry that not above six or seven thousand had seen a shot fired before.² The English infantry was largely composed of second battalions—*i.e.*, those which had been used as depôts or feeding centres for the battalions fighting at the front in the Peninsula. The great proportion of the Germans consisted of raw troops; but both English and Germans fought well *in the defensive positions* they occupied, although in the Duke's opinion it would have been hazardous to have used them for manœuvre under fire. Had he had his old Peninsular Army, he has left on record that he would have attacked Napoleon on the 18th June, instead of allowing the latter to attack him.³

The subordinate leaders fighting under the Duke of Wellington were, as a rule, well-known soldiers

---

[1] There are numerous instances of this, among others his conversation with Mr Thomas Creevey at Brussels on the 19th June: "He praised all our troops, uttering repeated expressions of astonishment at our men's courage." See 'The Creevey Papers,' vol. i. p. 237.

[2] 'Wellington Despatches,' vol. xii. p. 509, letter to Lord Bathurst, dated 25th June: "I really believe that, with the exception of my old Spanish infantry, I have got not only the worst troops, but the worst-equipped army, with the worst staff that was ever brought together." The Duke told Sir John Jones in 1819 when conducting him over the field of battle that he had only about 35,000 men on whom he could rely. He probably meant infantry, and 35,000 is the number he had available after deducting the Dutch-Belgians. He expressly stated to Sir John Jones that "the Belges" all quitted their ground. See 'History of the Corps of Royal Engineers,' vol. i. p. 382. In a letter written on the 2nd June to Sir H. Wellesley he estimates the numbers he would have to invade France with at 70,000 to 80,000. Plainly, therefore, he looked upon a large portion of his troops as useless. See 'Wellington Despatches,' vol. xii. p. 438.

[3] See 'History of the Corps of Royal Engineers,' vol. i. p. 383.

of proved capacity, such as Lord Hill, Picton, C. von Alten, Grant, Vivian, Vandeleur, Kempt, Pack, Arentsschildt, Ompteda, &c. The one exception was the Prince of Orange. This young gentleman was then twenty-two and a half years old.[1] He had been attached for a short time in an unofficial position to the Duke towards the end of the war in the Peninsula, but until 1815 he had never commanded troops in the field. His contributions to the campaign were, however, not without some importance. He rode into Brussels on the 15th from the outposts where he must have heard the sound of firing, without taking the trouble to ascertain what it really meant; it was largely his fault that the information from Mons on the 15th June was so late in reaching Wellington; he contrived to get the 69th cut up at Quatre Bras by telling them the French cavalry was not coming on when it was; finally, at Waterloo, he ordered Ompteda to execute a ridiculous counter-attack which terminated in disaster and the death of the brave man who led it. The Prince was a man of courage; but courage without judgment, knowledge, or perception, forms but a poor equipment for a leader on the battlefield.

The part played by the troops he commanded has formed the subject of much discussion. In the period immediately following the war no one seems to have claimed for the Dutch-Belgians any great share in the

[1] His brother, Prince Frederick of the Netherlands, who commanded the Dutch-Belgians at Hal on 18th June, was under nineteen! Prince Bernhard of Saxe-Weimar was in his twenty-fourth year, but had had some experience of war in Germany and in 1814 in the Netherlands.

success which crowned the exertions of the Allies at Waterloo; but after some years had elapsed various Dutch and Belgian writers began to take up the cause of their countrymen, and there now exists a mass of literature devoted to showing that the part played by them was more important than it was at one time held to be. The specific points on which these arguments rest will be dealt with as they occur in the narrative; it will suffice now to consider only the general aspect of the case, and to describe the Dutch-Belgian army as it really was.

The whole force consisted of thirty-one battalions, seven regiments of cavalry, eight batteries of artillery; of these seven battalions, two regiments, two batteries were Belgian, the rest Dutch.[1]

The spirit of these troops [the Belgians] was about the same as that of the population from which they came.

The Belgians desired the independence of their country; they desired it the more ardently because they had been promised it. General von Bülow said in a proclamation posted up at Brussels on the 4th February 1814, "All the peoples we have liberated up to now have expressed their desire to participate in the great cause, everywhere they have flown to arms, have organised, and gone onward. Let Belgium, formerly so flourishing, arise again. Her independence is no longer doubtful, but she should merit it by forming military levies which will fight for liberty and honour." Unhappily the Belgians did not respond to this invitation. They took no interest in the common cause of Europe, and left the Prussian and Russian armies the task of driving out the French.

---

[1] The Nassau troops are not included in this total. The Dutch-Belgian artillery was in seven batteries and two half-batteries.

The Powers called on to decide on their lot saw no reason to look upon them as Allies, but rather as adversaries, and disposing of Belgium by the right of conquest gave her to Holland.

Very satisfied at having been delivered from the oppressive domination of the French, under which they had so cruelly suffered, much discontented to find their country annexed to Holland, the Belgians in 1815 took no part for either belligerent. They remained as indifferent to the cause of Napoleon as to that of the allied nations.[1]

---

[1] The author of the above lines seems to me to express so completely the situation, his view is so thoroughly confirmed by all contemporary evidence, that I have thought it worth while to quote it at length. My readers will be somewhat surprised to learn that the writer is among the latest of those who have attempted to show that in reality the Dutch-Belgians contributed considerably to the defeat of the French army. See 'Les Belges à Waterloo,' by Louis Navez, p. 11. The day after Wellington arrived at Brussels he states that he had "a very bad account of the —— troops." The blank exists in the original, but perfectly obviously from the context applies to the Dutch-Belgians. See 'Wellington Despatches,' vol. xii. p. 291. It may be here remarked that the Duke had constant difficulties with the King of the Netherlands about the disposition of his troops,—difficulties which were only overcome when Wellington was made Generalissimo of his army. See 'Wellington Despatches,' vol. xii. p. 312.

The King objected to the Dutch-Belgian troops being mixed with the British ('Supplementary Despatches,' vol. x. p. 42, and 'Wellington Despatches,' vol. xii. p. 291), although the Duke thought it best to do so, as they would thus be serving alongside of better troops than themselves.

He objected to his troops garrisoning the fortifications, although his newly raised forces were better adapted for this purpose than to take the field, especially as the inhabitants were not well disposed towards the Government. See 'Supplementary Despatches,' vol. x. p. 32.

Wellington wrote on the 28th April ('Supplementary Despatches,' p. 167): "I have had the greatest difficulty in making this, and, indeed, every other arrangement with him. With professions in his mouth of a desire to do everything I suggest, he objects to everything I propose." He wanted to keep all his troops together although the Duke objected, "as placing in too great a mass all the youth and treason of the army. . . .

20   THE CAMPAIGN OF 1815

The attitude of the Dutch-Belgian troops was thus a fairly complete reflection of that of the civil population from which they came, and there is an absolute agreement among those who were in the country at the time—and better able therefore to judge of the feeling then existing than those who have written years afterwards—that the inclination of the inhabitants was, if anything, somewhat in favour of the French, especially in Belgium, and that this feeling was strong in the army. Nor is this to be wondered at. For years the kingdom of the Netherlands had belonged to France, her sons had fought in the ranks of the Grand Army, and many had risen to distinction. Sentiment would therefore tend to bind them to the Emperor rather than to the King of their newly-formed country. There had not been enough time to awaken a patriotic spirit in the newly-formed army. For a great part of the infantry had been raised in 1814 from soldiers formerly serving in the French ranks,

He is surrounded by persons who have been in the French service. . . . I would not trust one of them out of my sight, and so I have told him."

The Duke had to ask for English or Dutch officers who had not been in French service to command the most important places, 'Wellington Despatches,' p. 324. Writing to the Adjutant-General on the subject of enlisting the Belgians, Wellington pointed out that there were 30,000 to 40,000 men who had served in the French Army in various parts of the country "who will not enlist in the Belgian army and who would enlist in ours. They would desert us, however, &c.," *ibid.*, p. 416.

The Netherlands War Ministry, with General Janssens at the head, was in bad hands: all the heads of the branches were known to be attached to the system of the revolution and to France. The military administration in Belgium, under General Tindel, was equally as bad. The Belgium troops are bad and cannot be relied on. See 'Supplementary Despatches,' pp. *15, 16, 182.*

who had been dismissed to their homes after the fall of the Empire.[1] Of the thirty-two infantry battalions mobilised by the Netherlands, eleven were newly-raised militia who were practically all recruits of a few months' standing. In the others about two-thirds of the men had served under Napoleon, the remainder were recruits. The cavalry was also largely made up of men who had served in the French army. Nearly all the officers had served under the Emperor, a great many of them in the Imperial Guard, — nearly all had the Legion of Honour.[2] The more purely Dutch troops differed but little in quality nor much in feeling from their Belgian comrades.

Thus composed, it is not wonderful that desertion was rife in the Dutch-Belgian army. On the 12th April 120 hussars deserted from Mons. Von Brockhausen, the Prussian Ambassador, in his report of the 25th April, stated, "there is great difficulty in keeping the battalions of Dutch troops up to their full numbers.[3] In the headquarters at Nivelles there is great complaint of desertion, which often diminishes the battalions by half. Deserters do not go to the French but back to their own homes,

---

[1] 'Les Belges à Waterloo,' p. 10.

[2] 'Les Belges à Waterloo,' p. 11. Napoleon estimated one Englishman as the equivalent of one Frenchman, but judged two Dutchmen, &c., only equal to one Frenchman ('Commentaires,' vol. v. p. 117). He further expected that if the Allies were beaten Belgium would rise and join the French army. He had sources of information—*i.e.*, traitors to their national cause, in the Belgian army (*idem*, p. 119). Both Wellington and the Prussians complained of the French proclivities of the Netherlands Ministers.

[3] See Lettow-Vorbeck, 'Napoleon's Untergang,' vol. i. p. 206.

from which they are sent back to their battalions."[1] On the 19th April he writes, "The worst may be feared from the Belgian corps, whose attitude appears to be very doubtful." The quality of the troops may be judged from one fact — their numbers had grown from 10,000 to 29,000 in two months, from the 1st April to 1st June. The number of old soldiers in the ranks no doubt gave the regiments a fairly smart appearance on parade;[2] but their conduct during the two battles and their behaviour during the invasion of France showed that a large proportion of the men were deficient in discipline and had no desire to fight.

The Duke of Wellington's evidence on the first point is quite clear and decisive. On the 27th June, from his headquarters at Vermand, the Commander-in-Chief wrote to General ——[3] as follows:—

I much regret that I am obliged to complain of the conduct of the troops of H.M. the King of the Netherlands

---

[1] This was not true of all. Marbot, in his 'Mémoires,' vol. iii. p. 402, says, "The Belgian soldiers . . . arrive in bands of fifteen and twenty." Their numbers were sufficient to form a corps of just upon 400 by the first part of June. Napoleon had anticipated they would desert, and had early in April issued an appeal to them to do so.

[2] The Duke of Wellington, after inspecting the Dutch-Belgian troops on the 24th and 25th April, appears to have been pleased with their outward appearance, though even then he doubted their loyalty. See 'Supplementary Despatches,' pp. 167, 168.

[3] The name is left blank in the original. See 'Wellington Despatches,' vol. xii. p. 513. It is interesting, with regard to this letter of Wellington's, to point out that Colonel de Bas, in his work entitled 'Prins Frederik der Nederlanden en zijn Tijd,' gives on p. 1234, vol. iii., the text of a General Order issued at Haine St Pierre, 21st June, calling attention to plundering. On the 23rd June the Dutch-Belgian Adjutant-General issued another order (de Bas, *op. cit.*, p. 1232, vol. iii.) in which among other things he animadverts on the fact that "many soldiers and even officers have left the

THE DUTCH-BELGIANS 23

who are under your orders; but it is so bad that it is impossible not to remark it and complain of it.

1. The troops do not march in a military manner. Neither soldiers nor officers remain with their sections. There is not a house on the road which is not full of them, and the road from one resting-place to another is covered with them.

It is absolutely necessary that the officers should march with their companies, and I hold them responsible that all arrive together at the end of the march. You will have the goodness to report to me every day that the roll of each company has been called, and how many are absent from each battalion.

2. In consequence of this disorderly marching of the Netherlands troops it is impossible to depend upon them for anything. Yesterday I ordered that a brigade should march to Peronne at daybreak to co-operate with the English brigade in the attack on that place. I met the Netherlands brigade at nine o'clock in the evening, when they had just commenced their march; the place having been taken by assault by the English Guards more than an hour previously.

3. The troops of His Majesty the King of the Netherlands pillage and steal wherever they go, even the headquarters, the house where I lodge myself, not being excepted.

They force the safeguards, carry off the prisoners from the gendarmerie which I have formed for the police of the army, at the point of the bayonet. . . .

Your troops enter a village and destroy and pillage everything. . . .

I order you, General, to put in execution my order of the

---

ranks without leave and gone to Brussels, and some even as far as Antwerp, spreading a false alarm on the way." In the order of the 19th June it is laid down that "each regiment or battalion shall send two officers and the necessary number of non-commissioned officers to Brussels to collect the stragglers there." Comment on these two orders is unnecessary.

20th June at once; I also order you to have the rolls of the companies called every hour, at which every officer and soldier is to be present.

He then goes on to mention certain specific cases of indiscipline among the officers of a very flagrant kind, and finishes by ordering them to be sent to The Hague under arrest. Finally, he says—

I will not command such officers as these. I have been long enough a soldier to know that marauders and those who encourage them are worth nothing before the enemy, and I will have nothing to do with them.

This was written by the Duke of Wellington after his experience of the Dutch-Belgian soldiers both in battle and on the march, and it shows quite clearly what his opinion of their value was.

There is, moreover, a large amount of evidence which shows quite clearly that both after Quatre Bras and before Waterloo the rear of the army was crowded with Dutch-Belgians who had abandoned their colours. The Prince of Orange, doubtless inspired by a feeling of patriotism, which may be held to palliate the somewhat crude device, in making the returns of the killed and wounded includes the missing with the former, giving the losses at 2085 officers and men killed or missing, and 2051 wounded.[1]

---

[1] See Wellington's 'Supplementary Despatches,' vol. x. p. 557. De Bas says at p. 798 that the casualties of the 3rd Dutch-Belgian Division at Waterloo were 13 officers and 731 men, total 744; and he gives the losses of their cavalry during the 16th, 17th, and 18th June, at 520 officers and 1076 of the lower rank, total 1128. Plotho in his book, 'Der Krieg des verbündeten Europa gegen Frankreich im Jahre 1815,' p. 73 of the Appendix, gives a return of the casualties signed by the Dutch-Belgian

Now what is required for the Dutch-Belgian case is precisely what the Prince omits to give—*i.e.*, the number of the missing, which may be described as a more polite term for runaways.

The King's German Legion formed an important part of Wellington's army; unfortunately, it was no longer the same force which had fought so gallantly under Wellington in the Peninsula, for a large number

Adjutant-General van der Wijk, and dated 1st July 1815. According to this return the casualties in the three days' fighting of the 3rd Dutch-Belgian Division were 16 officers and 671 men, about the same as de Bas gives. But of the total 687, 342 were missing. He further gives the loss of the Dutch-Belgian cavalry on the three days at 49 officers and 1261 of lower ranks. Of the total, a little in excess of de Bas, 448 were missing. The "slightly wounded" are returned by van der Wijk in case of the 3rd Division at a total of 143 out of 294, in the case of the cavalry at 297 out of 614. The question is, What does "missing" mean, and what was the nature of the injury to constitute a slight wound? Also, Why does de Bas not give the numbers of the missing?

Any one who is interested in the question of the conduct of the Dutch-Belgian troops in the Waterloo Campaign should read Professor Oman's article in the 'Nineteenth Century,' vol. xlviii. p. 629 *et seq.* He gives therein a number of references to eye-witnesses of the struggle whose testimony it is impossible to impeach. To this may be added the account of Commissary-General Tupper Carey, present at Waterloo, whose recollections are published in the 'Cornhill Magazine,' June 1899, and to Lieutenant-Colonel Basil Jackson's 'Notes and Reminiscences of a Staff Officer,' pp. 39, 45, 47.

The latest apologists for their countrymen appear to forget that declamation is not refutation, and that their arguments are mere rhetoric, without any solid basis of fact. Personally, I can never see why the Dutch-Belgian troops should have fought for a cause in which they had no particular interest, while the recollection of past French service must certainly have tended to influence them unfavourably to it. No one would think of impugning the courage or loyalty of the superior officers. Chassé was a man of proved bravery, as his conduct from the days in which he won the sobriquet of "General Baïonnette" down to his last command, the citadel of Antwerp in 1832, shows. Others possessed as high a courage. But going down lower in the military grades there can be no doubt that those who had little to gain from the war in too many instances preferred their personal safety to the cause of their sovereign. I do not wonder at it.

of the old soldiers had been disbanded at the beginning of the year, and their places taken by an insufficient number of recruits, so that the battalions were considerably under strength. The cavalry of the legion was, however, in good condition, and formed a first-rate force. The legion had been for years drilled and trained on English lines, many of the officers were English, and it was to all intents and purposes an English force.

The Hanoverian troops, so far as the infantry is concerned, consisted of 7½ battalions of regular soldiers and 15 battalions of landwehr, and were largely unseasoned troops.[1] The cavalry did not particularly distinguish itself, but the artillery was good.

The Brunswick troops were composed almost entirely of new levies, which had not had time to become a thoroughly consolidated soldiery, but which fought well at Waterloo.

The troops furnished by the Duchy of Nassau were in two parts. Five battalions consisted of old soldiers who had formerly served in the French army, and who had been for some time in the pay of the Netherlands Government, with Prince Bernhard of Saxe-Weimar in chief command. In addition to these, there were three battalions of militia which formed a special contingent under General Kruse, which joined Wellington's army early in June.

---

[1] A number of officers and non-commissioned officers of the King's German Legion, rendered superfluous owing to the smallness of the battalions, were sent to do duty with the Hanoverian troops, thus giving these comparatively raw troops a very valuable stiffening. See Beamish's 'History of the King's German Legion,' p. 323; also 'Wellington Despatches,' vol. xii. pp. 330, 392.

THE ARMY AS A WHOLE

It will be seen, therefore, that the Duke of Wellington's army was of a very heterogeneous character. Why it did so well was due to two causes,—the battles of the 16th and 18th were chiefly defensive, and the troops were ably handled by their great leader, in whom a large proportion of them had perfect trust. At the battle of Waterloo the Duke of Wellington showed himself at his best, and proved that he was without doubt the greatest battle-fighter of his age, who from first to last in his military career had never failed to secure tactical victory " nor ever lost an English gun."

The Anglo-Allied force was distributed as follows:—

1st Corps, Prince of Orange	25,000	Soignies, Enghien, Nivelles, Rœulx	Headquarters, Braine-le-Comte.
2nd Corps, Lord Hill	24,000	West of the 1st Corps, to the Scheldt	Headquarters, Ath.
Reserve Corps, under the Duke himself	21,000	Brussels.	
Cavalry, Earl of Uxbridge	14,000	Ninove, Grammont, &c.	
Artillery and Engineers among the Corps	10,000		
Garrisons	12,000		
	106,000, with 204 guns.		

By this disposition Wellington watched the whole length of frontier assigned to him, and guarded both his right (of which he was specially careful, as his best line of communications lay through Ostend)

28   THE CAMPAIGN OF 1815

and his left which joined on to the Prussians.[1] The reserve being centrally placed at Brussels where the headquarters were, he could assemble two-thirds of his entire force at any point within twenty-two hours of its being threatened by the enemy.

The Prussian troops, under Field-Marshal Blucher, were, in round numbers, 124,000 men, of whom 12,000 were cavalry, with 304 guns. Nearly half the infantry consisted of landwehr—viz., 66 out of 136 battalions. Of these sixty-six, twenty-four were newly formed; the remainder had been allowed to return to their homes after the termination of the late war, and had just been called out again. Among the twenty-four newly-levied battalions six came from Westphalia, which had not formerly belonged to Prussia.

Of the seventy line battalions, eighteen were of new formation, among them two regiments from the late Grand Duchy of Berg, which had served for many years in the French army, and had just been filled up by conscription from the former appanage of Murat.

To complete the line regiments in March it had been found necessary to levy 8000 recruits from the new provinces between the Rhine and the Meuse, and many of the men thus raised only joined their regiments shortly before hostilities began. The equipment of the infantry was very deficient, some of the regiments still wore the uniforms of their old allegiance, and the

[1] Wellington had two lines of communication with England, the one by Antwerp, the other by Ostend. The first was reached by the Scheldt, the navigation of which was difficult to sailing-ships. The second had the advantage of water communication by canal as far as Ghent, which much facilitated the carriage of supplies.

landwehr was terribly deficient in clothing, and contained in its ranks many quite useless men. There were in some regiments muskets of three different calibres; knapsacks, pouches, and belts were often of many different patterns and colours.

The cavalry was in even a worse condition. It was composed of ten old and ten new regiments of the line, with fifteen regiments of landwehr, of which two had only just been formed. The new units had been formed by putting together three squadrons each from different regiments. Most of the officers were changed just before the mobilisation, and the commanders had very often only taken over their duties at the moment they had to advance against the enemy.

The outbreak of war found the artillery also in a state of change. Guns and carriages were available, but there was not enough equipment, nor were there sufficient gunners, and the deficiency had to be made up by untrained infantry soldiers. In such circumstances it is not to be wondered at when Marwitz says this army in accordance with all human probability was bound to be beaten.[1]

The Prussian army was divided into four corps:—

1st Corps,	Zieten	33,000	Charleroi.
2nd ″	Pirch I.	34,000	Namur.
3rd ″	Thielmann	25,000	Ciney.
4th ″	Bülow	32,000	Liége.

124,000 men, with 304 guns.

The Prussian headquarters were at Namur, and the troops were so cantoned that each army corps could

[1] The foregoing is taken from Lettow-Vorbeck, p. 200 *et seq.*

assemble at its own headquarters in twelve hours, or the whole army at any one of them in twenty-four hours.[1]

The line occupied by the Allies in their Belgian cantonments, extending from Liége to Tournay, measured about a hundred miles. The main line of Wellington's communication was by road to Ghent and thence by canal to Ostend, but he had a subsidiary line from Brussels to Antwerp and thence by the Scheldt to England. The Prussian line of communications went through Liége, Aix-la-Chapelle to Cologne, and until operations commenced ran by the road from Namur along the Meuse.

The leaders of the allied armies were both men of great war experience. The Duke of Wellington, then in his forty-seventh year, was at the height of his renown as a soldier.[2] He alone of all European generals had been uniformly successful in his operations against the French. Junot, Massena, Soult, and Marmont had all been defeated by him, and the crushing disaster he inflicted on Joseph and Jourdan at Vitoria, one of the most important battles in the whole series of wars from 1793 to 1815, coupled with the decisive character of his operations against Soult in the South of France in 1814, had placed him in the very highest rank of military commanders.[3] This was the reason which led the Allies in Congress at Vienna to beg him to assume the command of the

[1] This was the official view, but the IV. Corps was too far off to render it possible.

[2] He was born in the same year as Napoleon; "Providence," said Louis XVIII., "owed us that reparation."

[3] Vitoria brought Austria into active hostilities against Napoleon.

troops in Belgium even before he had obtained the permission of his own Government, because they believed from his record he was the best man in Europe to meet Napoleon.

Lettow-Vorbeck considers that Wellington's strategical ability stood on a far lower level than his tactical capacity or than his powers of statesmanship. "One may say that Wellington was more of a diplomat than a general, and he had to thank his diplomatic cleverness for his high military fame; but it must not be forgotten that the Duke, when he was offered the command of the army in the Netherlands, was a personage who stood high in European opinion, on whom the Monarchs of England, Portugal, and Spain had heaped up titles and honours."[1]

With the masterly campaigns of 1812, '13, and '14 to his credit, it is simply ridiculous to speak thus of the English commander, while to say that his strategy was based on the ideas of the pre-Napoleon era is only excusable through ignorance. Like most of his countrymen, Lettow-Vorbeck has apparently never studied the English operations in the Peninsula. But we know what Napoleon himself thought of the "Spanish ulcer," and prefer his opinion to that of the German writer. In the contemporary records it is easy to see that Wellington as a general occupied the highest position in European opinion. But just as the Germans habitually fail to recognise that Marlborough was a great military genius, and invariably attribute the whole of his successes to Prince Eugen, so do they refuse to admit the capacity of the great

[1] Lettow-Vorbeck, p. 216.

Duke.¹ Quite otherwise was the view of Napoleon. During the passage from France to England in 1815 on board the *Bellerophon* he stated to Bertrand: "The Duke of Wellington is fully equal to myself in the management of an army, with the advantage of possessing more prudence."²

Wellington was chosen by the statesmen at Vienna to command the heterogeneous collection of armed men in Belgium because he was universally recognised as the best man for the post, and for the same reason was subsequently placed at the head of the Army of Occupation. Houssaye's appreciation of the position is a far more just one, when he speaks of him as "that generalissimo on whom reposed all the hopes of Europe."³

Blucher, who commanded the Prussian army, was well calculated to aid and support the great Englishman. Loyal and brave, gifted with an extraordinary vigour for his age (seventy-one), he had shown in previous wars that he at any rate was not afraid of Napoleon. This was precisely the quality in which most of the Continental generals failed.⁴

---

[1] Marlborough planned the march to the Danube in 1704, anticipating the Emperor's campaign of 1805; from Wellington's brain sprang the great idea of the march round the right flank of the French in Spain in 1813, a plan which was as overwhelming in its results as was Napoleon's passage of the St Bernard in 1800.

[2] See Maitland's 'Narrative,' &c., p. 222.

[3] See Houssaye, 'Waterloo,' vol. i. p. 480. The Emperor of Russia, who directed the negotiations which took place with regard to the measures to be taken against Napoleon, when urging the Duke to go to Belgium, is reported to have said, "You must once more save us."

[4] Lord Westmorland, in his 'Memoir of the Operations of the Allied Armies,' &c., p. 32, speaking of Blucher and the Prussian army in the war of 1813, says: "The spirit of its great commander, Marshal Blucher,

THE PRUSSIAN LEADERS   33

Moreover, Blucher possessed in Gneisenau and Grolmann, the first his Chief of the Staff, the second his Quartermaster-General, two staff officers of great reputation.

Grolmann's ability has scarcely received the recognition which has been freely given to Gneisenau. Yet it is impossible for any one who studies this campaign not to recognise the great part he played in it. Gneisenau's capacity has been fully recognised. Although he never held any important command, it is usually claimed for him that his was the inspiring mind which planned the general outline of the Prussian movements. As his illustrious chief said when he was given the honorary degree of Doctor by the University of Oxford in 1814, the authorities ought to have made him at least an Apothecary, as the maker of the pills which he (Blucher) administered! The old hussar hardly understood what the doctor's degree meant, but his utterance precisely expresses the relationship between him and his assistant.[1] But it would not be fair to deprive Blucher of all share in the conduct of the war. If Gneisenau thought out the lines of action possible, on Blucher devolved the task of determining which should be taken. "Like the poor cat i' the

pervaded the whole; he was ever foremost in attack, decisive and resolute in his determinations; wherever in the course of the war offensive movements are to be traced, wherever the enemy is attacked and pursued, Marshal Blucher will almost always be found to have directed them."

[1] Gneisenau was a man of disagreeable temperament, and his intercourse with Blucher appears to have been purely official. The old Marshal was a man given to strong views and strong language, not always of a character suited to the drawing-room. His roughness of speech appears to have grated on his Chief of the Staff, who, moreover, thought he should have held the actual leadership. See Lettow-Vorbeck, pp. 140, 159, 160.

C

adage," Gneisenau was far too fond of letting "I dare not wait upon I would." This mental weakness he had clearly shown in 1814, and he showed it again after the battle of Ligny.[1] Moreover, on the day of battle Blucher was the actual commander, and his determination, tactical insight, and personal influence were all of the highest importance in determining the issue of the fight.[2]

To Grolmann the successful issue of the campaign was largely due. For it was his influence which chiefly brought about the decision to retire on Wavre, and to his wise judgment was owed the order for Bulow's attack on the 18th June, when Gneisenau's hesitation caused some delay on the part of the Prussians.[3]

Wellington had no one acting exactly in the capacity of Chief of the Staff, for the Quartermaster-General, Colonel Sir W. De Lancey, merely worked out the march routes in accordance with the instructions of the Duke, who was the head not only of the army in the field but also in all administrative matters. The staff of the Anglo-Allied army was by no means efficient. As the Duke himself says, "I might have expected that the Generals and Staff formed by me in the last war would have been allowed to come to me again; but instead of that I am overloaded with people I have never seen before; and it appears to be purposely intended to keep those out of the way whom I wished to have. However, I'll do

---

[1] See Lettow-Vorbeck, pp. 159, 160. Also *post*, p. 178.
[2] See *ante*, pp. 32, 33, footnote.
[3] See *post*, pp. 176, 177, and also pp. 255, 256.

the best I can with the instruments which have been sent to assist me."[1]

It is impossible to draw any exact comparison between Napoleon and the English commander: their careers were subjected to vastly different conditions; but both over a long series of years had shown that, whatever their relative merits, they were both far above any of their military contemporaries.

Yet it must be admitted that neither displayed on the only occasion on which they met in the field the conspicuous ability each had shown in previous campaigns. Napoleon formed a plan of campaign of the highest merit, but failed in its execution. Wellington, on the other hand, failed somewhat in his General Idea, as he obstinately declined to recognise the evidence in favour of the line of operations actually chosen by Napoleon, preferring to believe on the strength of a report from Paris that the Emperor would move against the Anglo-Allied right; but he redeemed his initial error by the masterly handling of his troops on the battlefield.

The Emperor's shortcomings have been attributed by many of his admirers to his health. It is possible he was no longer the man of Austerlitz and Jena, which is not to be wondered at, considering the life he had led. But he had shown in 1814 that he was still the foremost general of his time. Nor can it be alleged that a man who could remain in the saddle for nearly eighteen hours on the 15th June could have been suffering from ill-health to such an extent as to injure his mental capacity. He started

[1] See 'Supplementary Despatches,' vol. x. p. 219.

at 3 A.M. on that day, and seems to have remained on horseback, except for brief intervals, till nearly 9 P.M. He was then very tired, and threw himself on his bed for a few hours' rest. He intended to rise at midnight, probably to issue orders for the next day, as was his usual custom,[1] but does not appear to have done so, and his fatigue appears to have been sufficiently great on the 17th as to have kept him in bed when he ought to have been up and doing.

Of the three commanders, Napoleon and Blucher both possessed a quality which in Wellington was conspicuously wanting. They knew how to appeal to their soldiers in words which reached their hearts and emboldened their spirits, and both stood on familiar terms with the men they led to battle. Napoleon could issue a stirring proclamation which roused the enthusiasm of his soldiers, or could use the familiar "tu" in talking to a private, thus showing him and his comrades that no individual, however obscure, was beneath the Emperor's care and attention. Blucher was no orator in the generally accepted sense of the word; but if it be oratory—and surely it is in the highest sense—to have the power of moving men by spoken words, however brief, old "Marshal Forwards" possessed this gift in the highest degree.

When at the battle of the Katzbach he unexpectedly found the French on the right bank of the river, he addressed his troops as if the situation was what he had expected and desired. Riding among them he

---

[1] Napoleon usually dined about six, then went to sleep, and, rising after a few hours' rest,—by which time the reports from the various corps had come in,—issued his orders for the next day.

cried, "Now lads, I have got enough Frenchmen on this side—Now forward!" As the fight progressed, with bayonet and musket-butt, for the rain prevented the flintlocks acting, the troops who at first had been depressed cried out to him, "I say, Father Blucher, things are going well to-day, eh?"

A man who stood on this intimate and trusted footing with his men might well appeal to them, as he did on the 18th June, with the absolute certainty that they would answer up to his exhortations. "Lads, we *must* get on! I know it is said we cannot, but we *must!* I have promised my brother Wellington—I have promised him, do you hear? You won't let me break my word, will you?"[1]

On the other hand, the attitude of the British troops towards their commander was one of confidence but not of love, and an anecdote told me by the late General Sir Edward Hamley, who had it from the lips of one of the officers concerned, illustrates perfectly the feeling about him amongst the British officers and men. On the morning of the 18th June two distinguished artillery officers were watching the parade of the French troops on the other side of the valley. Seeing the numbers opposed to them, and probably thoroughly well aware of the value of a large portion of the soldiers in their army, the one said to the other, "We're in a deuce of a mess here!" Said the other, seeing the Duke riding by close to them, "Yes, but here comes the —— that can get us out of it!"

---

[1] See 'Leben des Fürsten Blücher von Wahlstadt,' by Varnhagen von Ense. 2nd ed., pp. 185, 186, 447.

The organisations of the three armies varied considerably. For the first time Wellington divided his troops into army corps: the first consisting of four infantry divisions, the second of three and an infantry brigade. Each division had two batteries of artillery, but no cavalry was attached either to the divisions or to the corps: the reserve, which he retained under his own personal command, may be looked on as a third army corps.[1] There was a special body of reserve artillery attached to this reserve.[2] The whole of the British and King's German Legion cavalry was kept in one mass of seven brigades, under the Earl of Uxbridge, to which six batteries of horse artillery were attached. The proportion of guns to infantry was small—viz., two per thousand. The battalions of infantry and regiments of cavalry varied considerably in strength—some of the former being over 1000 men, some under 500. The cavalry was about one-fifth of the infantry.[3] The companies of sappers and miners were not attached to the field troops.

[1] See 'Wellington Despatches,' vol. xii. p. 317: "In the Peninsula I always kept three or four divisions under my own immediate command, which, in fact, was the working part of the army, thrown as necessary upon one flank or the other." This was similar to Napoleon's method of using his Guard.

[2] The British batteries were mostly armed with five 9-pounder guns, and one 24-pounder howitzer. One horse battery, Bull's, had 24-pounder howitzers only, and two of the horse batteries had 6-pounder guns instead of 9-pounders, while Whinyate's battery had a rocket section attached to it. The German batteries had the same formation as the British. The Dutch-Belgian, six guns and two howitzers.

[3] The army corps organisation was largely administrative, and appears to have been instituted chiefly with a view of distributing the good and bad troops equally throughout the army. At Waterloo parts of the 1st Corps were used at either end of the line. Possibly this was because the Duke preferred to have his troops commanded by tried commanders like Hill, Alten, and Picton, rather than by the Prince of Orange.

PRUSSIAN ORGANISATION

The Prussian army corps were formed of four infantry brigades, each with a cavalry regiment and a six-pounder battery attached to it. In addition there were corps troops consisting of reserve cavalry, reserve artillery, and engineers. The first named comprised two or three brigades of cavalry, with one or two batteries of horse artillery. The reserve artillery included three batteries of 12-pounders, one 6-pounder, and one 15-pounder howitzer battery.[1] Each army corps should have had two field engineer companies, but these and many other units required by the establishment were not present when hostilities broke out. The number of guns per thousand infantry was three, and the cavalry amounted to about one-eighth of the infantry.

The French army corps comprised for the most part four infantry divisions, each with an 8-pounder battery of eight guns attached to it, besides a light cavalry division with a horse battery of six 8- or 6-pounders, and an artillery reserve of one or more batteries of eight 12-pounders.[2] The reserve cavalry was organised in four corps, each of two divisions, of two brigades, with two batteries of horse artillery armed with 6-pounders. There were three to five companies of engineers to each army corps, and the Guard had a certain number of sappers and sailors attached to it. The proportion of guns to infantry

---

[1] Each battery had eight guns. The 6-pounder batteries had each six 6-pounder guns and two 15-pounder howitzers. The 12-pounder batteries had six 12-pounder guns and two 20-pounder howitzers. The 15-pounder howitzer batteries had eight 15-pounder howitzers.

[2] Each battery had two howitzers among its eight (or six) pieces, each about equivalent to our 24-pounder howitzer.

was four per thousand. The cavalry amounted to about a fourth of the infantry force.

For the invasion of France the combined Powers had available about three-quarters of a million troops; but they could not all be ready before the 1st July, on which date it was expected the Russians would reach the Rhine.[1] Their plan of operations, based on the result of the previous campaign, was to march on Paris.

Wellington, who would have about 100,000 Anglo-Allies, and Blucher with 120,000 Prussians, were to advance from Belgium, by Maubeuge and Avesnes. Kleist, who commanded a small German force of 25,000 men, from the little States of Germany, had for his objective the reduction of the fortresses in the north-east of France, and was then to aid the other invaders.

Barclay de Tolly with an army of 170,000 Russians was to enter France between Thionville and Metz, and march by Châlons-sur-Marne and Reims on Paris. Schwartzenberg with 250,000 Austrians was to cross the Rhine in two columns, the right at Mannheim and Germersheim, the left at Bâle and Rheinfelden, force back the troops opposing him, and mask or take the fortresses that lay across his road. The right column was to keep up communication with the Russians, and the united force of Russians and Austrians was to move on Châlons, and then towards Paris.

Besides these armies, there was a Swiss corps of observation, 25,000 men, which, though nominally

[1] The bulk of the Russian troops had to come from Poland.

NAPOLEON'S PLANS

intended to guard the neutrality of Switzerland, might help to swell the invading force should the Allies be successful.

In Northern Italy there were two armies, one of Austro-Sardinians, 60,000 men, the other of Sardinians, 10,000 strong, which were at first to be directed on Lyons, and afterwards to support Schwartzenberg's left.

When Napoleon found that the Allies declined to treat with him and that war was inevitable, two alternative courses presented themselves — he could wait till the Allies invaded France, and beat them in detail, as he had done the previous year, or he might advance against them before they had time to concentrate their masses against him. No doubt the first plan presented many advantages from the military point of view. The longer he waited the more troops he would have and the better his chance of beating his enemies. For he could then adopt the same line of action as in 1814, but under more advantageous circumstances. He had given orders for Paris to be defended by provisional fortifications, and the fortresses of the east of France were being prepared for resistance. Thus the Allies would have to leave a large proportion of their strength to watch the latter and their communications, thereby diminishing their field army, while Napoleon would have had available at least 200,000 men to manœuvre against them.

But there was one grave objection to this course. It would have exposed France once more to all the sufferings of invasion, and it was very doubtful if the people would have acquiesced in such a proceeding, or whether they would not have sacrificed the Emperor to gain peace.

Moreover it was practically impossible for him to be successful in the long-run, as the Allies would, without doubt, bring far more regular troops into the field than he could hope to dispose of.

Napoleon therefore determined to choose the alternative course and attack the Allies. He selected Belgium as the field of operations,—because there lay the nearest forces of his opponents; because the inhabitants of that country were believed favourable to him; because it was important to defeat the English, who formed the backbone of the alliance against him, while the heterogeneous character of the forces under the Duke of Wellington rendered victory more probable, and a great success at the beginning of operations was necessary to rouse the enthusiasm of the French nation and strike dismay into the hearts of his opponents.[1] Moreover, by occupying Belgium and seizing the defiles of the Rhine, he could act on the flank of the armies advancing from Central Europe against him, while the so-called Armies of the Rhine and Alps held them in front. Such a course offered the only real chance of victory.

Napoleon having determined to invade Belgium, could do so in three different ways—

1st. He might enter between the Lys and the Scheldt, or west of the former river, and sever Wellington's communications with Ostend, which were of especial value to him in the summer on

[1] To Carnot he said, "Il me faut un coup d'éclat."

account of the canal to Ghent allowing stores to be transported by water-carriage. Moreover, the Scheldt to Antwerp was difficult of navigation for sailing vessels, while Ostend could always be reached in a few hours from England. The objection to this line of operation was that it would force back the Anglo-Allies on the Prussians. The French would then have to form to a flank to fight them, with their backs to the sea. Moreover, the roads were few, and the progress of the troops would be much impeded by inundations about Ghent and Oudenarde.

2nd. He might aim at the Prussian communications between the Meuse and the Moselle; but here the roads were very bad and the country (chiefly the Forest of Ardennes) not suited to the maintenance of a large force. His advance in this direction would, as in the first case, lead to the concentration of his enemies and to his having to fight them in a position parallel to his communications.

3rd. He might advance by one of the three great roads which led direct on Brussels, *viâ* Tournay, Mons, or Charleroi. Of these, that by Mons was the highroad from Paris to Brussels; but both this and that by Tournay were blocked by the fortresses at these places, which had been hastily put in a state of defence by Wellington. There remained then the road by Charleroi; a little consideration will show that it was the best for the Emperor's purpose. For—

1. It was the most direct route to Brussels.
2. It struck the Anglo-Allied and Prussian armies at their point of junction—*i.e.*, the weakest point in the front of the two armies.

3. The line of communication between the two armies being gained by the capture of Quatre Bras, the Allies would have no good road by which to rejoin one another than that from Louvain-Brussels[1] or Wavre-Brussels.

The Prussians being somewhat the more advanced in position, it is obvious that Napoleon would attack them first while guarding against any attempt of Wellington to support Blucher. After beating the latter, he could concentrate against the Anglo-Allies and defeat them. It was indeed an excellent plan, but contained one false assumption: he thought that the Allies in 1815 would, like the Sardinians and Austrians in 1796, fall back each along their own line of communications, and thus render it impossible for them to act in concert against him after the first defeat inflicted on them. Now there never was any reason to think that either Blucher or Wellington would do anything so foolish. Their object was to crush Napoleon. For this purpose they had to keep together, and their numerical superiority was so great that as long as they did so the defeat of the Emperor was practically certain, and one battle would in all probability terminate the struggle. No great risk was run by the allied armies occupying the positions they actually did, if it were the firm intention of their commanders to keep within supporting distance of one another whatever happened. For behind them the rich country back to the Scheldt was certainly capable of supporting both forces for the short

[1] Blucher, when moving from Wavre to Waterloo, sent his trains back to Louvain.

time which might be required before they attacked Napoleon in concert. Moreover, the road back to Antwerp was effectually covered by the two armies, and there was therefore no reason why they should separate, as both could be subsisted from this base. The map shows that the line from Wavre to Liége was just as good a line of communications for the Prussians as the one from Namur to that place, and the line through Louvain-Tongres to Maestricht was also available. Thus the Prussians, if temporarily obliged to rely on Wellington for supplies, would be able to regain communication with their own base the moment the combined efforts of themselves and the Anglo-Allied army compelled Napoleon to retreat.

Napoleon then chose the line of operations which on the whole was best, and this being the case, it follows that it was the one which the Allies should have thought the most probable for him to select. But early in April we find Wellington considered that the Emperor would enter Belgium between the Sambre and the Scheldt. At the end of the month he seems to have modified his opinion somewhat, so that he thought the enemy might advance "between the Lys and the Scheldt, or between the Sambre and the Scheldt, or by both lines." On the 11th of May he seems to have thought that the French would act on the defensive, as they were taking defensive measures, "such as breaking up roads, bridges, &c." On the 13th June he wrote to Lord Lynedoch of reports that Bonaparte was likely to attack, but adds, "I think we are too strong for him here." By this time Mons and Tournay were capable of defence, and blocked the roads through these places, rendering rapid movement by them impossible, and this would certainly have become known to Napoleon. There remained then only the road *viâ* Charleroi, or the outside routes beyond the Lys on the one side or beyond the Meuse on the other. Neither of these would, as we have seen, have been so favourable as that by which the Emperor actually advanced, and yet there can be no doubt that by the former it was that Wellington expected him to come, and to the day of his death he maintained his opinion. Why was this? The only reasons apparently were that his best line of communications lay through Ostend, that Louis XVIII. was at Ghent, and that he wished, for political reasons, to cover Brussels. The Duke seems to have dreaded an attempt to carry off the King. But the capture of a sovereign who had abandoned his capital without a struggle on the approach of the Emperor does not seem likely to have been a factor of much importance in deciding the question at issue. Most certainly had Napoleon moved against Wellington's right flank, he would have been much hampered by the restored fortresses and the rivers, over which Wellington possessed fortified points of passage, while he would have had to deal with the Anglo-Allies supported by the Prussians.

But putting the question of the line of operations aside, were the actual dispositions of the Allies good, spread as they were over ninety miles, while from the French frontier to Brussels was only fifty? Napoleon thus had but a very short distance to go to attack the Prussians, and it was certain he could do so before Wellington would be in sufficient strength to support them effectively, unless his troops were concentrated as soon as it was known that the French were in force on their side of the frontier. Wellington says, the dispersion was right so far as the Anglo-Allies were concerned, as it was necessary for the purposes of supply.[1] Now it was no doubt imperative to ensure the proper feeding of the army, but it is impossible to believe that in so rich a country it was necessary to keep it for this purpose so scattered as to risk defeat in detail. It must, however, be remembered Wellington originally meant to invade France on the 1st June, and that he put off doing so because the Allies were not ready to invade France from the Rhine.[2] The outspread cantonments would have favoured an offensive concentration on the frontier for invasion. Moreover, he did not believe Napoleon would dare to attack him and Blucher, thinking, as the events subsequently showed, they were too strong for him; and further, until the actual

[1] Wellington appears to have fed his troops easily enough, but there is no doubt the Prussians experienced considerable difficulty in doing so. With them ready money was scarce, and although Wellington arranged with the King of the Netherlands that he should supply the necessary food for the Prussian army,—the Prussian Government settling later on the debt thereby incurred,—still considerable friction arose between the Prussians and the Netherlands authorities, and this increased to such an extent that Blucher at one time threatened to withdraw from the advanced position he had taken up on the strength of the promises of the King of the Netherlands. Wellington, however, was happily able to overcome the difficulties, but only by the exercise of considerable pressure on the monarch. See 'Supplementary Despatches,' vol. x. p. 368.

[2] Wellington had wished to assume the offensive from the moment he arrived at Brussels. See 'Wellington Despatches,' pp. 296, 297, 304.

attack took place, the information pointed to a feint on the Prussians, the real attack being delivered on the English from the direction of Mons.[1]

But, at any rate, as soon as an attack became probable, and we know that the concentration of the French army on the frontier was known some days before at Brussels, the Allied forces should have been drawn in, so that they might have been better able to support one another. It is not too much to suggest that from the 13th June the 4th Division from Oudenarde and the 1st Dutch-Belgian Division from Sotteghem might have been moved to Grammont; the 1st Division might have marched to Nivelles; the 1st Brigade of the 2nd Dutch-Belgian Division united with the 2nd, which already held the highroad from Charleroi to Brussels, about Quatre Bras; while the Reserve should have come to Waterloo.[2] Wellington could then have acted with equal facility to the right, left, or front.

If, however, the disposition of the Anglo-Allied army was bad, that of the Prussian was worse. Two corps, Thielmann's at Ciney and Bülow's at Liége, were beyond the field of any possible or at least probable operations. Had the former been at Sombreffe and the latter at Hannut they would have been infinitely better placed to resist invasion, and the line of communications might have been from Maestricht to Tongres and thence to Namur or Hannut, by which route it would have been less liable to injury than by

---

[1] See *post*, p. 60.
[2] Compare this suggestion with Wellington's orders issued on the 15th June, *post*, p. 96.

POSITIONS OF THE ALLIES

Namur-Liége.[1] The evil of an exposed line of communications was well known to the Prussians, who had suffered from it in 1806, and it is surprising, therefore, that they should have chosen one liable to be cut at an early period of the operations had Napoleon advanced by the country between the Meuse and the Moselle.[2]

It is desirable to draw attention to the bad arrangement on the right flank of the Prussians and the left flank of the Anglo-Allies. From the first, Zieten was told in case he could not hold the outpost line to retire to Fleurus. Now the disposition of his advanced troops was such as to render him responsible for the frontier line as far as Bonne Esperance, yet as soon as he was attacked in any force he was to abandon the whole of this position to the west of the Charleroi road and take a flank position at Fleurus—*i.e.*, he was to retreat by a line parallel to his front. Behind Zieten's troops there was nothing but the Nassau brigade stationed at Genappe, Villiers-Perouin, and Hautain-le-Val, the nearest support to which was the remainder of the 2nd Dutch-Belgian Division at Nivelles. Surely it would have been better for one or the other of the two commanders to have had a considerable force

---

[1] Ciney and the country east of the Meuse might have been watched by cavalry.

[2] That Gneisenau knew it to be dangerous is proved by the fact that the moment the army was ordered to concentrate against the French attack, he ordered it to be abandoned for the old Roman road. See *post*, p. 65. The plain truth is that Gneisenau had not emancipated himself from the old strategical notion of guarding everything, which is purely defensive in its origin. Napoleon's idea was to concentrate his forces, and to seek in the offensive the truer and more powerful method of defence.

on the Charleroi-Brussels highway. If the Prussians were to hold it, Zieten should have been supported by another corps. If Wellington was to be responsible for it, he should have had at least a division at Quatre Bras. But the fact of the matter is, both commanders were so certain Napoleon would not attack, because they thought it was too dangerous for him to do so, that they preferred arrangements, the main object of which was the invasion of France, and which had very little regard to a French irruption into Belgium.

On the whole, then, it must be conceded that, against a man of Napoleon's known capacity for rapid movements, both Wellington and Blucher were to blame for continuing in their widely spread-out cantonments when they knew the French army was being concentrated against them. It is difficult to admit that these were vital to the question of supply, and even if they were not dangerous, they gave the Emperor a valuable gain of time, as owing to the short distance he would have to move, he would probably be able to attack the Allies before they were concentrated.[1] If he did not mean to assume the offensive, why should he have concentrated troops on the frontier? Their presence there was proof positive of his intention to do so.

Napoleon's plan of campaign was masterly, but the same cannot be said of the general arrangements he

[1] Reference to the General Map will show that Napoleon's centre at Beaumont was distant only nineteen miles from Gosselies, which may be taken as a point which, when reached by the Emperor, would put him within striking distance of either Wellington's or Blucher's army, while the outer wing of each of these was over forty miles from this point.

THE DISPOSITION OF THE FRENCH

made of the whole army he had available. He once more fell into the error of 1813 by trying to guard too much, and he spread forces along the Eastern and Southern boundaries of France far too feeble to stop any advance of the large armies the European Powers could bring against them; while against the Anglo-Allied force of 106,000, and the Prussian of 124,000, he left himself only 124,000 men. Had he diminished his numbers on the Eastern frontier and added them to the Army of the North, he would have put himself much more on an equality with the troops of Wellington and Blucher. Of what use was it wasting men on the Spanish frontier or on the Var? The distance of both these points from the decisive theatre of operations would render any hostile advance from either useless, as in neither case would it have any effect on the operations in Belgium, on which his fate depended. How could Rapp with 20,000 men stop Schwartzenberg and Barclay de Tolly with 420,000? Half of his men would have been far better employed under the Emperor, and it seems quite possible that the latter might have augmented the troops he used in Belgium by at least 20,000 more men taken from those he wasted on the more distant frontiers of France.

CHAPTER III.

THE SITUATION AT THE COMMENCEMENT OF THE CAMPAIGN—THE EVENTS OF THE 15TH JUNE.

SEVERAL English engineer officers were engaged on the permanent defences of Belgium at the time Napoleon reached Paris, and Lieutenant - Colonel Carmichael Smyth, the Commanding Royal Engineer, at once set to work to improve the existing fortifications. Ostend, Nieuport, Ypres, Oudenarde, Tournay, Mons, were repaired and strengthened, and by the beginning of June all these strongholds were in so efficient a state as to render siege operations necessary for their capture.[1]

On the French side of the frontier the triple line of fortresses were also prepared for war.[2] The front row, Calais, Dunkerque, Saint Omer, Lille, Condé, Maubeuge, and Philippeville, were completely armed, provisioned for six months, and provided with adequate garrisons of selected National Guards. The second and third lines behind those mentioned were also in a state of adequate preparation to afford considerable resistance. The frontier was carefully guarded, the

---
[1] For details see 'Supplementary Despatches,' vol. x. p. 721 *et seq.*
[2] See 'Commentaires de Napoléon Ier,' vol. v. p. 102.

THE FRENCH CONCENTRATION 53

passages over it from the sea to the Ardennes occupied by strong detachments, and demonstrations were made to attract the attention of Wellington to the western end while the movement of concentration was being carried out, by which the Army of the North was brought together opposite the point where the Emperor intended to break into Belgium.

We have seen (see *ante*, p. 14) that the corps destined to form the invading force extended in a long line from Metz to Lille, the Guard being at Compiègne and Paris. Napoleon proposed to gather them together between Philippeville and Maubeuge, and then to advance on Charleroi. There was no danger of the Allies discovering the concentration of the more centrally placed corps, as there had been much marching to and fro of troops during the last two months.[1] The only movements likely to arouse suspicion were those of the 4th Corps from Metz and of the 1st Corps from Lille. Every precaution was taken in these two cases to prevent any information leaking out about them.[2]

Gérard, who commenced his march from Metz on the 6th June, was ordered to Philippeville; but he was not to tell any of his officers his destination, he was to take care that no one left Metz, and the gates of the city were to be kept closed. The frontier towards the Ardennes and the Eifel was watched by National Guards and Volunteers, to cover the movement.

---

[1] See Dörnberg's letter of the 9th April, 'Supplementary Despatches,' vol. x. p. 52.
[2] The zone of strategical deployment on the frontier was covered by woods, which extended from Fosses to the Sambre. See General Map.

D'Erlon moved from Lille on the 9th with the greatest secrecy — all intercourse over the frontier being forbidden and the frontier posts increased. The National Guards who took up these duties were ordered to make such demonstrations against the outposts of the Anglo-Allied troops as would lead Wellington to suppose that the main advance was to be against his right.

Reille set out from Valenciennes on the 11th June, as d'Erlon approached this town, and the two moved towards Maubeuge. The 4th Corps marched from Mézières to Philippeville, while the rest of the troops were directed to Beaumont, the cavalry being pushed to the front and to the right of the mass of troops thus concentrated. The last of the Imperial Guard marched from Paris on the 8th. Napoleon left the capital on the 12th June, and reached the army on the 14th June, the anniversary of Marengo and Friedland. On the night of this date the positions of the different corps were as follows:—

The Left—*i.e.*, the 1st and 2nd Corps were bivouacked at Solre-sur-Sambre and Leer, and held the passages over the Sambre.

The Imperial Guard, the 3rd and 6th Corps, forming the Centre of the army, with the Reserve Cavalry and the pontoon equipment and the Headquarters, were at Beaumont.

The Right, consisting of the 4th Corps and a division of cuirassiers (Delort's), was at Philippeville.[1]

[1] The whole of the 4th Corps did not arrive at Philippeville till the morning of the 15th, while Delort's cavalry did not come up till the afternoon of that date.

STATIONS OF THE ANGLO-ALLIES

The stations of the Anglo-Allied army on this date were as follows [1] :—

FIRST ARMY CORPS.

1st British Division	Headquarters—Enghien.
3rd British Division	Headquarters—Soignies, Braine-le-Comte, and the country towards Enghien.
2nd Dutch-Belgian Division	Headquarters—Nivelles, the 2nd Brigade holding Hautain-le-Val, Frasnes, and Villers-Perouin.
3rd Dutch-Belgian Division	Headquarters—Rœulx and towards Binche.

SECOND ARMY CORPS.

2nd British Division	Headquarters—Ath, holding the roads towards Tournay and Mons.
4th British Division	Headquarters—Oudenarde. The 6th Hanoverian Brigade at Nieuport.
1st Dutch-Belgian Division	Headquarters—Sotteghem, holding the road from Grammont to Ghent.
Dutch-Belgian Indian Brigade	Headquarters—Alost.

THE RESERVE.

Round Brussels.

THE CAVALRY.

The British and King's German Legion Cavalry, with the Hanoverian Brigade, were at Gramont and Ninove, and in the villages along the Dender. The 1st Hussars, King's German Legion, of the 6th Brigade watched the country in front of Tournay, on the right of the Dutch-Belgian cavalry at Rœulx, Mons, Maubeuge, who guarded the frontier to the Prussian outposts at Bonne Esperance, near Binche. The Brunswick cavalry was at Brussels.

---

[1] Full details of the three armies will be found in the Appendix. The positions of the troops of the three armies are given on the General Map.

Dörnberg was at Mons, where he acted as intelligence officer.[1]

The I. Prussian Corps, with its headquarters at Charleroi, was posted with its 1st Brigade at Fontaine L'Evêque; the 2nd Brigade at Marchiennes on the Sambre; the 3rd Brigade at Fleurus; the 4th Brigade in Moustier on the Sambre; the Reserve Cavalry was at Sombreffe, and the Reserve Artillery, Gembloux. Its outposts extended from Bonne-Esperance along the frontier through Lobbes, Thuin, Gerpinnes, to Sossoye.[2]

The II. Corps had its brigades posted as follows: the 5th Brigade, with the headquarters of the corps, at Namur; the 6th Brigade at Thorembey-les-Beguignes; the 7th Brigade in Heron; the 8th Brigade in Huy; the Reserve Cavalry in Hannut; and the Reserve

---

[1] There were numerous French Royalist and English emissaries across the frontier, among the latter the well-known scouting officer Colquhoun Grant. See *post*, p. 166, footnote.

[2] It is obvious from the length of the line occupied by the I. Corps, and from the Reserve Artillery and Reserve Cavalry being kept well in rear, that it was not intended to offer any great resistance to the French advance. Moreover, none of the bridges were prepared for demolition. Zieten's instructions on this point are: "As the bridges are made of stone and cannot be destroyed, and are not to be occupied by guns, the defence must be limited to a powerful fire of skirmishers." See 'Militair-Wochenblatt,' for 1846, p. 19. No defence of this kind could possibly hope to keep the French back long, nor did it. That more serious steps were not taken to defend the Sambre was the fault of Blucher and Gneisenau, or more probably of the latter only. Lettow-Vorbeck justly points out (p. 246, *op. cit.*) that from the Sambre to Sombreffe was only about half the distance of the latter place to Liége, where the IV. Corps was. A sufficient reason either for a more serious defence on the Sambre, or for bringing the IV. Corps nearer to the rendezvous point. Gneisenau's dispositions were like those which Napoleon so strongly animadverted on. "It is good against smugglers, but this system of war has never succeeded." See 'Correspondance de Napoléon Ier,' 20/1/1814.

STATIONS OF THE PRUSSIANS 57

Artillery along the road to Louvain. The advanced posts of this corps continued those of Zieten's corps from Sossoye to Dinant.

The III. Corps had its headquarters at Ciney, where also was the 10th Brigade. The 9th Brigade was at Asserre; the 11th Brigade at Dinant; the 12th Brigade at Huy; the Reserve Cavalry between Ciney and Dinant; the Reserve Artillery between Ciney and Asserre. The advanced posts extended from Dinant as far as Fabeline and Rochefort.

The IV. Corps had its headquarters at Liége, where was also the 13th Brigade. The 14th Brigade was at Waremme; the 15th at Hologne; the 16th at Liers; the cavalry was at Tongres, Dalhem, and Looz; the Reserve Artillery at Gloms and Dalhem.

For some months past there had been repeated rumours, and even definite statements, that the Emperor was about to invade Belgium. As far back as the 30th April Wellington had thought it desirable to concentrate the cantonments of his troops "with a view to their early junction in case of attack."[1] But

---

[1] This memorandum is as follows:—

SECRET MEMORANDUM.

For H.R.H. the Prince of Orange, the Earl of Uxbridge, Lord Hill, and the Quarter-Master General.

BRUXELLES, 1815.

(1.) Having received reports that the Imperial Guard had moved from Paris upon Beauvais, and a report having been for some days prevalent in the country that Buonaparte was about to visit the northern frontier, I deem it expedient to concentrate the cantonments of the troops with a view to their early junction in case this country should be attacked, for which concentration the Quarter-Master General now sends orders.

(2.) In this case, the enemy's line of attack will be either between the

time went on and the Emperor made no movement; and as their own armies strengthened and improved, both Wellington and Blucher began to think that attack was improbable. Gneisenau, in a letter of the 9th June, said, "The enemy in the meantime will not

Lys and the Scheldt, or between the Sambre and the Scheldt, or by both lines.

(3.) In the first case, I should wish the troops of the 4th Division to take up the bridge on the Scheldt, near Avelghem, and with the regiment of cavalry at Courtrai, and fall back upon Audenarde, which post they are to occupy, and to inundate the country in the neighbourhood.

(4.) The garrison of Ghent are to inundate the country in the neighbourhood likewise, and that point is to be held at all events.

(5.) The cavalry in observation between Menin and Furnes are to fall back upon Ostende, those between Menin and Tournay upon Tournay, and thence to join their regiments.

(6.) The 1st, 2nd, and 3rd Divisions of infantry are to be collected at the headquarters of the divisions, and the cavalry at the headquarters of their several brigades, and the whole to be in readiness to march at a moment's notice.

(7.) The troops of the Netherlands to be collected at Soignies and Nivelle.

(8.) In case the attack should be made between the Sambre and the Scheldt, I propose to collect the British and Hanoverians at and in the neighbourhood of Enghien, and the army of the Low Countries at and in the neighbourhood of Soignies and Braine-le-Comte.

(9.) In this case, the 2nd and 3rd Divisions will collect at their respective headquarters, and gradually fall back towards Enghien with the cavalry of Colonel Arentsschildt's and the Hanoverian brigade.

(10.) The garrisons of Mons and Tournay will stand fast; but that of Ath will be withdrawn, with the 2nd Division, if the works should not have been sufficiently advanced to render the place tenable against a *coup-de-main*.

(11.) General Sir W. Ponsonby's, Sir J. Vandeleur's, and Sir H. Vivian's brigades of cavalry will march upon Hal.

(12.) The troops of the Low Countries will collect upon Soignies and Braine-le-Comte.

(13.) The troops of the 4th Division and the 2nd Hussars, after taking up the bridge at Avelghem, will fall back upon Audenarde, and there wait for further orders.

(14.) In case of the attack being directed by both lines supposed, the

ALLIES PREPARE TO ADVANCE

attack us, but will fall back to the Aisne, the Somme, and the Marne to concentrate his forces," and on the 12th he wrote, "the danger of attack has almost disappeared."[1] On the 13th Wellington wrote to Lord Lynedoch saying it was reported Bonaparte was joining the army with a view to attack the Allies, but that he did not think his departure from Paris was likely to be immediate, and, he added, "I think we are now too strong for him here."

In the meantime Blucher was chafing with the delay, and was anxious to advance to invade France as soon as possible. Originally it had been intended to do so at the beginning of June, then in the middle, and finally the 1st July was named as the date for the Allies advance.[2] These postponements were due to the fact that the forces invading France from the East would not be able to do so before this date, and, considering the preparations Napoleon was known to have made, it was thought more prudent to

---

troops of the 4th Division and 2nd Hussars, and the garrison of Ghent, will act as directed in Nos. 3 and 4 of this Memorandum; and the 2nd and 3rd Divisions, and the cavalry and the troops of the Low Countries, as directed in Nos. 8, 9, 10, 11, and 12.

WELLINGTON.

De Bas, p. 1159, gives the same document, which he says is at the British Museum, and that a copy exists in the Military History Archives in The Hague, that in both cases it is dated 13th or 15th June, and that it is not given in the 'Wellington Despatches.' This is an error. It will be found in vol. xii. p. 337 of the Despatches, without date, and on p. 338 a covering letter to Lord Uxbridge, dated 30th April. It is strange that the Dutch officer should have overlooked this. Plainly the dates he gives are quite wrong.

[1] See Lettow-Vorbeck, vol. i. p. 192.
[2] Wellington had from the first favoured an advance into France.

wait until the events on the Eastern frontier would compel his attention to the movements in that quarter as well as to those of the Allies from Belgium.

From the 6th June onwards, however, the rumours became more persistent. The information received from day to day at the headquarters of the Anglo-Allied and Prussian armies was as follows:—

6th June.[1]

REPORTS TO BLUCHER.	REPORTS TO WELLINGTON.
	Dörnberg reported that according to French papers Napoleon had left Paris that day. The Prince of Orange reported information received from the French General Albert, to the effect that the Allies would be attacked on the 8th or 9th, if they did not attack on the 7th. He also sent into Wellington a report from General Behr, from Mons, of information obtained through an agent of Louis XVIII. that Napoleon was leaving Paris on the 6th, and was going to Avesnes, that he intended to make a feigned attack from Maubeuge, while the real attack would be made between Lille and Tournay against Mons. This information was sent by Wellington to Blucher.

8th June.

A French General, Bournonville, reported that Napoleon would wait attack between the fortifications, being afraid of the superiority of the Allies' cavalry. Zieten reported that the French posts had retired from the frontier nearer to Maubeuge.	Dörnberg reported it was probable Napoleon would go straight to Laon, that the Young Guard were expected the previous night in Valenciennes and the Old Guard at Maubeuge.

---

[1] Taken from Lettow-Vorbeck, and from the 'Wellington Despatches.' Places named are on the General Map or Map No. 2.

INFORMATION RECEIVED BY ALLIES

9th June.

The Prussians received information of the movements of both the 3rd and 4th French Corps.

Various rumours received as to Napoleon's movements—according to one he was going to Strasburg, according to another he had arrived at Valenciennes or Maubeuge.

Dörnberg reported guns were heard in that direction, probably a salute on the Emperor's arrival. Van Merlen reported Napoleon had come to Maubeuge, and that he had been received with a salute of 101 guns, and that the Allies would be attacked that day.

Zieten said the movements of the enemy (probably alluding to the withdrawal of the French posts from the frontier) seem to have been caused by the arrangements made for a camp of the Prussian troops there.

10th June.

Zieten confirmed the report of the arrival of Napoleon at Marienbourg, and reported that Gerard was approaching Maubeuge.

Wellington thought Napoleon was on the frontier, and that he had gone towards Lille. Dörnberg reported Bonaparte had left Paris with 80,000 men on the 6th, and that he was at Laon.

11th June.

Some people think Napoleon will attack on the 10th from Rocroi.

Wellington felt sure from information received that Napoleon was still in Paris on the 7th. Dörnberg reported from information received from Colonel Dillon, a Netherlands officer, that Napoleon had been for the last five days in Valenciennes, and that yesterday he had gone to Avesnes, and the sound of guns he heard in Maubeuge and Valenciennes was on account of the arrival of the Eagles which had been distributed in Paris on the 1st June.

Müffling wrote to Blucher that he did not think Napoleon would attack immediately, and that Wellington awaited the advance with the greatest calmness, as he was now ready for him.

12th June.

The III. Corps reported that Vandamme was with his corps at Philippeville.

Zieten reported that at Givet, Roty,[1] Marienbourg,[1] Couvin, there were considerable masses of troops —strength unknown.

Gneisenau wrote to Hardenberg that "the fear of attack is almost passed away."

Dörnberg reported that Reille had reached Maubeuge, that a division of Guards had reached Avesnes, where the headquarters were. Bonaparte was expected every minute. Jerome was in Solre-le-chateau. Soult had passed through Maubeuge. Between Philippeville, Givet, Mézières, Guise, and Maubeuge, the French army was estimated at 100,000 men by the man who brought the information. Grouchy had been inspecting during the last two days a very considerable body of cavalry near Hirson. The general opinion held in the army (French) is that as soon as Bonaparte arrives in Avesnes he will attack. On the same date Baron Roison, who had a country seat on the frontier, reported that preparations were being made for attack on the 14th, the anniversary of Marengo. Lord Uxbridge reported from Ninove that Bonaparte's headquarters were in Laon on the 10th, and he intended to attack immediately. On the other hand, it is said troops have been sent by rapid marches to La Vendée.

13th June.

Steinmetz reported from Fontaine L'Evéque at midnight (12th-13th) to Zieten that Bonaparte was with the Guards in Maubeuge, that the 2nd Army Corps had arrived there, and that four battalions had crossed the

Dörnberg reported that there was apparently no doubt that the whole of the French army was assembled round Maubeuge. The Prince of Orange reported that the French headquarters were at Avesnes, as

---

[1] Probably Rocroi and Martembourg.

INFORMATION RECEIVED BY ALLIES

Sambre and moved towards Merbes-le-chateau, and that Labuissière was also strongly occupied. This information came from a drum-major who had deserted, who also stated that the attack was to be made either on the 13th or 14th. This information was not sent on to Namur until the 14th.

Later in the day Zieten reported that there was a large body of troops, 60,000 men, of whom 38,000 were National Guards, between Givet, Martembourg, Thuin, Maubeuge, without any artillery; that Jerome was in Beaumont, Murat in Avesnes, and that Napoleon was expected. From Ciney Clausewitz reported Vandamme had not left Rocroi.

also a division of the Guards. Napoleon was daily expected. At 8 P.M. General Behr, from Mons, reported to the Prince of Orange that Van Merlen, coming from the outposts, reported large bodies of troops were in the neighbourhood of Maubeuge.

14th June.

Zieten reported that in consequence of the information received the previous midnight he had warned the brigades commanders to draw in their troops so as to be able to assemble the whole corps at the shortest notice. He also reported that he had received information from Van Merlen that only weak outposts were in front of him, and that the light of the watch-fires seemed to show considerable forces were by Thirimont[1] near Beaumont, and by Marpent between Maubeuge and Solre-sur-Sambre. At 10 o'clock in the evening Hardinge sent this information to Brussels, adding, "General Gneisenau believes in the report from different sources of the arrival of two divisions of the 4th Corps at Sedan and Mézières. Here the opinion is held that Napoleon intends to assume offensive operations."

Dörnberg at 9.30 A.M. reported that the troops at Maubeuge seem only to have been inspected, as yesterday they moved in various directions, part towards Beaumont and part to Pont-sur-Sambre. At three o'clock he reported Napoleon's military kitchen was yesterday in Avesnes; he had not arrived himself. The whole of the French troops are assembling near Beaumont and Maubeuge, 80,000 at the former place, 100,000 at the latter; the cavalry pickets in front of Valenciennes are relieved. Napoleon left Paris during the night of the 11th-12th. The Prince of Orange reported at 5 P.M. from Braine-le-Comte, "Everything here quite unchanged. Müffling reported to Gneisenau that according to the news received at Brussels that night the whole of the enemy's army will be assembled to-day at Maubeuge." Van Merlen also sent similar information direct to Namur.

---

[1] Probably Thuillies.

It will thus be seen that by the 14th it was fairly evident that the enemy was assembled between Philippeville, Beaumont, and Maubeuge. But Wellington, influenced by the report of the 6th June—for this is the only possible explanation—still thought it probable that the attack would be directed against his right, and did not think it well to move till Napoleon's plan became more evident.[1]

The Prussian commander, however, judged the information he had received sufficient to justify a preliminary concentration. But still Gneisenau does not seem to have thought attack imminent, for the instructions sent to Bülow at mid-day on the 14th were merely to the effect that the enemy was concentrating about Maubeuge with a view to assuming the offensive, and the commander of the 4th Corps was therefore to make such arrangements as would enable him to assemble his troops in one march at Hannut. The orders to Thielmann were of a similar character—*i.e.*, for a drawing in of the outspread troops and not for a movement of concentration of the whole army.

But later in the day, probably a little before eleven, further information was received which induced Gneisenau to issue at 11.30 P.M. more definite instructions.[2] Thielmann was now told that the

---

[1] In the early part of May Napoleon seems to have had some idea of doing this, as will be seen by reference to his 'Correspondance' letters to Davout of the 13th and 22nd May. Also it must be remembered that a French concentration at Maubeuge pointed just as much to an attack on Mons as to one on Charleroi. This is evident from the General Map.

[2] See Lettow-Vorbeck, vol. i. p. 197. Deserters of some importance seem to have been the cause.

THE ORDERS TO BÜLOW

enemy had concentrated on the frontier and probably intended to assume the offensive. The army was therefore to concentrate to meet it, and the III. Corps was to come to the left bank of the Meuse near Namur, merely watching Dinant and the country towards Givet with a detachment (one battalion, two squadrons) which was to communicate with the outposts of the II. Corps (of equal strength) on the left bank of the Meuse near Namur, to which point both detachments were to fall back if necessary. Pirch I. was to assemble the II. Corps between Mazy and Onoz, leaving a battalion in Namur. Zieten already had his instructions, and knew what he was to do if attacked —*i.e.*, to concentrate at Fleurus.

To Bülow, who was senior in rank to Gneisenau, somewhat vague instructions were sent, couched in such courtly phrase as to lose all definite character. He was on the 15th to concentrate his troops in close cantonments at Hannut and establish his headquarters there, "as the information received makes it probable that the enemy had concentrated opposite to us, and that we have forthwith to expect him to assume the offensive," the line of communications was to be by the old Roman road, and no longer by that which ran along the right bank of the Meuse. All corps were told to send their sick to the rear, and that the headquarters remained for the present at Namur. But Gneisenau omitted to inform Wellington of the intended concentration of the Prussian army, and left the Duke in total ignorance of the orders he had issued. Possessing, therefore, no news from the Prussian side beyond the general statement of Hardinge that at Blucher's headquarters it was believed Napoleon intended to assume the offensive, the Duke gave no orders for any movement to be made by his forces.[1]

Napoleon's orders for the advance on the 15th were as follows. They form an excellent example of his ideas as to the arrangement of troops for a march.

The centre column was to be headed by the 3rd Corps. Its light cavalry under General Domon was to move off at 2.30 A.M. and send reconnoitring parties of not less than fifty men in all directions to scour the country and carry off the enemy's posts. Vandamme (commander of the 3rd Corps) was to see that it was provided with ammunition. It was to be followed by Pajol's 1st Corps of the Reserve Cavalry, which was to act as a support to Domon, Pajol being in command of both. The Horse Artillery battery of the cavalry of the 3rd Corps was to follow behind the leading battalion, and the corps was to assemble at 2.30 A.M. and move off at 3 o'clock. The whole of its baggage was to come behind the 6th Corps, which was to move off at 4 A.M. to follow the 3rd. Every division was to have its battery and ambulance, all other vehicles to follow in rear with those of the 3rd Corps. The Young Guard was to parade at 4 and

---

[1] Although Wellington felt it undesirable to move prematurely, the same argument did not apply to the Prussian III. and IV. Corps, which, being badly placed, would under any circumstances have to be drawn in nearer to headquarters for defensive purposes. It is impossible to excuse Gneisenau's failure to inform the Duke that he was about to concentrate his army. See Pollio's 'Waterloo (1815) con nuovi documenti,' p. 151. It is the more remarkable, as Gneisenau had sent Colonel Pfuel into Brussels on the 13th June to arrange the plans of mutual co-operation.

NAPOLEON'S ORDER FOR THE 15TH

march off at 5 A.M., following the 6th Corps. The chasseurs of the Old Guard were to follow at 5.30, and the grenadiers at 6 o'clock. Grouchy was to mount the cavalry corps nearest to the road at 5.30, and the other two were to follow at an hour's interval. The whole were to move by the lateral roads so as to avoid incommoding the infantry.

Reille was to move off at 3 A.M., march the 2nd Corps on Marchiennes, and cross there, first repairing the bridge if necessary.

D'Erlon was to follow Reille, placing himself on his left as soon as possible, cross the Sambre at Thuin, occupy it with a division which was to throw up a bridge-head there and at the Abbaye d'Aulne, both on the left bank. He was to send reconnoitring parties towards Mons and Binche, but not over the frontier. He was to leave a cavalry brigade behind to keep up communications with Maubeuge.

The same order of march was to be observed for the artillery, ambulances, and baggage as ordered for the 3rd Corps, and the baggage of the 1st and 2nd Corps was to march on the left of the 1st Corps.

The 4th Corps, if its divisions had been united in front of Philippeville, was to move on Charleroi, keeping in touch with the 3rd Corps, and reconnoitring toward Namur. Gérard was to march ready for action, and leave the baggage at Philippeville. He was to order the 14th Cavalry Division which was due to arrive at Philippeville on the 14th to accompany him to Charleroi, where it was to join the Reserve Cavalry to which it belonged.

Reille, Vandamme, Gérard, and Pajol were to keep

in frequent communication and arrange for their troops to arrive in a united mass in front of Charleroi.

The sappers of these three corps were to follow the first light infantry regiment to improve the roads, bridges, streams, &c.[1]

The marines, the sappers of the Guard, and the reserve were to follow the first regiment of the 3rd Corps.

The pontoon equipment was to furnish three bridges to throw over the Sambre, and the portion told off for this purpose was to follow the sappers of the 3rd Corps, the remainder marching with the reserve park of the artillery.

The Emperor would move with the advance-guard of the centre, and it was his intention to pass the Sambre before noon, with the whole of the army.

These orders have been justly considered as a perfect model of their kind. To military students they are especially valuable as showing all the steps required for the movement of a large force. The front is to be covered by cavalry, furnished by one body (Domon's division) supported by another (Pajol's). The artillery is kept well to the front in the columns, which are kept stripped as it were for battle, all trains not required for fighting being kept behind.

The flanks were specially protected (14th Cavalry Division on the right, a brigade of the 1st Corps Cavalry on the left). The march was to be facilitated by using as many roads as possible consistent with the object of the march, and by the construction of bridges where necessary.

[1] The roads towards the frontier had been broken upon the French side.

BAD ARRANGEMENT OF COLUMNS 69

The communications were to be protected by bridge-heads (Thuin, Abbaye d'Aulne), in accordance with Napoleon's habitual practice.

There is only one point on which the dispositions of the Emperor may be unfavourably criticised, and that is the direction of the 3rd, 6th, and Guards Corps with the bulk of the cavalry on Charleroi, while the 4th Corps was also sent to the same point. Here only one bridge was available, and it is evident that the whole of these troops could not have passed quickly by it. We shall see later that the 4th was diverted to Châtelet, which afforded some relief; but it would have been decidedly better had Napoleon kept to his original plan of forming his Right of the 3rd and 4th Corps, thus removing the former from the Centre. As it was, the passage of the troops at Charleroi was considerably delayed, and not nearly the whole reached the right bank of the Sambre on the 15th. The blame for this change seems to be due to Soult, who held the idea that the troops were to advance in two columns, and when Napoleon ordered a reversion to the three, as he originally intended, it was too late for the 3rd to join the 4th Corps at Philippeville, and it was allowed to remain with the Centre.[1]

The Prussian troops available to meet the French attack consisted of the I. Corps, distributed as follows: The 1st Brigade, with its headquarters at Fontaine L'Evêque, covered the ground from Binche to the Sambre; the 2nd, at Marchiennes, held the river line to Charleroi and Châtelet; the 3rd, at Fleurus, the debouches over the river at Farciennes and

[1] See Lettow-Vorbeck, pp. 222-24.

Tamines; the 4th, at Moustier, protected the Sambre nearly to Namur. The Reserve Cavalry, about Gosselies, the Reserve Artillery at Gembloux. When driven back, the various brigades were to concentrate on Fleurus, where Zieten was to await the development of the enemy's plan. He was also to inform Wellington and Blucher as quickly as possible.[1]

The French began the movement at 3 A.M. by the advance of their left, Bachelu's division of Reille's corps leading. Pushing back the Prussian outposts, the 5th Division reached Marchiennes about ten o'clock. By mid-day the bridge over the Sambre at Marchiennes was carried, and Pirch II. fell slowly back towards Charleroi, in accordance with his orders. Reille, delayed by the narrowness of the bridge, did not get his corps across till well on in the afternoon.[2] D'Erlon, coming after the 2nd Corps, did not begin crossing the Sambre till 4.30 P.M.

Gérard's corps moved late from Philippeville, as part did not arrive till the morning of the 15th, and only reached its point of rendezvous (Florennes) at 7 A.M. It was directed at first on Charleroi, but after Bourmont's desertion (he was the Lieutenant-General commanding the leading division, the 14th), on Châtelet, to help the Emperor in the attack on Gilly. Whether

---

[1] See Ollech, p. 45. The actual line occupied by the Prussian outposts was as follows: the 1st Brigade held the line from the south of Binche, where its outposts joined on to those of the Dutch-Belgians, to Lobbes on the Sambre; from here the 2nd Brigade held the line Thuin, Ham-sur-Heure, Gerpinnes; from Gerpinnes to Denée was watched by a cavalry regiment, and from this place to Dinant the outpost line was furnished by the 4th Brigade.

[2] The Prussian outposts had been driven from Thuin, and this point captured by Jerome.

the desertion was the cause of this change in direction or not must remain a doubtful point; but anyhow the order enjoining it being sent off at 3.30, reached Gérard after he had started for Charleroi, and thus the change of route delayed him, so that he only reached Châtelet late in the day, and the whole of his corps did not cross the river that night.

The centre moved last, and its advance was delayed by the 3rd Corps, which was in front of the column, and which had received no orders, the aide-de-camp who took them on the previous evening having fallen off his horse and broken his leg. A second messenger was not sent, and thus Vandamme was without instructions. This blocked up the route by which the 6th Corps and Guards were to advance on Charleroi. Pajol, with his cavalry, however, pushed on, and drove the Prussian outposts back on Charleroi, which he reached between 9 and 10 A.M. Having no infantry with him, he was unable to capture the bridge there until reinforced by Duhesme's division of the Guard about eleven or twelve o'clock, which the Emperor sent on by a rapid march along a by-road, when he heard of Vandamme's delay. Pirch II. with his brigade fell back toward Gilly. Pajol sent the 1st Hussars up the Brussels road, and went with the other two of his divisions after Pirch.

Napoleon reached Charleroi with Duhesme's division, and sent Gourgaud up the Brussels road with the 1st Hussars. He returned about two o'clock and reported that Gosselies was strongly held. The Emperor then ordered Reille to advance on this village. To guard himself from attack from the north he sent some infantry with a battery up the road, and shortly afterwards supported these by the Light Cavalry of the Guard. He also ordered d'Erlon to march on Gosselies to help Reille. As the troops of Grouchy and Vandamme came up they were pushed up the road towards Gilly.

Reille moved on Gosselies, but was vigorously resisted by the 1st Brigade of Zieten's corps and by the cavalry. Steinmetz was for a time in considerable danger, being on the west of the Piéton when the advanced troops of Reille's corps were at Jumet, but after some severe fighting he contrived to draw off his men by Gosselies and Heppignies to Fleurus, where he joined the rest of the I. Prussian Corps.

In the meantime Pirch's brigade (the 2nd) of Zieten's corps had been slowly retiring to Gilly, where it was joined by a part of Jagow's (the 3rd) brigade from Châtelet. The ground was favourable for a rear-guard action, and the woods which exist beyond Gilly prevented the French ascertaining accurately the force before them. Grouchy did not care to act in these circumstances, and went back to the Emperor for orders. Napoleon himself rode out to the front, gave verbal instructions to Grouchy to take command of the right wing, and then returned to Charleroi to hasten up Vandamme. But considerable delay arose in making the arrangements for the attack, and the Emperor once more went forward to the front of the column.

It was now 6 P.M., and too late to carry out a decisive combat; but the remaining daylight sufficed to drive the Prussians back with loss on Fleurus, where Zieten was able to concentrate his whole corps, holding the village with two battalions, his main body, however, being in rear of it towards the Nivelles-Namur roads. During the day's fighting the I. Corps lost 1200 men.

To return to the left wing. Ney, who joined Napoleon at Charleroi about three o'clock, was ordered by him to take command of the two corps forming it, and Lefebvre-Desnoëttes' Light Cavalry Division, and told to advance along the road to Brussels.

Ney arrived at Gosselies, probably at 4.30, just as Reille's men were forming for the attack on Steinmetz's brigade, which occupied the village with a portion while the rest was falling back towards Fleurus. It was not the aim of the Prussian commander to do more than draw off his men, and, after a brisk counter-attack, which forced back the leading French troops, he retired toward Heppignies with some loss, followed, but scarcely pursued, by Piré's cavalry. Ney now sent on Lefebvre-Desnoëttes with the Guard Light Cavalry, supporting it with Bachelu's division, which he sent to Mellet. It seems probable that Ney told Lefebvre to reconnoitre as far as Quatre Bras, and to occupy it if possible with a cavalry post.

The first opposition Lefebvre met with was from a battalion and a battery at Frasnes covering the front of Prince Bernhard's brigade, which was billeted in the neighbourhood of Quatre Bras.

The Nassauers, their left flank threatened by a turning movement, fell back and took up a position in front of Quatre Bras and in the Bossu wood, and here they were joined by the rest of Prince

Bernhard's brigade. But it was getting late, Lefebvre had no infantry or guns with him, and thus being unable to press the enemy to any extent, broke off the combat and took up post at Frasnes for the night. From this village at 9 P.M. he sent back the following report to Ney[1]:—

FRASNES,
15<i>th June</i> 1815, 9 P.M.

To the MARSHAL PRINCE OF THE MOSKOWA.

MY LORD,—When we arrived at Frasnes, in accordance with your orders, we found it occupied by a regiment of Nassau infantry of about 1500 men and 8 guns. As they observed we were manœuvring to turn them, they retired from the village, where we had practically enveloped them with our squadrons. General Colbert even reached within musket shot of Quatre Bras on the high road[2]; but as the ground was difficult and the enemy fell back for support to the Bossu wood, and as he fired with great vigour from his 8 guns, it was impossible for us to carry it.

The troops which were found at Frasnes had not advanced this morning and were not engaged at Gosselies. They are under the orders of Lord Wellington, and appear to be retiring towards Nivelles. They set a light to a beacon at Quatre Bras and fired their guns a great deal. None of the troops who fought this morning at Gosselies have passed this way; they marched towards Fleurus.

The peasants can give no information as to a large assembly of troops in this neighbourhood; only that

---

[1] These documents, which are in the French War Office, are now for the first time published *in extenso*. They are the actual reports of the two principals concerned, viz., Lefebvre-Desnoëttes and Ney, explaining what each did in pursuance of the orders received.

[2] Colbert commanded the lancers of Lefebvre's division.

there is a park of artillery at Tubise, composed of 100 ammunition waggons and 12 guns; they say that the Belgian army is in the environs of Mons, and that the headquarters of the young Prince Frederick of Orange are at Braine-le-Comte. We took about fifteen prisoners, and we have had ten men killed and wounded.

To-morrow, at break of day, if it is possible, I shall send to Quatre Bras a reconnoitring post to occupy that place, for I think that the Nassau troops have left it.

A battalion of infantry has just arrived, which I have placed in front of the village.[1] My artillery not having rejoined me, I have sent orders for it to bivouac with Bachelu's division; it will rejoin me to-morrow morning.

I have not written to the Emperor, not having anything more important to tell him than what I am telling your Excellency.—I have the honour, &c.,

LEFEBVRE-DESNOËTTES.

I am sending you a non-commissioned officer to receive the orders of your Excellency.

I have the honour to observe to your Excellency that the enemy has shown no cavalry in front of us; but the artillery is light artillery.[2]

---

[1] This battalion was evidently the one sent on from Bachelu's division. Houssaye says, p. 130, that when Lefebvre arrived in front of Frasnes (about 5.30 P.M.) and found infantry and artillery there, he sent back for infantry. There is no mention of this in Lefebvre's report to Ney; on the contrary, he implies that the battalion had just arrived at Frasnes as he returned there, and he evidently had not expected it. He had no artillery, as we see from his report. Prince Bernhard had, therefore, only to deal with cavalry. This accounts for the very few casualties among the Nassauers, who only lost forty men killed and wounded (see de Bas, p. 539). Prince Bernhard had about 4400 men and 8 guns, Lefebvre 1800 cavalry and no guns, but he contrived to push back the Nassauers. It may be inferred they made no very strenuous resistance.

[2] About fifty of the 1st Silesian Hussars had retired towards Quatre Bras, and were taken to that point by Perponcher on the 16th.

Now it is clear from the fact that Lefebvre reported in writing to Ney a detailed account of what he had done from the beginning, that the Marshal was not present during the fight. Had he been there the report would only have commenced from the time he left the scene of action. Where Ney was, it was impossible to say—possibly he went to Mellet, to Bachelu's division, and may have sent on from there the battalion to aid the cavalry when he heard the sound of firing.

However this may be, at 11 P.M. he sent in a report to the Chief of the Staff as follows:—

GOSSELIES,
11*th June* 1815, 11 P.M.

To HIS EXCELLENCY THE MARSHAL CHIEF OF THE STAFF.

SIR,—I have the honour to report to your Excellency that in accordance with the orders of the Emperor I advanced to Gosselies this afternoon to dislodge the enemy from this point with the cavalry of General Piré and the infantry of General Bachelu. The enemy made only a slight resistance. After an exchange of 25 to 30 cannon shots he fell back by Heppignies on Fleurus. We have made 500 or 600 Prussian prisoners from the corps of General Zieten.

Here is the position of the troops:

General Lefebvre-Desnoëttes with the Lancers and Chasseurs of the Guard at Frasnes.
General Bachelu with the 5th Division at Mellet.
General Foy with the 9th Division at Gosselies.
The Light Cavalry of General Piré at Heppignies.
I do not know where General Reille is. General

NAPOLEON'S ORDERS TO NEY

Count d'Erlon has sent to inform me that he is at Jumet with the greater portion of his Army Corps. I have just sent him the instructions prescribed by your Excellency's letter of to-day's date. I annex to my letter a report of General Lefebvre-Desnoëttes.

(Signed) THE MARSHAL PRINCE OF THE MOSKOWA,
NEY.

The report probably expresses the carrying out of the orders given to him by Napoleon.

The tenor of these has been much disputed. The version usually accepted is as follows :—

"Good morning, Ney ! I am very glad to see you. You are going to have command of the 1st and 2nd Army Corps. I am giving you also the Guard Light Cavalry, but don't use it. To-morrow you will get Kellermann's Cuirassiers. Go and push back the enemy along the Brussels road, and take post at Quatre Bras."

There is one great objection, at any rate, to the details of this order—viz., that a general of the capacity of Napoleon, if it is to be believed, gave Ney troops and then told him not to use them! It is too large a demand on our credulity.[1] Napoleon meant Ney to use the Guard Light Cavalry, which the Emperor had sent on before the Prince of the Moskowa

[1] See Houssaye, pp. 122, 123. There are, as a matter of fact, as many witnesses against this so-called order as there are for it. Soult has distinctly stated that this order was not given till the 16th. Jomini takes this view—see his letter to Ney's son in 1841, published in his 'Précis politique et militaire de la campagne de 1815,' placed at the end and headed "importante." This book was not issued till 1841, though the preface is dated 1839. Ney's report seems finally to settle the question.

arrived at Charleroi, he did use it, and Napoleon on the 16th did not blame him for having done so.

In the bulletin issued at Charleroi on the 15th June it is stated that "Ney had his headquarters at Quatre Bras in the evening." Some authors, therefore, insist that Napoleon must have ordered Ney to occupy this point, but it does not require a very intimate acquaintance with Napoleon's bulletins to know that it is quite impossible to rely upon them. To "lie like a bulletin" has become a proverb, and to base an argument merely on what Napoleon said in a bulletin would be to rest it on a very insecure foundation. A little consideration of Ney's report shows that he was told to push back the troops reported by Gourgaud to be holding Gosselies. Lefebvre's duty was to *reconnoitre* to Quatre Bras, a very different task from *seizing* it, which was inadvisable on the 15th.

For Napoleon knew he would meet the Prussians first, and in his letter to Davout of the 14th June he distinctly anticipates doing so,[1] and his object was to crush them before he attempted to defeat Wellington. He believed that his advance had taken Blucher by surprise, and that the latter would not be able to bring the whole of his corps against him, and he would thus have the opportunity of defeating them in detail. Now even on the 16th he estimated the Prussians in front of him at only 40,000 men.[2] This was due to the position of their original

---

[1] See 'Correspondance Militaire,' letter to Davout of 14th June.

[2] See 'Correspondance Militaire,' instructions to Marshal Ney, issued on the 16th June from Charleroi.

cantonments—he probably knew where these were, and that Thielmann's corps was at Dinant. When this corps was ordered to move to Namur on the evening of the 14th, outposts were left behind, and these formed, with those of the II. Corps, a continuous chain from Dinant up the Meuse to its junction with the Sambre. The patrols sent out by Gérard's corps would most likely have reported that there were outposts in that direction; this would lead Napoleon to believe that, apprehensive of some movement in this direction, Blucher had not brought up the III. Corps, and he knew that Bülow's was far away back at Liége. From Dinant to Sombreffe is 29 miles, from Liége to Sombreffe is 48 miles, hence allowing that he had only Zieten and Pirch to deal with, and deducting the losses which the former had sustained on the 15th, there could not be more than 40,000 or 50,000 Prussians about Sombreffe. Napoleon, therefore, acted throughout the 15th and 16th on the assumption that the Prussians could not bring at the best more than two corps to oppose him. As he systematically underestimated the enemy before an action and exaggerated their numbers afterwards, to make the task seem easier to his troops before, and more glorious for them after, a battle, so in this case he would put them at only 40,000 before the fight. Knowing Wellington's wide spread-out cantonments, he judged that the latter would not be able to concentrate his whole force before he had defeated the Prussians, and he intended to hold Wellington off while he was doing so.

This was the General Idea of his proposed operations both on the 15th and 16th. What, then, would be the part to be played by his Left on the first date? Plainly, while it should be in a position on the 16th which would keep Wellington back and allow Napoleon to defeat the Prussians, yet on the 15th it would have been undesirable to push it too far to the front, until it became more certain what the course of action on the morrow would be. To send Ney to Quatre Bras on the 15th would have been to invite disaster if Wellington contrived to concentrate sufficient numbers against him. Napoleon must have been aware when he gave him his orders that d'Erlon was pretty far behind, and that Ney had only Reille's corps with him. Moreover, Lefebvre's report shows the Emperor thought there was some large force of the Anglo-Allies not far from Quatre Bras. It would have been wrong, therefore, to have given Ney any definite orders to hold it, and it seems certain that the instructions to the Prince of the Moskowa were only to move up the Brussels road, push back any force that might be found about Gosselies, and reconnoitre with his cavalry to Quatre Bras. The Emperor would then judge from Ney's reports what the position was on his left, and issue orders accordingly. Now this, we have seen, is what was done, and Napoleon appears to have been content with Ney's conduct on the 15th, for he certainly addressed no word of complaint to him in his letters of the 16th June. At 3 P.M. the troops had been on their legs nearly twelve hours, Bachelu had marched twenty miles, and would have had five more to go to reach

Quatre Bras, only this division could have got there, certainly not a sufficiently large force to hold it strongly, and the others were five and more miles behind.[1]

When night fell the French were placed thus: Reille's corps held the Brussels road; Bachelu's division being at Mellet, covered by Piré's cavalry; the Light Cavalry of the Guard at Frasnes; Foy's division at Gosselies; Jerome's half a mile behind this village; and Girard's at Wangenies. The last had been sent against Steinmetz, by order of the Emperor, at 8 P.M., and was now left to keep touch with the French right wing. D'Erlon's corps had Durutte's and Donzelot's divisions between Jumet and Gosselies, Marcognet at Marchiennes, Allix at Thuin. Jacquinot had one brigade at Jumet, the other at Sobray. Of the right, one division only of Gérard's corps had crossed the Sambre at Châtelet. Pajol and Exelmanns were between Lambusart and Campinaire; Kellermann at Châtelineau. Vandamme's corps held a line from Wainage to the Soleilmont Wood. In the centre, the Guard alone had passed the river. Lobau's entire corps, and Delort's cavalry division, being still on the right bank of the Sambre.

The report from the right flank, sent in by Vandamme to the Emperor, was that the Prussians, whom

---

[1] Napoleon in his criticism of Rogniat's book, 'Considerations sur l'art de la Guerre' (see 'Commentaires,' vol. vi. pp. 145-6), distinctly states that to have occupied Sombreffe would have spoiled his plan, as Blucher would not then have fought at Ligny. If he did not wish to push his Right Wing to Sombreffe, most certainly the Left Wing would not have been ordered to Quatre Bras, as this would have still more betrayed his plan of action. This, combined with the evidence of Ney's report, is a plain contradiction of the Emperor's statement that he ordered its occupation.

he estimated at twelve to fifteen thousand men, were in full retreat, having left only cavalry outposts in Fleurus. By Pajol Napoleon was informed that he would have taken Fleurus if Vandamme had lent him some infantry. Both, therefore, agreed that the enemy had retired.

The Prussian corps were situated as follow: The I. Corps at Fleurus; the II. at Onoz and Mazy; the III. had reached Namur; the IV. was still round Liége. Bülow had judged from Gneisenau's orders that no great haste was needed, and had therefore only ordered preparations for an early march to Hannut the next day.

The Anglo-Allied troops were, to all intents and purposes, in the posts they had previously.

On the 15th the Prince of Orange left his headquarters at Braine-le-Comte at five in the morning and rode to van Merlen at St Symphorien. He was told that the French dispositions were the same as yesterday. After issuing a few minor orders, he rode straight back to Brussels, where he had been asked to dinner by the Duke.[1]

---

[1] De Bas, 'Prins Frederik der Nederlanden en Zijn Tijd,' vol. iii. part ii. p. 532, states that the Prince was back at Braine-le-Comte at 8.30, that he changed his clothes and rode off to Brussels at 10.30 with Captain Lord George Russell (one of his English aides-de-camp). But Sir William Berkeley, who was a staff officer at Braine-le-Comte, states distinctly that the Prince rode out at five and had not come back at 2 P.M. See 'Supplementary Despatches,' vol. x. p. 480.

De Bas says (p. 533) that de Constant Rebecque determined to keep the Prince's absence secret and to act on his own authority. Now it must have been known that the Prince had been invited to dine with Wellington, and that he and some of his staff had been invited to the Duchess of Richmond's ball. If he had returned to Braine-le-Comte and stayed there an hour, it is incredible that he was not seen by some of his staff and that he told no

About 3 P.M. a rumour reached Brussels that there had been an affair of outposts, and that the French had been repulsed. This was told to the officers of a regiment (either the Royals or the 92nd) when they were at dinner, by some Belgian gentlemen.[1] The first authentic news of the French attack came shortly after. It had been sent in to Braine-le-Comte by General Behr from Mons, and reached the Prince's headquarters "a few minutes before twelve."[2] It was to the following effect: That he had received information from van Merlen, who informed him that General

one that he was going on to Brussels. He must have talked to some one about his visit to the outposts, and the fact that he had nothing of importance to report would have been noted. But plainly nothing of the kind occurred, or it would have been alluded to later in reporting to Wellington. But if, thoughtlessly as a young man might, he had originally merely said he was going out to the outposts, and had then gone on straight to Brussels, Constant, not knowing whether he was coming back or not, might very well have said he did not know where the Prince was, feeling that his absence was very unfortunate at such a crisis, and thinking he might at any moment return. If the Chief of the Staff knew his Commander had gone to Brussels, what object was there in concealing the fact? Plainly the former did not know where the latter was, but to conceal the culpable remissness of the Prince in saying only that he was going out to the outposts, and then not returning as was expected, he pretended he was at Braine-le-Comte. The statement that the Prince returned to Braine-le-Comte is unworthy of credence, and it is plainly contradicted by the action of his Chief of the Staff. The latter sent off a message from Behr to Brussels on the chance that the Prince might have gone there, or in the hope that some one might open the communication and give it to Wellington. But he did not know where the Prince was.

[1] See Operations of the 5th Division by an Officer of the Division, in the 'United Service Journal,' 1841, part ii., p. 172. This relation was thought sufficiently important to be translated into the 'Journal de l'armée belge' in 1841, and from this into the 'Militair Wochenblatt' in 1846. According to many authors the Prince of Orange had heard firing when at the outposts in the morning. Was this rumour due to him or some member of his staff who came with him to Brussels?

[2] De Bas, p. 533.

Steinmetz commanding at Fontaine L'Evêque had just sent an officer to say the 2nd Prussian Brigade had been attacked that morning, and that the alarm guns had been fired all along the line. Apparently the attack was directed on Charleroi, where a lively fire of musketry was heard. All was quiet in front of the advanced posts of van Merlen, and the same was the case with those in front of Mons.[1]

Constant in his diary states that he sent in the report to the Prince as soon as he received it.

> I am sending this news immediately to the Prince at Brussels, and at the same time the order to General Perponcher to assemble his 1st Brigade on the Quatre Bras side of the Nivelles road and his 2nd Brigade at Quatre Bras itself. To General Chassé and to General Collaert their divisions, the first at Fayt, the second at la Haine.[2]

Löben-Sels gives the time these orders were sent out as 3 o'clock in the afternoon.[3] But if Constant

---

[1] See 'Supplementary Despatches,' vol. x. p. 481. There is no time of despatch given on this report, but it is plainly the one which General Constant received, and which, he says, he sent on at once to the Prince.

[2] De Bas quotes from this diary, which is among the State Records at The Hague. See p. 534. Pflugk-Hartung states, see p. 378, that Colonel de Bas informed him that the diary is in Constant's own handwriting, and that it appears to have been written at the time, but that later additions have been made to it.

[3] Löben-Sels' 'Précis de la Campagne de 1815 dans les Pays-Bas,' p. 128, Prince Bernhard denied that he had any orders during the day. If Constant did not send them to Perponcher till 3 P.M., the time he gives for doing so, they could not have reached the Prince before he had started for Quatre Bras.

did not send on the report to Brussels till 3 P.M. it could not have reached there till half-past five or six, whereas from the Duke's own statement he obtained the first news from the Prince of Orange, who came to dine with him at three o'clock. It seems, therefore, that Constant was speaking very generally when he used the word immediately, and that he did forward the report fairly soon after it reached Braine-le-Comte, although the orders were issued later.

Shortly after Behr's message came to Braine-le-Comte a report arrived from Dörnberg, which was as follows:—

> *Major-Gen. Sir W. Dörnberg to Lord FitzRoy Somerset.*
>
> MONS, 15*th June* 1815, ½-*past* 9 *o'clock in the morning.*
>
> MY LORD,—A picket of French Lancers has been placed again at Autreffe, on the Bavay Road; but at Quivrain there are only National Guards, with a few gendarmes.
>
> A man who was yesterday at Maubeuge says that all the troops march towards Beaumont and Philippeville, and that no other troops but National Guards remained at Maubeuge. He thinks that near 40,000 men have passed that place.
>
> I have sent towards Pont sur Sambre, where, I believe, a corps remains.
>
> I just hear the Prussians were attacked.[1]

This report contained nothing of importance, and

---

[1] See 'Supplementary Despatches,' vol. x. p. 481.

added but little to the information sent in by Behr shortly before, and of which the British Assistant-Quartermaster-General was fully aware, as he was in the room with Constant when it arrived.[1]

Now it was known that the Prince was absent, and as Behr's report had gone on to Brussels there was no special object to be gained by sending Dörnberg's on at once. But then came further information from General Chassé at Haine St Pierre and from van Merlen at St Symphorien, the latter now sending direct to Braine-le-Comte. The news which both officers despatched about eleven was much to the effect of Behr's message; but van Merlen also stated that Steinmetz was retiring from Binche to Gosselies, and that if pressed the I. Corps would concentrate at Fleurus. This threefold information from the Dutch-Belgian advance posts was sufficiently important to be forwarded. Some consultation naturally took place; Sir George Berkeley was asked by Constant to forward the substance of the new reports from Merlen and Chassé; with it he sent on Dörnberg's letter.

Berkeley's letter to Lord FitzRoy Somerset is dated Braine-le-Comte, 2 P.M., and in it he states that the Prince

> having set out at five o'clock this morning for the advanced posts, and not being returned, I forward the enclosed letter from General Dörnberg. General Constant desires I would inform you that the reports just

---

[1] See de Bas, p. 533.

received from different quarters state that the Prussians had been attacked upon their line in front of Charleroi ; that they have evacuated Binche, and meant to collect first at Gosselies.

Everything is quiet upon our front; and the 3rd Division of the Netherlands is collected at Fay.[1] He sends you also the copy of a letter from the Commandant at Mons.

Thus Constant made sure that the Duke would get all the information received, even if the messenger who took in Behr's report had not succeeded in finding the Prince of Orange.

Berkeley's letter, which started not later than 2.30, must have reached the Duke about 5.30, as there was only 21 miles for it to go in full daylight. Some authorities have stated it did not reach Brussels till much later, but there is absolutely no foundation for this statement. The two reports from Braine, coupled with one which, as we shall see latter, arrived from the Prussians, determined Wellington to issue the first series of orders.

Zieten first became aware of the French advance at 4.30 A.M., when the sound of guns and musketry was heard on the right flank — *i.e.*, the attack of Reille's men on Steinmetz's troops at Thuin. He at once informed Blucher, and fired off the alarm guns which formed the signal for the various brigades to assemble.[2] At 8.15 A.M., further reports having

[1] Fay or Fayt.
[2] Both Damitz and Clausewitz state that Zieten sent in a report to Wellington about 4.30 A.M. Ollech and Lettow-Vorbeck copy this statement, but give no evidence for it. This does not seem to have been the case, no trace of it having arrived at Brussels is to be found, while the

come in, he sent in to the Prussian Commander-in-Chief to say that Thuin was captured and the outposts at Montigny-Lestigneis driven back.[1] The enemy was advancing on the left bank of the Sambre, and that the French were too strong to permit isolated fights, and the 1st and 2nd Brigades were therefore being withdrawn to the line Gosselies-Gilly. This would enable them to cover the retreat of the 1st Brigade from Thuin. Napoleon was present with the whole of his Guards, and therefore serious attacks were to be expected at this point. The enemy showed a large amount of cavalry. The enemy was not advancing in the direction of Nalines. He added that he had sent this information to Wellington, and had asked him to concentrate on Nivelles in accordance with the information he had from Müffling the day before.[2]

words of the same report actually sent to Blucher show that it was eminently improbable that Zieten did so. The despatch runs as follows :—
"Since half-past four, gun and musket shots have been heard on the right flank. No report has yet come in. As soon as information is received I shall not fail to let your Highness know. I am ordering the troops into their positions, and if necessary shall concentrate at Fleurus."
It is scarcely credible that any commander would have sent in so bald an announcement to anybody but his own Chief. See Lettow-Vorbeck, footnote, p. 252. Charras's statement that Wellington received at nine o'clock a despatch from Zieten is a mistake. This was the time of sending off, not the time of receipt. See 'Wellington Despatches,' vol. xii. p. 473.

[1] Lettow-Vorbeck suggests as the name of this place Les Tigneu. It seems to me quite clear that Montignies-le-Tilleul is the place.

[2] This information was brought by Colonel Pfuel. It is difficult to prove absolutely that definite arrangements had been come to between Wellington and Blucher as to the exact movements which were to be made by both, taking into consideration the various lines by which Napoleon might advance, but it is probable that without going as far as Müffling suggests, some general understanding existed, and judging from the despatch sent

ZIETEN'S REPORTS

Zieten's first report, sent off from Charleroi at five o'clock, reached Blucher about nine o'clock, and Blucher replied that he had ordered the II., III., and IV. Army Corps to concentrate, and that the II. would be at Onoz and Mazy, the III. at Namur, and the IV. at Hannut by the evening. Zieten was to closely observe the movements of the enemy and the direction and strength of the columns, and to watch the neighbourhood of Binch and the Roman Road. Zieten's next report to Blucher—*i.e.*, the one sent off at 8.15—reached the latter about half-past eleven. Gneisenau at once sent the substance of it to Müffling for Wellington's information, and added that Zieten had been told to closely observe the enemy, and if possible not to fall back farther than Fleurus. The Prussian Army would be concentrated at Sombreffe the next morning, and the Prince intended to accept battle there. The Headquarters would leave for Sombreffe in a couple of hours, where information would be awaited from Müffling as to when and where Wellington would concentrate and what he determined to do. The line of communication between

by Zieten to Blucher on the 15th June at 8.15 A.M., it would seem that the possibility of an advance against the centre of the Allied forces—*i.e.*, by the Charleroi road—had not been left out of consideration, and that in this case Wellington proposed to gather his forces together about Nivelles, holding on to Quatre Bras, while Blucher would assemble his about Sombreffe. Plotho, page 20, gives Nivelles, and so does Müffling in his letter to Blucher in the evening of the 16th June. That Quatre Bras was to be held is proved by the position of Prince Bernhard's troops, and by the fact it was there that the brigade was to assemble in case of alarm. See de Bas, page 1148, where the rendezvous of the 1st and 2nd Brigades of Perponcher's Division are given as Nivelles and Quatre Bras. It was with this knowledge that Perponcher's Division was sent to the latter place by de Constant Rebecque.

the two armies should now be opened through Genappe.

It has been very much disputed as to whether Zieten's information or Gneisenau's letter reached Müffling first. From Charleroi to Brussels is about 34 miles, from Namur to Brussels is about 41 miles. It would be reasonable therefore to suppose that Zieten's would reach first. It appears probable that it did, and that it arrived in Brussels some time after three, and was taken to Wellington about 4 P.M. It doubtless took an unconscionably long time to reach Müffling, and various reasons have been given to explain this, none of them very trustworthy,—among others Wellington's statement that the officer who brought it was stout. But be this as it may, the despatch took six hours to go a distance of 34 miles. Had Zieten's information been sent in with proper speed it could easily have reached Brussels by half-past one or two in the afternoon, but it is perfectly certain that no news from the Prussians did reach Wellington until after he had received the information sent from Braine-le-Comte by Constant. The suggestion that the news from Namur, which did not arrive there till twelve, reached Wellington before Zieten's despatch, is—on the score of the greater distance it had to come and the fact that it left Namur three hours after Zieten's left Charleroi—scarcely credible.

The most probable sequence of the news from the front to Brussels appears to be as follows:—

(1) Behr's report, sent on from Braine-le-Comte by Constant, to the Prince of Orange at

Brussels. This reached Wellington a little after three.[1]

(2) Zieten's report from Charleroi, sent off at nine o'clock, which reached Müffling about half-past three and Wellington about four.[2]

---

[1] This is quite clear, Wellington says so, see his despatch, and it is probable, because Constant sent it off after twelve, probably about 12.30.

[2] Müffling states this in 'Passages from my Life,' p. 229. This is confirmed by Hügel, one of the Prussian envoys at Brussels. See Pfister, 'Aus dem Lager des Verbundeten,' p. 366. It is worth while to quote this at length. General Hügel was a Prussian representative at Wellington's headquarters, whence he reported the course of events to Berlin. At six o'clock on the 15th June he wrote a report, of which, unfortunately, the whole is not given in Pfister's book, but he states: "At this moment (apparently referring to some earlier time) a Prussian hussar rides in to General Müffling, who lives close to me, and brings him information which Müffling at once imparts to me, that in the forenoon Napoleon had attacked the Prussian Army on the Sambre near Thuin. Result not yet known. Müffling has just come back from the Duke. The Crown Prince of the Netherlands has reported that on our left flank a considerable cannonade is heard.

"Wellington at once ordered all his corps to march through the whole night and concentrate. Müffling allowed me to read Zieten's report. He was obliged, in consequence of the considerable superiority of forces, to withdraw his outposts to about Fleurus."

It will be observed that—

(1) The report is one from Zieten.
(2) It is brought in by a hussar.
(3) Müffling has come back from the Duke.
(4) The letter to Berlin is written after Wellington has determined to issue orders.
(5) The time of the letter is 6 P.M.

It follows that, as Müffling states, the first intimation *was* Zieten's report, not the copy of the same sent off by Blucher. A quite reasonable explanation of the time it took—about six and a half hours—to reach Brussels is to be found in Wellington's statement about the "fattest officer," which the Duke doubtless got in conversation with Müffling, to whom he was sent by Zieten. He also appears to have been rather a stupid one. For it is plain that he rode through the Nassau outposts at Frasnes and through Genappe where Prince Bernhard was without saying one word

92   THE CAMPAIGN OF 1815

(3) Berkeley's letter, with Dörnberg's report and further information from Chassé and van Merlen, which reached Wellington some time after five.¹

(4) Gneisenau's letter from Namur to Müffling, sending on Zieten's information of 8.15 A.M., saying what Blucher was doing, and asking Müffling what Wellington's intentions were. This arrived about six.²

Now, it will be observed that the total sum of the information received by Wellington was that the

about the French attack or mentioning the important news he carried. Müffling's letter to Blucher, sent off at seven o'clock, in which he states "the news has just arrived that Lieutenant-General Zieten has been attacked" (see Pflugk-Hartung, p. 55), plainly refers to the report which Gneisenau sent from Namur after he had received Zieten's of 8.15 A.M. It was brought in by two aides-de-camp (zwei adjutanten), who reached Brussels about half-past five or six, being seen by the officer of Pack's brigade about the latter time in the park.

¹ The message had only 21 miles to go. Damitz, giving no authority, says it did not reach till midnight (see Damitz, vol. i. p. 105). It is ridiculous to imagine it took eight or nine hours to do the distance. The argument of Pflugk-Hartung, that because the officer of Pack's brigade says a dragoon arrived about 10 P.M., that therefore he must have brought Berkeley's letter, is such a case of extreme special pleading that it may be rejected. Nor does his suggestion that Müffling confirms this view carry any more weight. There are so many assumptions necessary to account for the orderly bringing this report being eight or ten hours on the road, of which six and a half were broad daylight, that it is more probable that the assumptions are entirely without foundation, and that the message took some two and a half to three hours. Pflugk-Hartung is willing to believe two Prussian officers rode over 40 miles in four hours (see Pflugk-Hartung, p. 53), but thinks a British orderly would take eight to do about 20. Damitz is plainly wrong in his statement, and Dörnberg's despatch, as will be seen by reference to p. 85, contains no such definite information as he suggests.

² See the officer of Pack's brigade, 'United Service Journal,' 1841, part ii., p. 172.

THE PRUSSIAN SHORTCOMINGS 93

French were apparently moving on Charleroi, and that they were doing nothing in the neighbourhood of Mons; *but at time of issuing his first orders on the evening of the 15th June, absolutely no information of any kind later than 9 A.M. had reached him from Charleroi as to the fighting there.* He had no idea as to whether the Prussians were holding their own, nor did he know anything whatever about the French movements later than the hour named.

For Zieten failed to send any further intelligence, and did not even inform Prince Bernhard, who first knew of the French attack merely by the vague reports of fugitives from Charleroi, who began to arrive at Genappe about 11 A.M. Now, Blucher depended on the Commander of the I. Corps to send all information to Wellington, and naturally concluded the latter would carry out the instructions given him and keep the Duke fully informed of the movements of the enemy.[1] It is therefore entirely due to the faulty arrangements of the Prussians that no information reached the Anglo-Allied Commander as to the result of the fighting in which they had been engaged from dawn of day.

It was impossible that Wellington could have had any information from Quatre Bras at the time the orders were issued, for even if Prince Edward of Saxe-Weimar had reported to Brussels when he himself

---

[1] Zieten had been told to keep Wellington posted with his movements and with all that took place on his front. This he had carefully done, and evidence shows that up to the 15th the Commander of the Prussian 1st Corps had sent into Brussels all the information that his outposts collected, but failed to do so when hostilities commenced.

moved with his brigade to Quatre Bras, the news could hardly have come to Brussels before the Duke issued them. Such a message, if sent, might have arrived about 8 P.M. But so far as existing evidence goes, the Prince only sent information to his immediate commander, Perponcher, at Nivelles, and he only did this at 9 P.M. He has himself left on record that he received no orders, and that his advance to Quatre Bras was simply due to a report from the officer commanding the advanced post at Frasnes that the French were advancing in force. This appears to have reached Prince Bernhard about 4 P.M.[1]

Wellington therefore could, until some definite information arrived, do nothing more than order his troops to be in readiness. The little news that he had received showed that an attack was being made against the Prussians, but this did not preclude a French advance against Wellington.

When Müffling brought Zieten's despatch to him he said, "If all is as General von Ziethen supposes, I will concentrate on my left wing"—*i.e.*, the corps of the Prince of Orange. "I shall then be *à portée* to fight in conjunction with the Prussian army. Should, however, a portion of the enemy's forces come by Mons, I must concentrate more towards my centre. For this reason I must positively wait for news from Mons before I fix my rendezvous. Since, however, the departure of the troops is certain, and only the place

[1] See 'Das Leben des Herzog Bernhard von Sachsen Weimar-Eisenach,' by Starklof, vol. i. p. 180 *et seq.*

of rendezvous remains uncertain, I will order all to be in readiness," &c.[1]

Then came the news from Mons, but it was still quite indefinite. Wellington, however, determined to prepare his troops to move and to draw in those portions of his extreme right which could not be required there if the Emperor were using the larger part of his troops against the Prussians. For this would involve the reduction of any attempt on the Anglo-Allied right to very small proportions.[2] Wellington's statement, with regard to the reasons for issuing the orders, is quite clear and is contained in his despatch.[3] He states:—

(1) He did not hear of the attack on the Prussian posts at Thuin and Lobbes till the evening.

(2) He immediately ordered the troops "to prepare to march."

(3) Afterwards he ordered them "to march to their left as soon as he had intelligence from other quarters to prove that the enemy's movement upon Charleroi was the real attack."

(4) After these orders, when he got some further news confirming the first, he "directed the whole army on Quatre Bras."

This we shall see is exactly what did occur.

---

[1] See Müffling's 'Passages,' &c. p. 229. Zieten's name was spelt as given.

[2] It must always remain an unsolvable problem to explain why Wellington thought Napoleon would divide his forces. It was an idea totally foreign to all the Emperor's ideas of war.

[3] The despatch will be found in the Appendix.

The orders issued were to the following effect [1]:—

General Dörnberg's brigade of cavalry and the Cumberland Hussars to march on Vilvorde, and bivouac on the highroad near that town.

The Earl of Uxbridge will please to collect the cavalry this night at Ninove, leaving the 2nd Hussars looking out between the Scheldt and Lys.

The 1st Division [to remain at Enghien, ready to move at the shortest notice.[2]

The 2nd Division] to collect this night at Ath and adjacents, ready to move at the shortest notice.

The 3rd Division to collect this night at Braine-le-Comte, ready to move at the shortest notice.

---

[1] The original orders were lost with the papers of Colonel De Lancey (see 'Wellington Despatches,' vol. xii. p. 474). Those printed here were not the orders sent out, but the memorandum written by Wellington and given to the Quartermaster-General on which to found them. This, too, was lost with Colonel De Lancey's papers. Those given above are taken from the two editions of Wellington's Despatches, the one of 1839 the other of 1852. Those of the former are stated by Colonel Gurwood to "have been collected from the different officers to whom they were addressed." (See vol. xii. *op. cit.*, p. 474.) In vol. viii., 1852 edition, it is stated they were furnished by Sir De Lacy Evans, who made copies from the originals given by the Duke to De Lancey, he being with the latter officer at the time the orders were issued. (See the 1852 edition, vol. viii. p. 142.) The time noted on the Duke's memorandum is 5 P.M. in the 1852 edition. This is impossible, and is probably merely a mistake in printing of 5 for 6. The writing commenced about seven, and the orders were all out in about two hours (see Jackson in 'United Service Journal,' 1841, p. 542, and also 'A Week at Waterloo,' by Lady De Lancey, pp. 43, 44). Jackson was a lieutenant in the Staff Corps, and was engaged in writing them. Allowing an hour for the collection of the officers for this purpose would make the time of the Duke's memorandum about six.

[2] The portion between brackets is omitted in the earlier impressions of the 'Wellington Despatches.' A good deal of writing has been wasted on the apparent omission of the Duke to issue orders to the 2nd Division, which would have been saved had the writers taken the trouble to investigate the question which has the above very simple solution.

THE DUKE'S ORDERS

4th Division at Grammont, except the troops beyond the Scheldt, which are to move to Oudenarde.

5th Division and the 6th Division to be ready to march at a moment's notice.[1] The brigade at Ghent to march to Brussels in the evening.

The Duke of Brunswick's corps to collect this night on the road between Brussels and Vilvorde; the Nassau troops to collect at daylight to-morrow morning on the Louvain road, both ready to march in the morning.

The Hanoverian Brigade of the 5th Division to collect at Hal, ready to move at daylight towards Brussels, and to halt between Alost and Assche for further orders.

The Prince of Orange is requested to collect at Nivelles the 2nd and 3rd Divisions of the Army of the Low Countries, and should that point have been attacked this day, to move the 3rd and 1st Divisions upon Nivelles as soon as collected. This movement is not to take place till it is quite certain that the enemy's attack is on the right of the Prussians and left of the British.

Lord Hill will be so good as to order Prince Frederick of Orange to occupy Oudenarde with 500 men, and to collect the 1st Division of the Army of the Low Countries and the Indian Brigade at Sotteghem, ready to march at daylight.

The Reserve Artillery, &c., to be in readiness to move at daylight.[2]

---

[1] The 5th Division was at first ordered to march off to Waterloo at 4 A.M., subsequently this departure was accelerated by two hours. (See 'United Service Journal,' 1841, part ii., p. 173. The 10th British Brigade, which formed part of the 6th Division, was at Ghent.

[2] Shortly before issuing these orders, however, it would seem that Wellington judged from the information which had reached him that the French attack had not developed further, for the Prince of Orange sent a letter to Braine, which reached there about nine o'clock, to say that the troops might return to their quarters in accordance with the usual custom, unless it was thought undesirable, and that they were to assemble again at four in the morning, that the Duke wished him to spend the evening at Brussels, and he would not therefore leave there before twelve or one

Apparently the Duke later on received some further information, for the following After Orders were issued at 10 P.M.[1]

The troops in Brussels (5th and 6th Divisions, Duke of Brunswick's and Nassau troops) to march when assembled from Brussels by the road of Namur, to the point where the road to Nivelles separates; to be followed by General Dörnberg's brigade and the Cumberland Hussars.

The 3rd Division of infantry to continue its movement from Braine-le-Comte upon Nivelles.

The 1st Division to move from Enghien on Braine-le-Comte.

The 2nd and 4th Divisions from Ath and Grammont also from Oudenarde, and to continue their movements on Enghien.

The cavalry to continue its movement from Ninhove upon Enghien.

The above movements to take place with as little delay as possible.

The After Orders being issued, Wellington went to the ball given by the Duchess of Richmond, at which many of the senior officers of the Anglo-Allied Army were present, his object being to encourage the loyal supporters of the cause of Europe, and show the doubtful friends or covert enemies that he regarded the

o'clock. For some time past the troops had assembled every morning in complete readiness to march off, and were therefore always available for movement in any direction.

[1] What this was, or whether the After Orders were merely due to Wellington thinking that the absence of further news of French movements showed the main attack was in the Charleroi direction, it is impossible to say. It may be that he did get news direct from Quatre Bras as to the advance of the French in that direction,—some of the Prussians who ran away and brought the news to Genappe very likely went on to Brussels.

rumours current as to the French movements with equanimity.

When the guests had sat down to supper an important despatch was brought to the Prince of Orange from Braine-le-Comte by Lieutenant Webster, one of his aides-de-camp.

The despatch in question, sent by Constant, dated Braine-le-Comte, 10.30 P.M., ran as follows:[1] "Captain Baron von Gagern has just arrived [at ten o'clock according to Constant's note-book] from Nivelles, reporting that the enemy had pushed up to Quatre Bras." Constant has therefore ordered Perponcher to support the 2nd Brigade by the 1st Brigade of his division. He had also sent an officer to Nivelles and Fay to find out the position of affairs at the former place, and to warn Chassé and Collaert, so that they could join together and support the 2nd Division (Dutch-Belgian) if necessary.

Constant had throughout the day shown a complete and masterly appreciation of the situation. In the morning, when the first reports came in from De Behr, Merlen, and Chassé, he had ordered "Perponcher to assemble his 1st Brigade near Nivelles toward Quatre Bras, and the 2nd at Quatre Bras itself, while Chassé was to concentrate his division at Fayt, and Collaert his cavalry behind the Haine." The orders now issued to these officers formed an extension of his early views, and show a clear perception of what was required.

But the Duke had already by his After Orders given instruction for a movement tending to draw the right

[1] See de Bas, p. 542.

of his forces in towards the left, and as this had been done and it was night, there was no need to issue any new instructions till daylight, for the orders he had given would ensure his troops moving in the required direction. In the course of the next morning Quatre Bras would, as the result of Constant's orders, be held by the 2nd Dutch-Belgian Division, while the 3rd Dutch-Belgian Division and the Dutch-Belgian cavalry would support it. The 3rd British Division would be at Nivelles, and could move on to Quatre Bras if necessary. The Reserve would be marching on Waterloo, and could be ordered on to the same place. Of his right he would have during the day the 1st Division at Braine-le-Comte, the 2nd and 4th Divisions about Enghien, with the whole of the cavalry. Thus he could deal either with an attack up the Charleroi road on Quatre Bras or with one in the direction of Binche, either towards the line of division between the Prussian and Anglo-Allied armies or more towards the left and centre of the latter.

The Duke left the ball about 2 P.M. Previous to doing so he told the superior officers present what orders he had given, and his views on the situation.

Dörnberg, who had been at Mons, his mission there being terminated by the outbreak of hostilities, rode into Brussels, reached Wellington between four and five on the 16th, and found him in bed. The Duke sprang up, told him that in all probability there would be a fight at Quatre Bras, and instructed him to ride at once to Waterloo and order Picton to advance his division to Quatre Bras.[1]

[1] See Pflugk-Hartung, p. 292.

THE DUKE GOES TO QUATRE BRAS

From this we may deduce the fact that, as the result of his conversation with Dörnberg, coupled with Constant's last despatch, the Commander of the Anglo-Allied army had at last come to a definite conclusion that Quatre Bras was the point to concentrate his forces at, and he therefore issued orders to this effect. The Quartermaster-General did not ride out with the Duke, as he and his officers were engaged in giving out the new instructions.[1]

That the Duke had not appreciated the seriousness of the attack on Quatre Bras till so late a period, was of course due to want of information. But the force stationed there had held its own fairly well.

When Prince Bernhard heard from his advanced battalion at Frasnes that the French were coming on in force, he issued orders for his brigade to assemble at Quatre Bras. This was accomplished between five and half-past, and the Prince determined to support his advanced post, saying to his commanding officers: "Although I have no orders of any kind, I have never yet heard of beginning a campaign with a retreat, and therefore we will hold on to Quatre Bras."[2] This he did, and notwithstanding that his advanced troops were pushed somewhat back, he maintained himself in front of the cross roads from half-past six, when the fight began, till nine o'clock, when the French retired

---

[1] These orders, like the others, were lost with De Lancey's papers, but one is extant, viz., an order to Lord Hill, dated 7 A.M., to move the 2nd British Division on Braine-le-Comte, saying that the cavalry had been ordered to the same point. See Table facing p. 162.

[2] See Starklof, 'Herzog Bernhard von Sachsen Weimar-Eisenach,' vol. i. p. 181 *et seq*. Quatre Bras was the point ordered for the assembly of the 2nd Brigade. See de Bas, p. 1148.

to Frasnes. Prince Bernhard placed his outposts close up to the enemy, while the Bossu wood was held by a part of his troops, the remainder being kept at Quatre Bras. At 9 P.M. the Prince sent to tell Perponcher of his engagement. He was unable to give any information as to the strength or composition of the French, and stated that he was too weak to hold out long without assistance, that his troops wanted cartridges, and he expected to be attacked at daybreak.

This was the report sent on from Nivelles to Braine-le-Comte, alluded to on page 99. At Nivelles it was supplemented by information obtained from a French officer, who came over to the Allies in plain clothes, and who stated that Napoleon was advancing on Brussels with 150,000 men.[1]

To sum up. At the end of the day Wellington, governed by the idea that Napoleon would attack in two directions, his main attack being against the Anglo-Allies, and totally without information as to the result of the fighting against the Prussians, had taken steps purely tentative in character, adapted for either contingency, whereas Napoleon had made a determined movement along one line only. Luck had favoured the Duke to some extent, for Constant and Perponcher had judged the situation correctly and taken steps to stop the French advance. On the other hand, Dörnberg had sent in nothing but the vaguest news,[2] and the Prussians had completely failed to give Wellington any

---

[1] See Lettow-Vorbeck, p. 296.
[2] See *post*, p. 166.

THE PRUSSIAN FAULTS 103

information as to the result of the French advance against them. Knowledge of this was absolutely necessary before he could come to any definite determination as to his action for the morrow, and he did not obtain it till too late to issue orders on the night of the 15th-16th June. The conduct of Gneisenau becomes more blameworthy when, as we know, he had already determined to fight a pitched battle at Ligny.[1] He had failed, too, in his own staff arrangements,—for his orders to Bülow had been so expressed that the latter had thought it sufficient to reach Hannut on the 16th, and thus he was too late for the battle. Not only were Gneisenau's orders wanting in clearness, but the arrangements for delivering them to the commander of the IV. Corps were so bad that the latter did not get those of 11 P.M. of the 14th till 10.30 A.M. on the 15th. Then Bülow, having issued orders for the brigades of his corps to move within a short march of Hannut on the 15th, issued no further orders for the day, so that Hannut was not reached till early on the 16th. An order which Gneisenau sent to Bülow at 11.15 A.M. on the 15th, ordering him after a rest at Hannut to go to Gembloux at the latest on the early morning of the 16th, did not reach him, as it was delivered at Hannut, whereas Bülow was still at Liége, where this order eventually found him at sunrise on the 16th. It was then too late, and the IV. Corps, unable to reach Ligny, took no part in the battle.[2]

---

[1] See 'Das Tagebuch des Generals der Kavallerie, Grafen v. Nostitz,' p. 18. Nostitz was aide-de-camp to Blucher. Gneisenau and Grolmann adhered to their decision to fight at Sombreffe notwithstanding the risk involved.
[2] On the question of Bülow, see Pflugk-Hartung, pp. 252-267.

The movements of Napoleon's troops, if they had not completely realised his expectations, had yet put him in a favourable situation, for he had concentrated the bulk of his forces on the left bank of the Sambre, within striking distance of Blucher. He had driven back the Prussian covering troops, and, from the report sent in by Vandamme, he evidently had no great portion of Blucher's army opposed to him; while the report of Lefebvre showed that but a very small part of Wellington's force was anywhere near the Brussels highway. He had, as he thought, surprised the two commanders. The direction of the Prussian retreat led him to believe Blucher was falling back towards Namur, and Wellington had plainly not concentrated his troops against him. All was going well, he would defeat any Prussians who might try to stop him the next day, thrust back whatever force the English might bring against him, push on to Brussels by the 17th, and issue the proclamations he had already printed, with the Palace of Laeken as the place of issue!

CHAPTER IV.

THE EVENTS OF THE 16TH JUNE—BATTLE OF LIGNY
—BATTLE OF QUATRE BRAS.

(*See Plan.*)

DURING the night of the 15th Napoleon came to no decision as to the course to be pursued on the morrow. Ney had reported fully to him as to the position on the left flank, and the resting-places of the various divisions forming the 1st and 2nd Corps had been sent into Charleroi by d'Erlon and Reille.[1] From Grouchy he knew the position on the right flank. But, contrary to his usual practice, no fresh orders were issued that night.

It has been stated that Ney rode into Charleroi and spent part of the night with Napoleon. It seems improbable that he did so after sending such a detailed report, and the only reasons alleged in favour

---

[1] See reports of Ney and Lefebvre, *ante*, pp. 74-77. Reille had sent in a report at nine o'clock from Gosselies to Soult as to the position of his divisions. D'Erlon had also reported the same, saying that in accordance with the order of 3 P.M. he advanced on Gosselies, that Durutte's division was behind Gosselies, Donzelot's with a cavalry brigade in front of Jumet, Marcognet's division in Marchiennes, Allix's division in Thuin, and the other cavalry brigade at Solre-à-Bieme. He also asked permission to bring up the rearward troops. See Lettow-Vorbeck, p. 264.

of the statement are the short distance he had to go (4½ miles), and that he felt, as he had had very little conversation with Napoleon when he saw him in the afternoon, it was desirable to talk the situation over with him, find out exactly what the Emperor's intentions were, and get some details of the troops forming the left wing.[1]

Whether Ney did or did not go to Charleroi, one thing is certain, the conversation, if any, that he had with Napoleon could not have been a very enlightening one so far as the Emperor was concerned, for Soult had to write to Ney between 5.30 and 6 o'clock—*i.e.*, about four hours after the latter is said to have left Charleroi—to find out whether the 1st Corps had completed its movements, what was the exact position of both the 1st and 2nd Corps, of the two cavalry divisions attached to them, and what he had learned about the enemy in front of him. The same letter placed

---

[1] Heymès states distinctly that on the morning of the 16th he had to go round collecting the names of the colonels commanding the various units, and that, as Ney had no staff officers, he was obliged to use officers of the chasseurs and lancers of the Guard to take messages to d'Erlon. See Heymès, p. 557.

M. Houssaye throws doubt on the interview altogether. Heymès is the authority for it, and his account of events is so full of errors that it is impossible to rely implicitly on it. But it was made only a few years after the battle. He states as a matter of common knowledge that Ney supped with the Emperor, and that "tous les grands officiers du quartier imperial purent l'attester." No one denied it, and as at the time it was made the spirit of controversy ran high, it seems likely it would have been at once contradicted if it had not been true. According to Heymès Ney left Charleroi at 2 A.M. on the 16th. He could not have started to go there much before midnight, as his report was not sent in till eleven. He would then have reached Napoleon about 12.30, and this would only have given him about an hour with the Emperor. On the whole, therefore, it seems improbable that he went.

THE INSTRUCTIONS TO NEY   107

Kellermann's corps at Ney's disposal, and gave him instructions about the Light Cavalry of the Guard.[1]

Early in the morning, probably about six o'clock, Napoleon began to issue his orders for the day. A little later, about 7 A.M., Soult sent instructions to Ney to put the 1st and 2nd Corps in movement, and take up a position at Quatre Bras, sending forward reconnaissances on the roads to Brussels and Nivelles, from which latter place the enemy had probably retired.[2]

The Emperor himself also wrote to Ney, giving him full details of his intentions. The letter was taken by Count Flahaut, one of the Emperor's aides-de-camp. Ney was told that he and Grouchy were definitely constituted the leaders of the left and right wings respectively. The Emperor was sending Grouchy with the right wing towards Sombreffe, and he was himself going to Fleurus with the Guard: he would be there before mid-day, and would attack the enemy and clear the road as far as Gembloux. After that he would decide upon his plan, perhaps at 3 P.M., perhaps in the evening, but Ney was to be ready to march on Brussels immediately he received orders. He would be supported by the Guard, and the Emperor wished to reach Brussels the next morning. Ney was to move there in the evening if Napoleon made up his mind soon

---

[1] 'Documents Inédits,' p. 26. This letter was received by Ney before 7 A.M., as his reply to it bears this hour. See Houssaye, p. 192, footnotes 2 and 3. It was the first sent to him from the Imperial headquarters this day. The order with regard to Lefebvre was for him to be drawn back from the front ready to rejoin the Guard.

[2] This was Soult's second letter to Ney.

enough to let him know during the day, and he was then to push on three or four leagues (*i.e.*, between eight and ten miles), and be at Brussels the next day by seven o'clock. He was to dispose his troops so as to have one division about five miles in front of Quatre Bras if possible, the other six about that place, and one division at Marbais, which the Emperor could draw towards Sombreffe if he wished to. Kellermann with the 3rd Cavalry Corps was to be placed at the intersection of the Roman and Brussels roads, so that Napoleon could use him if necessary. As soon as Ney knew the Emperor's plan he was to call Kellermann up to join the left wing. Lefebvre-Desnoëttes with the light cavalry of the Guard had been with Ney the previous day; he was now to be replaced by Kellermann, but the latter was to be so placed that he could be recalled if wanted, and, as he did not want to subject Lefebvre to marching and counter-marching, he was to remain with Ney for a time with a view to the advance on Brussels. Lefebvre was to be covered by the light cavalry of the 1st and 2nd Corps so as to save the Guard, for if any skirmishing took place with the English it was better it should fall on the line.

The instructions wound up by saying that the Emperor had adopted as his general principle for the conduct of the campaign, the division of his army into two wings and a reserve. The left wing was to be composed of the eight divisions of the 1st and 2nd Corps, with their light cavalry and Kellermann's cavalry corps, the total being

THE INSTRUCTIONS TO GROUCHY 109

45,000 to 50,000 men. Grouchy was to have about the same force on the right wing. The Guard formed the reserve, and would be used with one wing or the other according to circumstances. Ney was always to command the troops under him, and instructions would be sent to the officers concerned so that there should be no difficulty about this; but if Napoleon was present, then he would send orders direct to them, also he might weaken one wing or the other to augment the reserve. Ney would understand how important it was to capture Brussels, as so rapid a movement would isolate the English army from Mons, Ostend, &c. The last phrase of the letter runs: "I desire that your dispositions should be so made that immediately on receiving orders your eight divisions may march as rapidly as possible, and without impediment, on Brussels."[1]

Two points are plainly indicated in these orders, the one that the Emperor did not expect to meet much resistance on the Brussels road, and that he was aware of the importance to Wellington of the Ostend line of communications.

Orders couched in similar language were taken to Grouchy by Colonel La Bédoyère. He was to command the right wing, consisting of the 3rd and 4th Corps, the Cavalry Corps of Pajol, Milhaud, and Exelmans, which would together number about 50,000 men. He was to move to Sombreffe immediately. Napoleon was moving his headquarters to Fleurus; Grouchy was

[1] This was the third letter to Ney. See 'Correspondance,' vol. xxviii. pp. 289-92.

to send to Gérard to tell him to come up straight from the Sambre to Sombreffe. Orders to this effect had also been sent from headquarters. As with the left wing so with the right: the general officers were to obey their new commander, except when Napoleon was present. The Emperor was coming to Fleurus between ten and eleven, and would then move on Sombreffe, leaving the Guards at Fleurus. He would not take them to Sombreffe unless it was necessary. He would attack the Prussians at Sombreffe, or even at Gembloux, and, having captured these positions, he would leave that night to operate with the left flank against the English. Grouchy was told not to lose a moment, because the sooner the Emperor could determine his plan the better for the operations. He was to communicate constantly with Gérard, so that he could aid him in attacking Sombreffe if it was necessary. Girard's division was within reach of Fleurus; but he was not to use it unless absolutely necessary, because it would have to march the whole night.[1] The Young Guard and its artillery was to be left at Fleurus. He was told that Kellermann was on the road to Brussels to join Ney, with a view to aiding the operations of the left wing in the evening. Grouchy was to report all the information which came in. The Emperor finished

[1] Evidently the Emperor intended Girard to rejoin his corps—*i.e.*, Reille's—otherwise this statement about the night-march would be meaningless; but it is odd that the Emperor, who knew where Girard was, and that he had indeed gone to Wangenies by his order, should still have ordered Ney to send one to Marbais (see *ante*, p. 108). Surely Girard's division would have been the one to use for this purpose. Did the Emperor mean Ney to send another division to Marbais? for plainly he intended Grouchy to use Girard if necessary, and, as will be seen later, did use him from the very first at the battle of Ligny.

THE INSTRUCTIONS CRITICISED

up by saying: "All the reports which I have show that the Prussians cannot oppose us with more than 40,000 men."

There were several points in these instructions worthy of notice. The Emperor plainly thought the Prussians had not come up in strength; he would attack them at Sombreffe or Gembloux—*i.e.*, drive them back towards Namur; he believed he could do so, and then move off to aid Ney. Girard was evidently intended to operate against the right flank of any Prussian force. The orders about the Guard are curious, as in one paragraph the whole of the Guard was to be left at Fleurus, apparently for the Emperor's orders, whereas in another Grouchy is told that the Young Guard is to be left there, thus implying that the rest is to move on Sombreffe.

Both this letter and the one to Ney were dictated by the Emperor himself and sent in supplement to Soult's orders, because Napoleon said the officers of the Chief of the Staff were badly mounted, and did not go as quickly as his!

Broadly speaking, therefore, on the 16th June Napoleon expected no great opposition from either the Anglo-Allied or the Prussian armies, certainly nothing of the nature of a pitched battle. Against the former Ney at first would have six divisions, while two (one from the 1st, one from the 2nd Corps) would at the outset be available for action with the right wing of the French army. Nor did indications of increasing forces opposite either wing alter in any way the conclusion the Emperor had arrived at. As he was on the point of starting for

Fleurus (eight miles from Charleroi), between 9 and 10 A.M., an officer of lancers arrived from the left wing and stated that the enemy were showing considerable strength near Quatre Bras. Soult at once wrote to Ney, told him to draw together the corps of Reille, d'Erlon, and Kellermann, and to beat and destroy any forces of the enemy which might present themselves. He added that as Blucher was at Namur on the 15th, it was not probable he had sent any troops to Quatre Bras, and that Ney, therefore, could only have to do with those coming from Brussels.[1]

The first intimation that Napoleon had received of the advance of the Prussians towards their chosen battlefield was in a report from Grouchy, sent from Fleurus at 5 A.M., that strong columns of the enemy were advancing from the Namur road towards Brye and St Amand. At six o'clock Grouchy again sent in to say Girard had reported from Wangenies that the Prussians were advancing in force towards the heights about the mill at Bussy. Neither of these messages caused the Emperor to think that Blucher

[1] This was Soult's third letter to Ney this day. Houssaye assumes quite gratuitously that this officer came from Girard, and gives as the reason for his belief Reille, who, in his relation of events, states: "About nine o'clock I received a report from General Girard informing me that he saw from Wangenies masses of Prussians beyond Fleurus; this was transmitted at once to the Emperor." Now Soult's despatch distinctly states Quatre Bras; obviously, therefore, Girard's report about troops at Wangenies had nothing to do with it. There were lancers both in Piré's cavalry at Wangenies and with Lefebvre at Frasnes. We know from Heymès that Ney used officers of the lancers for orderly purposes, and we know that the man who brought the information from Frasnes was a lancer officer. Probably, therefore, he was one from the Guard cavalry there. When Girard's report reached Napoleon he doubtless had also received news from Grouchy.

was advancing with his army to give him battle, for in writing his letter (the 3rd communication) to Ney, when he knew the contents of these two reports, he plainly attached no importance to them, or he could not have spoken as lightly as he did to both Ney and Grouchy of his intentions to brush aside any Prussian force he might encounter near Sombreffe.

When the Emperor reached Fleurus about eleven, Grouchy informed him that considerable bodies of the Prussians were taking position to the north of this village, and he had, therefore, done nothing more than occupy it.

At this time not only was *Zieten* in position of the chosen battlefield, but Pirch's corps was marching to Sombreffe, and reached this point at noon, and a short distance behind him was Thielmann with the III. Corps; thus what the Emperor estimated at a corps,[1] or at the most 40,000 men, was really double that number.

Blucher had from the first made up his mind to fight Napoleon. He believed he could beat him alone, and felt doubly certain that he could do so with Wellington's assistance. On the 15th June, at noon, he wrote to Müffling saying he intended to give battle the next day. In the evening he wrote to his King from Sombreffe, where he arrived at 4 P.M., that his army would be concentrated on the 16th, which would be the decisive day, and he wrote in the same sense to Schwartzenberg.[2] All this shows that Blucher firmly intended to fight under any circumstances, and is confirmed by the fact that his arrangements were all made

---

[1] See also *post*, p. 123. [2] See Lettow-Vorbeck, p. 276.

and his troops drawn up before Wellington arrived on the battlefield of Ligny.[1]

Although the precise terms are not known, there is no doubt that Blucher and Wellington had come to some understanding as to the way in which they should support one another in the event of Napoleon attacking them, taking into consideration the various lines of operation open to him. It is absolutely certain that two such practical commanders would have done so.

The first discussion on this subject probably took place on the 4th April, when Wellington met Gneisenau. On the 5th the Duke wrote to him that his desire was that arrangements should be made to assemble the whole Prussian and Anglo-Allied armies in front of Brussels, and for this purpose the former should take up cantonments between Charleroi, Namur, and Huy, so as to allow of a combined concentration in front of Brussels. There had also been a meeting between Wellington and Blucher at Tirlemont on the 3rd May, which the Duke considered very satisfactory.[2] It was the intention of the two commanders to invade France at the beginning of July, but doubtless the defensive measures to be taken, should Napoleon previously assume the offensive, were also discussed. Blucher had, if the French advance was a direct one on Brussels, determined to assemble his force about Sombreffe. A little consideration will show this was a rendezvous well adapted to meet all probable lines of French operation. Only if the

[1] See Ollech, p. 99.
[2] See 'Wellington Despatches,' vol. xii. p. 345.

Emperor chose to advance on Liége through the Ardennes was it unsuited. This was extremely unlikely, as the roads were bad and the country unfavourable to the movements of an army. Moreover, any prolonged advance in this direction would have offered a favourable opportunity to act against his communications. It is of course true that the Emperor might thus have cut Blucher's; but the latter could have lived on the country and on supplies furnished by Wellington for a few days, and the two armies would have united against him and have severed him from France. Let us then consider the other cases which might have arisen.

If the attack was directed against Wellington's right beyond the Scheldt, the Prussian army assembled at Sombreffe was a good position to support the Anglo-Allied army.

If the Emperor advanced, either by the Charleroi-Brussels road from Beaumont and Philippeville, against the right of the Prussians and the left of the Anglo-Allies; or by Maubeuge and Beaumont towards Binche, against the centre of Wellington's army, Sombreffe was equally well suited. For from it the Prussians could threaten the line of Napoleon's advance, and act against his communications.[1]

---

[1] There is good evidence extant that the last two lines of operation had been considered, and the measures necessary to meet either of them carefully worked out. In a memorandum on the arrangements of the I. Corps, signed by Zieten at Charleroi on the 2nd May, the two cases are discussed in detail. Probably Blucher had this document with him at the interview with Wellington on the 3rd May; he certainly approved of the proposed disposition in a letter to Zieten of the 5th May. See 'Militair Wochenblatt,' 1846, p. 15. It is also given in Siborne, p. 543.

It is plain from what has been said that the assembly point of Wellington's army was to be Nivelles in either case.¹ The Duke could not at first tell whether the attack on the Prussians was the main one, or merely a feint intended to divert his attention from the main one against him through Binche. With Prussians at Sombreffe, and the Anglo-Allies at Nivelles, it would have been madness for Napoleon to have advanced between them, without first driving one or the other out of the way. Thus, by concentrating at Nivelles, Wellington protected Brussels either from an advance by Binche-Rœulx, Braine-le-Comte, or by Nivelles or Quatre Bras, and stood in a position to help the Prussians. The orders he issued on the 15th are consonant with all this, and Prince Bernhard's advance to Quatre Bras from the neighbourhood of Genappe with his brigade was in accordance with the general plan of the Anglo-Allied commander. Moreover, if the French advance were directed on Braine-le-Comte, he would become aware of it while his troops were moving on Nivelles, and could stop them in time to deal with it.

Both the Allied army commanders appear to have considered the indirect defence by the occupation of a flank position preferable to a direct one, as it gave them command over more country; while it

---

¹ See *ante*, p. 89, footnote. It would seem probable that by the 15th June, knowing that the French were distributed from Maubeuge to Philippeville, he had given up the idea of an attack against his extreme right; but still, owing to the information he had received from Paris (see p. 60), believed that the main French attack would be delivered against him, not Blucher.

must be remembered that the defile of Genappe could have been defended by the Reserve and the Brunswick Corps, numbering some 20,000 men with 64 guns.

Nivelles is distant from Quatre Bras 6½ miles, from Brye to Quatre Bras is 5½ miles, the total distance 12 miles, not more than four to five hours' march, and the two armies assembled at these points were therefore distinctly within supporting distance of one another.

When Prince Bernhard reported to Perponcher at Nivelles that he had been engaged, the report was sent on to the Prince of Orange's headquarters at Braine-le-Comte, where it arrived about 10 P.M. De Constant Rebecque, appreciating the importance of Quatre Bras, ordered Perponcher to concentrate the whole of his division there early the next morning and hold his ground to the last extremity. He was also to send officers to the 3rd Dutch-Belgian Division, and to the Dutch-Belgian Cavalry Division, to acquaint the officers concerned with the situation.[1] Wellington's order to the Prince to collect the 2nd and 3rd Dutch-Belgian Divisions at Nivelles arrived at Braine-le-Comte at 11 P.M. on the 15th, and was sent on to Perponcher; but the latter, judging the situation more accurately than the Duke had done at Brussels, very properly disregarded it and carried out the first instructions that Constant had sent him.

Perponcher started at 2 A.M. on the 16th with the 27th Chasseurs, and pushing ahead reached Quatre

[1] See Siborne, p. 60; also Löben-Sels, p. 176.

Bras at 3 A.M., and at once took steps to drive back the French outposts. In this he was aided by some fifty Prussian cavalry of the 1st Silesian Hussars.[1] He was able to secure the southern edge of the Bossu wood, and to extend his troops to the east across the main road.

The Prince of Orange joined the force about six o'clock, and determined to take up a position as far forward as possible, to delay the French attack until reinforcements arrived. The farm of Gemioncourt was occupied, and in front of the line thus held from it to the Bossu wood fourteen guns were placed, while the two remaining were disposed near the right flank on the side of the Bossu wood. The Prince had no cavalry available, as the Prussian hussars, after the first skirmish, had gone off by the Namur road to join their regiment.[2] The total available strength, as the troops of the 2nd Dutch-Belgian division gradually came up, amounted to 6800 men with 16 guns.

Wellington left Brussels about 7.30, and reached Quatre Bras at ten o'clock. He had previously issued orders for a concentration of his troops towards Quatre Bras. But the delay which had occurred before a decision was come to prevented him carrying out the concentration as he had originally thought he could do. He stated on the 13th to Colonel Pfuel, who had come from Blucher to confer with the Duke,

---

[1] These hussars belonged to Lutzow's brigade, and had fallen back on the 15th towards the Quatre Bras-Nivelles road when driven back from the Prussian outposts.

[2] By this road Prussian cavalry kept up connection during the day between the two commanders. See Ollech, p. 137.

that he could concentrate his forces on his left in twenty-two hours. As a practical fact he did nothing of the kind. His hesitation to commit himself until he knew the direction of the Emperor's attack was natural and prudent, and the only course open to him in the circumstances. But Constant's despatch of 10 P.M. showed clearly that the French were advancing along the Charleroi highway. Yet even then he seems to have been half inclined to believe that the Emperor would move against his right, and the opinion he had originally formed continued to influence him up to and including the day of Waterloo.

The reputation of the great English commander stands high, but it must be candidly admitted that his persistency is difficult to justify, and savours more of obstinacy than sound judgment.

Perponcher's wise disobedience secured the position of Quatre Bras for the moment, and Ney's supineness in attacking gave the Anglo-Allied commander breathing time. But the danger was great, for had Ney captured this important place, as he easily might have done early in the day, he would have held in his possession the point of junction of the Anglo-Allied forces coming both from Brussels and from the West. Owing to the delay in issuing his concentration orders, the Duke would never have had during the day more than 27,000 men to use against Ney, of which only 20,000, the Reserve, were really reliable troops.

When Wellington arrived at Quatre Bras about ten o'clock he found Perponcher's men in position, and saw that the enemy was showing no sign of activity.

Shortly after reaching the front he wrote to Blucher, saying what he believed the positions of the various units forming the Anglo-Allied army were at the time of writing. This letter is as under:—

On the Heights behind Frasnes,
June 16, 1815, 10.30 A.M.

My dear Prince,—My army is situated as follows:

The Corps d'Armée of the Prince of Orange has a division here and at Quatre Bras, and the rest at Nivelles.

The Reserve is in march from Waterloo to Genappe, where it will arrive at noon.

The English cavalry will be at the same hour at Nivelles.

I do not see any large force of the enemy in front of us, and I await news from your Highness, and the arrival of troops, in order to determine my operations for the day.

Nothing has been seen on the side of Binche, nor on our right.—Your very obedient servant,

WELLINGTON.

Shortly after sending the letter Wellington rode over and consulted with his German comrade on the situation. He appears to have reached the windmill of Bussy about one o'clock, and here he found Blucher and his staff watching the approach of the French columns. A consultation took place as to what would be the best course to pursue, and the Duke asked Gneisenau his opinion. The latter replied that if the Duke could overthrow the French force in front and advance quickly, that would bring about the greatest result, as he would come on the rear of the French army. But the roads he would have to use were narrow, and therefore it would be more certain in effect if he held fast the force in front of him, and with the troops not required for this purpose advanced towards the Prussian right and the French left flank. The Duke replied: "Your argument is correct. I will see what is in front of me and how much of my army has come up, and act accordingly."[1] He left Blucher shortly afterwards and reached Quatre Bras about half-past two o'clock.

By the time Wellington had finished his conversation with Blucher, the army of the latter was practically formed up to resist the attack shortly to be made on it. The centre of the position occupied by the Prussians was formed by the village of Ligny, situated astride the brook which bears the same name. This in itself was some obstacle, and the buildings of the village were mostly stone and well adapted for defence. Enough does not seem to have been made of their capabilities, but this was due to lack of time and engineer troops. The right, which turned

---

[1] See Ollech, p. 127. Gneisenau thought at the time that only about 10,000 French were in front of Wellington. See Lettow-Vorbeck, p. 525. The Duke took with him Müffling, Dörnberg, and Sir Alexander Gordon, and some of his aides-de-camp. Dörnberg knew German, French, and English well, and his evidence is therefore valuable. It is given in Pflugk-Hartung, p. 293. After the very careful analysis given by this author of the various misstatements on this head made by every Prussian from Gneisenau to Lettow-Vorbeck (see *op. cit.*, pp. 234-52), it is impossible for any one to maintain the idea that Wellington promised unconditionally to come to Blucher's aid. Müffling, pp. 234-37, gives a clear account of the interview, and makes the Duke say, "Well, I'll come, provided I am not attacked myself." The evidence of those present — viz., Müffling and Dörnberg — is therefore quite clear and decisive.

back at right angles to the centre, rested on the village of St Amand, and beyond this were those of St Amand-la-Haye and Wagnelée, while in rear of these was the hamlet of Brye. The salient form of the Prussian front line much exposed it to fire, while the position sloped down toward the enemy, who was thus able to see all movements within it.

Zieten's corps held the front of the line. Three battalions of the 3rd Brigade were in St Amand. Brye had three from the 1st Brigade with a half battalion between it and St Amand-la-Haye, while the remainder of the brigade was in reserve behind St Amand. Ligny was held by four battalions of the 4th, and a half battalion of the 3rd Brigade. Behind this village was the rest of the infantry of the I. Corps and the Reserve cavalry, while the bulk of the artillery was in position on the slope between St Amand and Ligny.

The II. Corps was behind the I.; the 5th Brigade on the right at a small cluster of houses round a public-house, "aux trois Burettes." The III. Corps held the Prussian left at Tongrinne, with the 10th Brigade; the 9th and 12th Brigades being in second line at Sombreffe and Point du Jour, while the 11th kept the road which leads to Fleurus. The Ligny brook, where it flowed in front of Tongrinne and Tongrinelle, was difficult to pass, and thus formed a considerable obstacle to both armies on this side of the field.

When the Emperor arrived at Fleurus between eleven and twelve o'clock, and reconnoitred the field of battle in front of him from a windmill there, it seems probable that owing to the form

NAPOLEON'S DISPOSITIONS

of the ground and the crops which covered it he did not see much, if anything, of the II. Corps, and the III. Corps was only just coming up. Hence his assumption that he had only to deal with "a corps" of 40,000 men, and he determined to attack and beat it as soon as his troops were ready.

Unfortunately for him he had to wait some time. Gérard, whose whole corps had not crossed the Sambre at Châtelet on the 15th (see *ante*, p. 81), made no attempt to bring it over in the early morning, as he certainly might, and should have done, but waited for orders. These reached him at 9.30, and his corps was then set in motion.[1] It only reached the battlefield at 1.30 P.M.,[2] and was ordered to take position on the right of Vandamme's corps, which was then on the left of the Fleurus-Gembloux road, and in front of the first-named village. The Emperor now determined to hold back the Prussian left and envelope their right, thus effectually preventing all junction with the Anglo-Allies. Girard's division, which had been ordered up from Wangenies by Grouchy, was placed in support of Vandamme, and a wheel to the left was made by the whole army, bringing the latter with his divisions in front of St Amand, the 3rd, Habert's, facing the south end of the village. Girard was on Vandamme's left, his outer flank being covered by Domon's cavalry; Gérard was placed in front of Ligny, with Hulot's division thrown back to aid Grouchy's cavalry, which

[1] See Houssaye (p. 162), who justly points out that it was an extraordinary circumstance that Soult's order, certainly sent off between 7 and 8 A.M., took two hours to go 3¾ miles. The troops on the right bank had to cross the river by one narrow bridge.

[2] Houssaye (p. 161) says the head of the 3rd Corps arrived at 1 P.M.

was formed facing Tongrinne at right angles to the French line. The Guards were in reserve at Fleurus. Soult now wrote (at 2 P.M.) to Ney telling him that the Emperor was about to attack the "corps" in front of him, that he (Ney) was to attack and press back vigorously all the enemy in front of him, and then fall back so as to envelop "the corps which I have just mentioned to you." If the Emperor defeated this "corps" before Ney succeeded in his task, then his Majesty would manœuvre in Ney's direction so as to hasten his operations. Ney was to let the Emperor know how things were going with him.[1]

By the time the troops were in their new order it was nearly three o'clock. Napoleon had for some time been watching the Prussian movements, and it was now borne in on him that the "corps" was in fact the Prussian army. This, far from damping his ardour, seems to have made him think the situation was even better than he hoped for. Ney had, of course, no force of moment in front of him, and was probably already in motion to aid his master. "It may be," said he to Gérard, "that the fate of the war will be decided in three hours! If Ney executes my orders properly not a gun of this army will get off."[2] The corps has become an army, so much the worse for it and the better for Napoleon, who will destroy it at a stroke! Unfortunately the Prussian force amounted to 83,000 men, while the Emperor had not more than 65,000 at his disposal.

[1] Soult to Ney, Fleurus, 16th June, 2 o'clock. See Charras, p. 136. This was Soult's fourth letter to Ney.
[2] See Houssaye, p. 165.

THE BATTLE OF LIGNY

The attack was ordered to commence at once, the signal being three cannon-shots from the Guard artillery, which were fired about three o'clock.[1] Lobau, who had been left at Charleroi till the Emperor could decide whether he wanted him or whether he should join Ney, was now ordered up to Fleurus, which he reached about six. Just at this juncture a letter arrived from Ney to the effect that he had 20,000 men in front of him. Napoleon now saw that on the left wing also there was a larger force to deal with than he had hitherto believed probable. Still, recognising that the main object was to defeat the Prussians, he ordered Soult (at 3.15 P.M.) to write to the commander of the left wing telling him that the Emperor was attacking the Prussians between the villages of St Amand and Brye, and that the Marshal was at once to manœuvre so as to envelop the enemy's right and rear.[2] He added that the Prussians were lost if Ney acted vigorously, and that the fate of France was in his hands. He was not to hesitate an instant, but to move towards the high ground at Brye and St Amand to aid in gaining a victory which would probably be decisive.

The 1st Corps was then on the march to Frasnes, with Durutte's division last in the column. For d'Erlon had merely concentrated his corps on the road to Quatre Bras in the morning and waited for orders from Ney. These arrived about noon, telling

[1] See Houssaye, p. 167. This signal was a common practice with Napoleon. He used the same device at Friedland and at Waterloo.
[2] This was Soult's fifth letter to Ney.

him to move on Frasnes and to detach "the right division" and Piré's cavalry to Marbais.[1]

It seems probable that when the aide-de-camp carrying the order reached the 1st Corps the head of it had passed some way beyond the Roman road, and that the head of Durutte's division was near the road which leads to Villers-Perouin. It, being the right division, was about to move on Marbais with Piré's cavalry when the aide-de-camp took upon himself to order it to move towards St Amand, and ordered the rest of the corps to follow. Durutte marched by the road through Villers-Perouin on Wagnelée, and this brought him on the left flank of the French line, whereas the Emperor wished him to move to the heights of St Amand—*i.e.*, more in the direction of Brye.[2]

The Emperor had commenced the battle at 3 P.M. Lefol's division of Vandamme's corps attacking St Amand, formed in three columns covered by skirmishers. It succeeded in penetrating the village defences, driving back the Prussian 3rd Brigade; but, after falling back some little distance, Jagow re-formed his troops and supported by four battalions from the 1st Brigade advanced and forced his way into the village again.

Girard was sent against the hamlet and St

---

[1] See *ante*, p. 108, the orders sent by the Emperor to Ney.

[2] Durutte's division was last according to Captain Chapuis of the 85th Regiment, which marched at its head, and only became the leading division when it turned towards Villers-Perouin. See 'Journal des Sciences Militaires,' vol. x. p. 390. The name of the aide-de-camp who took the order has been much disputed, but it is quite immaterial. See Houssaye, p. 167, footnote.

Amand-la-Haye, and driving back the Prussians there turned to his right toward the village of St Amand, while Berthezène's division prolonged Lefol's left, advancing against St Amand. The position was becoming critical at this point of the field, and Blucher determined to make a strong effort to re-establish the battle. The 2nd Brigade (Pirch II.) was led down from its position in reserve on the flank of Girard's men and drove them back into La Haye, and even occupied a portion of this village. Girard now led another attack against the Prussians, but was himself mortally wounded and his troops thrust back over the Ligny brook. To aid the Prussian counter-attack Blucher had also sent Tippelskirchen with his brigade and the Reserve Cavalry of the 2nd Corps through Wagnelée against the French flank. But Vandamme had drawn to this flank Habert's division and Domon's cavalry. The French infantry drove back the 5th Brigade into Wagnelée, while the Prussian cavalry made little effort to support their infantry in the face of Domon's men.

Whilst this fighting had taken place Blucher had approached La Haye, and seeing the men of the 2nd Infantry Brigade falling back before Girard's troops he ordered a fresh attack. Inspired by the presence of their General, the Prussian troops turned on the enemy and drove them back into the hamlet of St Amand, and here for a time the action came to a standstill, for it was impossible to continue the movements against the French troops as Tippelskirchen's infantry and Jurgass's cavalry had both been driven back.

Meanwhile Gérard's troops had been engaged in attacking Ligny. Pecheux's division advanced in three columns covered by skirmishers, but, as in the case of Vandamme's assault, without any more artillery preparation than was to be obtained from the guns of the army corps while the infantry was advancing. All three columns obtained at first some slight success, but were ultimately forced back. The attack was then strengthened by a brigade from Vichery's division, and some 12-pounder batteries from the Guard joined the guns of the 4th Corps in cannonading the village. Once more the infantry advanced, and on this occasion succeeded in winning the buildings which were on the south side of the stream, bordering the open space along its banks where the church and churchyard stood. Then the French pushed forward to gain the houses on the far side of the open space, but were brought to a standstill by a hand-to-hand struggle of the fiercest kind. Still slowly but surely they gained ground, and pressing the men of Henckel's brigade at last drove them in disorder over the stream. But they made no more progress. For Henckel, putting in the last two battalions he had kept in support behind the village, and these being backed up by battalions of Jagow's brigade, hitherto in reserve at this point, the strengthened force of Prussians succeeded in thrusting back Gérard's men to their own side of the rivulet. The fighting by this time extended along the whole line from St Amand-la-Haye to Boignée, which Grouchy had gained with his cavalry. Hulot's division of the 4th

THE BATTLE OF LIGNY

Corps was now sent forward towards Tongrinelle and up the road leading to the Namur *chaussée*.

It was just on five o'clock; the French attacks on the Prussian right had failed,—in the centre they were brought to a standstill, and against the enemy's left the nature of the ground, and the fact that cavalry formed the chief attacking force available, made anything more than a holding fight impossible.

Nor did it enter into the Emperor's plans to do more on his right wing. For, having completed contact with the whole of the enemy's line, his mind was now made up as to the best direction for decisive action. He determined to penetrate the centre, and thus rending the army of the Prussians in two, surround and crush their right wing, and thrust the rest back along their line of communications towards Namur.

But to carry out this plan more troops were needed. For Lobau was not yet up, the troops in the front line were exhausted by the terrible struggle of the last two hours, in which 65,000 Frenchmen had tried to drive 83,000 Prussians from their place, and no help from Ney could be expected for some time longer. It was necessary, therefore, to use the Guard, and both horse and foot of this veteran body were brought up for the purpose. The infantry was to assault Ligny, Milhaud's cuirassiers were to accompany them in close support, and, when the infantry had won the village, they were to pursue the retreating Prussians and carry forward the attack till it burst through the Prussian line and completely isolated Blucher's right wing.

It was now 5.30 P.M., and the signal to advance almost given, when the Emperor was informed that a hostile column was coming down from the direction of Villers-Perouin on Vandamme's outer flank. Already the appearance of this force had had effect. For Lefol's men, exhausted by their efforts against the village of St Amand, and fearing attack from the new direction, were falling back in disorder, while Blucher's preparations for a great counter-stroke against Girard and Vandamme were almost completed. The attack on the Prussian centre was suspended, and half the Guard infantry with Subervie's cavalry sent to support the threatened wing, while an aide-de-camp went at a gallop to find out who the new-comers really were.

Meanwhile the Prussians, animated by their beloved commander, moved down to roll back the French left. Tippelskirchen's brigade, with Jurgass's cavalry division protecting its right flank, came through Wagnelée on to the hamlet, thus taking St Amand itself in flank; while the 2nd Brigade, reinforced by Brause's brigade from the II. Corps and six battalions of Krafft's brigade, attacked in front, the assault being prepared by the united fire of Zieten's reserve artillery brought into action against the village. At first the movement was successful, but the Guard advanced, and passing through the men of Hubert's division falling back to their original position, pushed onward against the advancing Prussians. Their determined advance reanimated the troops of Girard and Vandamme, and the whole going forward once more drove back the counter-attack and gained possession of the villages on the Prussian right.

And now the Emperor learned that the troops on the western horizon were d'Erlon's, but the same messenger told him that, recalled by the insistent command of Ney, the 1st Corps was retracing its steps towards the left wing. This d'Erlon had done, leaving only Durutte's division and Jacquinot's cavalry in observation near Wagnelée. Thus part of the force which the Emperor had ordered Ney to despatch to his assistance had arrived, and would be employed against the Prussian right wing.[1] But for some unexplained and inexplicable reason Napoleon made no attempt to retain the 1st Corps, although it must have been plain that these troops had come from the right wing to his assistance.

But there was yet time to win the battle by breaking in through the enemy's centre, and to this Napoleon devoted his efforts. All the Guard infantry available, eleven battalions in all, with Guyot's cavalry brigade and Milhaud's corps of cuirassiers, the Emperor led in person down to Ligny; leaving only Lobau's corps, which had shortly before come up, as his last reserve at Fleurus.

Against the Prussian right there seemed little hope of success: Ney had failed the Emperor, and the division of the 1st Corps left behind did nothing, although Jacquinot's cavalry, by demonstrating towards the group of house "aux trois Burettes," held in check Marwitz's Reserve Cavalry of the III. Corps brought towards this point to guard the

[1] See *ante*, p. 125.

flank.¹ On the Prussian left no great results were possible, but Grouchy had carried Tongrinelle and Hulot was attacking Potraux.

At Ligny, where, as we have seen, the Prussians had succeeded in thrusting back Gérard, both sides were much exhausted: Krafft's and Jagow's troops were at the end of their fighting powers, and Henckel's brigade had been withdrawn from the conflict. At this juncture Blucher learned by a message from Müffling that no help could be expected from Wellington. But the dying down of the fight which ensued as Napoleon gave pause to his troops at the moment when the approach of d'Erlon was for a time thought to be that of a hostile force, made the Prussian leader hope that victory was still possible.

Ligny was to be held, while gathering in all available reserves Blucher would himself lead them down on St Amand and, breaking through at this point, crush the French left and compel the Emperor to retreat.

On both sides then preparations for a final effort were in progress. The recapture of St Amand, and the report that the French were yielding ground, led Blucher to believe the time for the decisive counter-stroke had come. Taking the remainder of the 1st Brigade, two and a half battalions, which had not been engaged, and joining to them six from the 8th Brigade (Langen's), the last infantry reserve on the right flank of the battle, Blucher led them in person

---

¹ According to Chapuis of the 85th Regiment, the leading one of Durutte's division, an order was given to attack the Prussians. This is confirmed by Brue, who commanded the leading brigade, but Durutte refused to carry it out in the absence of d'Erlon. See 'Journal des Sciences Militaires,' 1863, vol. i. p. 390.

THE FINAL ATTACK

down against St Amand. These fresh troops were able to recover possession of the hamlet and part of the village of St Amand, but all further progress was stopped here by the Imperial Guard.

Unfortunately for outcome of the battle the employment of the Prussian reserves on the right flank deprived the Commander-in-Chief of troops he was soon to want badly for the safety of his centre. Here he had in second line only five battalions of the 8th Brigade left. The remains of Henckel's brigade, which had been replaced in Ligny by the 6th Brigade, even if they had been capable of further sustained effort, had been drawn back to Sombreffe, and the 12th Brigade, which had been called up from its position in reserve at Point du Jour, was too far off to be used to stem the new attack on Ligny, against which the Emperor directed the troops of the Old Guard, with Milhaud's cavalry corps and the heavy cavalry of the Guard.

To prepare the advance the whole of the available artillery of the Guard was joined to that of the 4th Corps, and the combined guns poured a heavy fire of shot and shell into the village. Against the east end was directed a column consisting of the 1st Grenadiers and 1st Chasseurs, while against the west end moved the remaining three battalions of the Grenadiers, the whole in double column of companies. In between these columns Gérard led forward once more the infantry of Pecheux, while Milhaud's cavalry followed the right column of the Guard, and Guyot's with the personal escort of the Emperor accompanied the left. The day had become dark, owing to a thunderstorm which broke just as the movement began, and served in some measure to cover it. But about half-past seven, as the clouds blew over and the field became clear, the French broke through the village, pressing the sorely tried Prussians back by dint of superior numbers and the force of veteran troops.

To meet the French attack Blucher had, as we have seen, hardly any infantry available. Practically, therefore, Blucher was limited to the Reserve Cavalry of the I. Corps. Drawing his sword, the gallant old Marshal placed himself at the head of the 6th Uhlans, commanded by Lützow (formerly head of the well-known Free Corps), and led them against the leading battalion of the left French column. This was the 4th Grenadiers of the Old Guard. Receiving with the utmost calmness the Prussian attack, they poured into the Uhlans a series of volleys at short range, which repelled the assailants with loss, and the success gained was confirmed by the cuirassiers, who charged and drove them back with great loss. Blucher's horse was shot under him, Lützow captured, and despite the efforts of the other regiments of Roëder's division, in a prolonged cavalry encounter which lasted till dark, the French pressed forward and pushed the Prussians back half-way to the Quatre Bras-Namur road. But they made no further progress, for in front of Sombreffe the 12th Brigade which had now come up was able to keep off all French attacks; and by Brye the 2nd Brigade took post, with a battalion of the 1st Brigade on the height to its left, to which other

THE PRUSSIANS ADVANCE 135

troops both cavalry and infantry joined on. Major-General Jagow taking command, was thus enabled to cover the retreat of the Prussian troops from this part of the field.

On the Prussian left flank the fighting had been indecisive. Hulot's division made little progress, but an attempt at a counter-attack by Lottum's cavalry was defeated and five out of six guns of the horse battery taken by Grouchy's horsemen.

Blucher had not been seen since he had left the headquarters staff to lead the cavalry attack, and in his absence Gneisenau ordered the retreating troops to fall back on Tilly, a point some two miles to the north-west of Ligny.

When the I. and III. Corps of the Prussian army began their retreat Thielmann drew back his corps to Sombreffe and Point du Jour, where it bivouacked. Between ten and eleven o'clock orders were received for him to retreat to Tilly if the roads were open, if not, to Gembloux; and Thielmann, considering the darkness and the disorganised state of his troops, determined to retreat on the latter place, which he reached about 6 A.M. on the 17th. Here he found Jagow with seven battalions of infantry, two cavalry regiments, and a battery, besides the ammunition columns of the I. and II. and of his own corps, which had fortunately been directed to this place on the 16th.

On the morning of the battle at Ligny, Bülow, in accordance with orders, had started from his cantonments round Liége to march to Hannut. He had scarcely reached this point at 1 P.M. when he received a further order to move through Gembloux to Ardenelle, a point close to the Roman road, about 2½ miles north-east of Sombreffe. But seeing that it would be too late to reach the battlefield, and finding the road much blocked with baggage and wounded, he determined to halt his troops close to the Roman road about Sauvenière and Baudeset. Here he reported his arrival to Blucher and asked for further instructions.

The three Prussian corps defeated at Ligny had suffered considerable loss, amounting to some 6000 killed, wounded, and prisoners, and sixteen to twenty guns.

The French casualties numbered about 8500.[1]

To return to the French left wing. The Prince of Orange, as we have seen, arrived at Quatre Bras about six o'clock. As the troops of the 2nd Dutch-Belgian Division came up he proceeded to put them into position. The main line taken up had for its centre the farm at Gemioncourt, with the Bossu wood on the right, while the left rested on the buildings of Piraumont. The position was not un-

---

[1] It is very difficult to determine accurately the numbers. The French, according to Houssaye's estimate (see 'Waterloo,' vol. ii. p. 189), amounted to the number given. Lettow-Vorbeck, p. 341, gives 12,000 for the Prussians. This seems exaggerated, but expresses doubts as to whether this included runaways. The number of prisoners taken by the French was distinctly small, hardly more than a few hundreds. The French attacked, and probably lost more than the defenders. The number of Prussian soldiers who left the colours, of which the greater part was furnished by those from the Rhineland, Westphalia, and the Duchy of Berg, some of whom had formerly been French soldiers, has been variously estimated at from 8000 to 10,000 men. If the killed and wounded be taken at about 6000, and the runaways near the smaller figure, we get a total of about 15,000,—the figure at which the losses are put by Gneisenau in his report to the king of the 17th June. See Ollech, p. 163.

THE BATTLE OF QUATRE BRAS 137

favourable for the defensive. At Quatre Bras was a group of houses and farm-buildings disposed round the four roads, and forming a considerable point of support there; stretching away to the left the Namur *chaussée*, which is partly in bank and partly in cutting, afforded a good defensive line. In front of this there was the farm of Piraumont, which acted as an outpost to check the French advance. The Bossu wood itself was filled with undergrowth, which made it a formidable obstacle; and in front of it there was the farm of Pierrepont, which afforded another advanced post. The farm of Gemioncourt, in the centre, also formed a good supporting point to this part of the line. From Piraumont to the edge of the wood was about 1900 yards, to the edge of the Bossu wood about another 1200. The number of troops available for its defence at the commencement of the action was 7200 infantry and 16 guns, consisting of Perponcher's division, with the exception of one battalion which did not come up till later. There is a slight ridge on the French side of Gemioncourt, and behind this farm there is a stream which flows through a pond and across the Namur road towards Sart-Dames-Aveslines. To defend the position, the Dutch-Belgian troops were distributed as follows:—

One battalion was placed in Gemioncourt, and another with five guns in front of it. To the right of this point there were four battalions, with Bijleveld's battery in front towards Pierrepont; the remainder of the division was in reserve at Quatre Bras, on the road leading to Namur.

On the morning of the 16th Ney seems to have waited for definite instructions from the Emperor before issuing orders to his troops, and it was not until Flahaut brought him the Emperor's letter at eleven o'clock that he gave them out. Then, in accordance with them, he ordered Reille to advance, with a view to placing the 5th Division at Genappe, the 9th Division in second line behind it, and the 6th and 7th Divisions at Quatre Bras.[1] The first three divisions of d'Erlon were to take post at Frasnes. The right division, with Piré's cavalry, was to hold Marbais. The 1st Cavalry Division was to cover the advance. Kellermann's cavalry divisions were to take post at Liberchies and Frasnes, the Guard cavalry of Lefebvre was to remain at the latter place. From all this it is plain that Ney, like Napoleon, thought he would be able to advance without much hindrance.

Reille had been told by Ney to obey any orders he might receive from the Emperor, but although he was shown the letter which Flahaut was taking to Ney he did not move forward, being somewhat troubled by a report from Girard, who was at Wangenies, that a considerable force of Prussians was advancing by the Namur road towards St Amand. Reille, therefore, wrote to Ney that he was waiting definite orders from him, and two hours were thus lost.

Some time after two o'clock, however, the divisions of Bachelu and Foy arrived, and in another half-

---

[1] It will not be forgotten that Girard's division was at Wangenies, and was to be used by Grouchy if necessary. See 'La critique de la Campagne de 1815,' par A. G., note 4, pp. 261-62.

THE BATTLE OF QUATRE BRAS 139

hour they were formed for the attack. Bachelu's division was sent against the left of the Allies' line, marching on Piraumont, with Jamin's brigade of Foy's division on the left—Foy's 2nd Brigade being for a time kept in reserve. The Dutch-Belgian troops had their front covered by skirmishers, but these, being few in number, were easily driven back by the advancing French troops, those on the left flank retiring on Piraumont, which was soon captured by the advancing French. Jamin's brigade was now inclined somewhat to the left, and drove back the 2nd battalion of the Nassau Regiment, and pushed the 5th Dutch Militia out of Gemioncourt. These troops were retiring towards the Bossu wood when they were charged by Piré's lancers and put to flight. On the Allied right, where Prince Bernhard held the Bossu wood with four battalions of his men, no fighting took place for a time, as Ney had not sufficient troops available for the purpose. Still the position was somewhat critical, as the centre and left of Perponcher's division had been driven back, and Foy's troops were advancing down the road.

But the arrival of reinforcements for the Anglo-Allies put a different complexion on the struggle. Merlen's brigade of light dragoons and hussars came up from Nivelles, and Picton's division, consisting of Kempt's and Pack's brigades of British troops, and Best's brigade of Hanoverian landwehr, from Waterloo. The English troops were at once formed along the Namur road,—Pack's brigade on the right, Kempt's on the left, and Best's in support behind them, with a battery of artillery on each flank. The left battalion of Kempt's brigade (1st/95th) was sent forward to hold the small wood just behind the brook on the Namur road, this being important for maintaining connection with the Prussians at Ligny. While this movement was going on, to stop the advancing French, Merlen's cavalry brigade was ordered to the front to support the Dutch infantry retiring from Gemioncourt. It was met by Piré's cavalry, and driven back in confusion to Quatre Bras, carrying with it the Duke of Wellington and his staff. Piré's lancers after defeating the Dutch-Belgian cavalry charged a Dutch battalion and overthrew it, and took, for a time, the eight guns in the central part of the battlefield.

Having possession of Gemioncourt and Piraumont, Ney held the ridge extending behind these two points, which favoured the assemblement of his troops, gave him a position for his artillery, and a good point of vantage for any further movement against the Allied centre.

By now the French had also received reinforcements, for Jerome's division had come from Frasnes —this freed Gauthier's brigade of Foy's division which had hitherto been in reserve, and it was moved up to join Foy. Jerome's division was sent against Pierrepont, from which the Nassau troops were driven back into the wood, which was then attacked, but the progress here was slow owing to the difficulty caused by the thick undergrowth. At this time also Ney received Soult's letter of two o'clock telling him to overthrow all in front of him, and to return against the Prussians in position at Brye.

The Brunswick corps now joined Wellington, thus for the first time placing him in numerical superiority to Ney. The numbers being for the Anglo-Allies 19,000 infantry, 2000 cavalry, and 30 guns, while Ney had 16,000 infantry, 1700 cavalry, and 38 guns.

To carry out the Emperor's orders, Ney ordered a general advance. To meet it the light companies of the regiments of Picton's division were sent forward to attack the French skirmishers covering the march of their main body. Wellington's troops held firm on the left, but on the right the Nassau and such Dutch-Belgian infantry as had sought refuge in the Bossu wood, when driven from Gemioncourt, were slowly pressed back—thus there was a gap left in the Allied forces between the Charleroi road and the Bossu wood. To fill this, Wellington ordered the Duke of Brunswick to send up a portion of his troops, and the latter accordingly ordered two battalions and two light companies to advance for this purpose, and supported them by the Brunswick cavalry, while two more battalions of infantry were in reserve behind the Namur road.[1]

The French troops were delivering their assault. Bachelu moved from Piraumont against the left wing. In the centre Foy marched with one brigade along the road, and the other on the eastern side

[1] The Brunswick corps was not complete, the 1st and 3rd light battalions and the guns not having come up. One battalion (the 2nd light) was also sent to aid the 95th, and two rifle companies were ordered into the Bossu wood. This left two battalions for the reserve. See detail of troops in Appendix.

of it. Jerome ordered Soye's brigade to attack the Bossu wood, while Bauduin's advanced between the wood and the road to meet the Brunswickers. Soye's brigade pushed back the defenders of the wood almost to its northern limit, where one battalion of the Nassau troops, however, contrived to hold on close to the Namur road. Bauduin's brigade received a charge of the Brunswick cavalry, but beat it back with considerable loss, the gallant Duke of Brunswick here meeting his death.

Supported by Gauthier's brigade, the French swept on towards Quatre Bras, accompanied by Piré's cavalry. On the right, Bachelu's division steadily advancing had almost reached the British line; but the 5th Division, which had been brought in front of the Namur road, received it with a deadly volley at point-blank range; Bachelu's men wavered, and Picton calling to his men to charge, drove them headlong back almost to Piraumont. The counter-attack, however, could get no farther, for the artillery fire from the divisional guns of the 5th French Division, and the volleys from the 108th Regiment of the line, which had been kept in reserve when the rest of the division advanced, first brought the English to a standstill, and then compelled them to retire. The chasseurs of Piré's cavalry now charged Kempt's three battalions, but were driven back with considerable loss. Meanwhile the lancers of the same division, after pursuing the Brunswickers, turned sharply round against the right of Pack's brigade, where were the 42nd Highlanders and the 44th Regiment. The 42nd were

CHARGE OF THE FRENCH CAVALRY

unable to form square before the charge reached home. Some lancers penetrated the regiment, but were soon killed, and the attack repelled. The 44th Regiment, the next along the line to the east, had also no time to form a square, but the rear rank faced about and drove off the Frenchmen by their fire. The attack of these two regiments had not involved the attention of the whole of Piré's lancers, and a portion of them were sent against the 92nd, but were roughly handled, and eventually the French cavalry drew back, some round the wood, others by the road they had advanced by.

While this fighting was proceeding Kellermann's cavalry joined Ney's force. The Marshal was much disturbed in mind by the little practical progress he had made with the fight, and by the messages he had received from the Emperor. At five o'clock Soult's letter of 3.15, telling him that the fate of France was in his hands, reached him, and that he was to direct his troops back to the heights of St Amand and Brye. The situation was a terrible one. Deprived by the wanderings of d'Erlon of the help of his corps, feeling, notwithstanding the supreme efforts his troops had made, that he was making no progress while the forces of the enemy were plainly being augmented, Ney was now told that the fate of France depended on him. Small wonder if he cried out, "See those English cannon-balls — would that they all would bury themselves in my body." At this time Kellermann came up. Carried beyond himself by the pressing nature of the crisis, Ney ordered him to charge, notwithstanding, as he pointed out to the Marshal, that the latter was asking him with a single brigade of cuirassiers to attack 25,000 men.

The Anglo-Allied troops were now strengthened by the 5th British Brigade and the 1st Hanoverian Brigade. They arrived about five o'clock, at a time when the position was very critical. For the Brunswick artillery had been very severely handled, and the Dutch-Belgian troops were rapidly abandoning the front, while the Brunswick cavalry were much discouraged by the death of their gallant Prince. The reinforcements raised Wellington's numbers to 24,000 infantry and 42 guns. Colin Halkett's brigade was brought into the space from which the Brunswickers had been driven back, while Kielmansegge's troops were directed along the Namur road to support the 95th Regiment on the extreme left. At this juncture the French infantry advanced again to a point just south of Quatre Bras. The 92nd who were stationed there charged and drove them back. Yet Pack's brigade was in sore stress, for it had been necessary to form the sadly diminished 42nd and 44th Regiments into one battalion, and the ammunition was nearly all expended. The 69th Regiment was therefore sent from Halkett's brigade to join Pack's men, while the remainder of his brigade, advancing over the ground between the Bossu wood and the road, relieved the Brunswick infantry, who rallied behind them. Pack, who had gone to the front to observe the movements of the French, saw that an attack was imminent, and that cavalry were coming on;

he therefore ordered his own men to form square, and sent instructions to the 69th to do likewise. For Kellermann, in accordance with Ney's orders, was preparing to attack, and had formed his two regiments in column of squadrons at double squadron distance, while Piré's lancers were in support.

The Prince of Orange now made his second important contribution to the history of this campaign. He told the commanding officer of the 69th Regiment that there was no chance of the cavalry attacking, and ordered him to re-form into line; this was hardly done when Kellermann's cuirassiers were on them, and these, striking the regiment in flank, succeeded in completely rolling it up, with a loss to it of 150 men and one of the colours. His Royal Highness gave similar orders to the 30th Regiment, but the commanding officer perceiving in time the advance of the French cavalry formed square, as also did the 73rd Regiment, and the fire of these two forced Kellermann to diverge to his right. The 33rd, which was the most advanced of Halkett's brigade, suffered severely from artillery fire, and fell back with the Brunswick regiment which it had advanced to support, taking up position on the outskirts of the wood. The French cavalry had thus succeeded in penetrating almost to the centre of the Allied troops, but could get no farther; for coming into the angle formed by the wood and the road they received the fire from the infantry on either flank, while a battery of the King's German Legion, which had just arrived, struck the intrepid horsemen in front with grape and case. Kellermann's men were driven back

K

in disorder, and in their flight they carried with them several battalions of Foy's division and of Bauduin's brigade. This confusion in the centre stopped Bachelu's advance, and it was now the turn of the Duke of Wellington to make a forward movement; for he had just received further reinforcements in the shape of the 1st British Division of Guards and some batteries of artillery. The light companies of the Guards were sent into the Bossu wood. Piré's renewed attempts to charge the Brunswickers and Halkett's men were all beaten, while a portion of the Guards were sent round the western border of the Bossu wood, and this with the general advance of the English line drove the French slowly back. By nine o'clock the action ceased, and Wellington's force occupied the ground from which they had driven their opponents.

At nightfall the position was as follows: The Emperor had gained a victory over the Prussians, of which he could scarcely gauge the extent owing to the darkness, though as usual he greatly exaggerated it. Ney had been defeated, but not severely, with a loss of 4500 men, the Anglo-Allied casualties being about the same.

Napoleon was no longer in the favourable position that he held the night before. Ney had made mistakes. These were: not reconnoitring early in the morning, not pushing on Bachelu's division to seize Quatre Bras, and not bringing up the two others of Reille's corps available to help it. He waited for Napoleon's orders, but under no conceivable circumstances could the Emperor have wanted him to keep his troops dis-

NEY'S MISTAKES 147

persed. Foy's and Jerome's divisions should therefore have been ordered up early in the day, and instructions sent to d'Erlon to come up. Had this been done Wellington would have had to assault the 1st Corps in position; and although he might have done so with success, because Ney's flank would have been open to attack from Nivelles, yet if d'Erlon's corps had been called up at daybreak, as it should have been, Ney would have possessed so large a preponderance of force as to have rendered Wellington's defeat certain in the end. Perponcher's men would have been driven off, and thus Wellington could have had merely the Reserve, which did not come up till three o'clock, followed by the 5th British and 1st Hanoverian Brigades at five, and the 1st Division, which only arrived at seven.

So far as the right wing is concerned, there is no doubt that Napoleon's best plan would have been to turn Blucher's right, as, if successful, that would certainly have compelled the Prussians to fall back towards Namur, and thus have separated them from Wellington. This appears to have been the Emperor's original idea, and the penetration of the centre was only had recourse to when he found that his force was not sufficient to enable him to complete the flank attack on his opponent's right. But this was largely Napoleon's own fault, and arose from the fact that he did not appreciate till after the battle was begun the strength of the Prussians opposed to him. Had he issued definite and proper orders to d'Erlon or Ney, the 1st Corps would have supported him. Had he called up Lobau sufficiently early, the 6th

Corps would have been available to strengthen his left. Doubtless the Emperor was misled by the reports of the 15th; but he was quite willing to believe what he hoped for, and thus remained fixed in the idea till too late, that merely a small force had to be dealt with. This also accounts to some extent for the delay in ordering the troops to the front in the early morning.[1] If the concentration movement on Fleurus had been started at daybreak, the battle would have been begun quite four hours earlier, before the Prussians were completely assembled for battle. Both Ney and Napoleon wasted precious hours on the morning of the 16th, the most momentous day of the campaign—delays from which the Imperial cause never recovered.

On the other hand, had Wellington been able to concentrate his troops more rapidly, Ney would have been severely defeated, and in all probability the French army would have been driven back beyond the Sambre. That he did not do so was due to defective information from his outposts. The blame for this must be divided between Dörnberg, the Prince of Orange, and the Prussians; but to the latter the greatest share is due, because they utterly failed to send Wellington any news during the day of the result of the fighting at Charleroi.

Gneisenau must bear the blame of the Prussian defeat, for it was owing to his bad staff arrangements

---

[1] It must not, however, be forgotten that the troops had a long and tiring march on the 15th, and Napoleon may have judged it well to give them more rest than usual, although such considerations had not had any influence in former campaigns.

THE LIGNY POSITION

that the IV. Corps did not reach the battlefield.[1] On him too must rest the blame for fighting on ground so ill adapted for defence, chosen deliberately by the Prussian Headquarter Staff for a pitched battle.[2] It covered, it is true, the line of communications by the Roman road to Liége; but it possessed two great disadvantages. The chief of these was the fact that the whole of the position was completely exposed to view and fire.[3] The second, that the III. Corps

---

[1] It is the custom to blame Bülow for not having used greater speed in carrying out the order of the 14th June to draw in his troops so that they could reach Hannut in one march (see *ante*, p. 65). But this order did not reach him till the 15th at 5 A.M., whereas, being sent off at noon on the 14th, it should have reached him between 4 and 5 o'clock (see Pflugk-Hartung, p. 253). Moreover, it was indefinite in character. Now whereas in any case Bülow was required to support the other corps, this order should have definitely told him to concentrate at Hannut at once, and should have been sent in duplicate. The IV. Corps would then have reached Hannut early on the 15th, and been up at Ligny in the early afternoon of the 16th.

[2] That it was chosen deliberately is proved by Nostitz, who says (p. 18, *op. cit.*): "Although in the headquarters the subject had been much discussed, and the danger of accepting battle in the position of Sombreffe had often been put forward by many persons, yet Generals von Gneisenau and von Grolmann adhered firmly to the idea. Count Groeben had carefully reconnoitred and surveyed the chosen battlefield, and had described in such lively colours its many advantages as to have given rise to an almost fanatical fondness for it, which the objections put forward by other members of the Headquarters, among them myself, could in no way modify." This is doubtless a fair representation of what occurred, but I take leave to doubt whether a young officer like Nostitz was ever allowed to give his opinion to generals like Gneisenau and Grolmann.

[3] See *ante*, p. 122. Wellington was of the opinion that the position was a bad one (see 'Notes on Conversations with the Duke of Wellington,' by the Earl Stanhope, p. 109). When he met Hardinge near the windmill of Bussy he said to him: "If they fight here they will be damnably mauled." At the interview with Lord Stanhope on the 26th October 1837, at which Hardinge was present, he explained that the Prussians were dotted "in this way" (like the fingers of a hand) "along the slope

was so situated as to be completely out of tactical unison with the I. and II. Corps. For although formed up almost at right angles to the line of the latter, the ground in front of it was not suited to counter-attack. Thus Thielmann's whole force was held at bay by cavalry and one infantry division. Surely, from the time the battle began, it would have been possible to have brought round at least two brigades to help the I. and II. Corps, while some of the III. Corps artillery might have been deployed to take in flank the French attacks on Ligny.

of the hill, so that no cannon-ball missed its effect upon them." Napoleon also thought the position a bad one. In the 'Commentaires,' vol. v. p. 144, he says: "The Prussian army was all massed on the amphitheatre which goes from St Amand and Ligny to the heights of Brye. The cannon-balls of the French army which missed the first lines struck the reserves; not a single round was wasted."

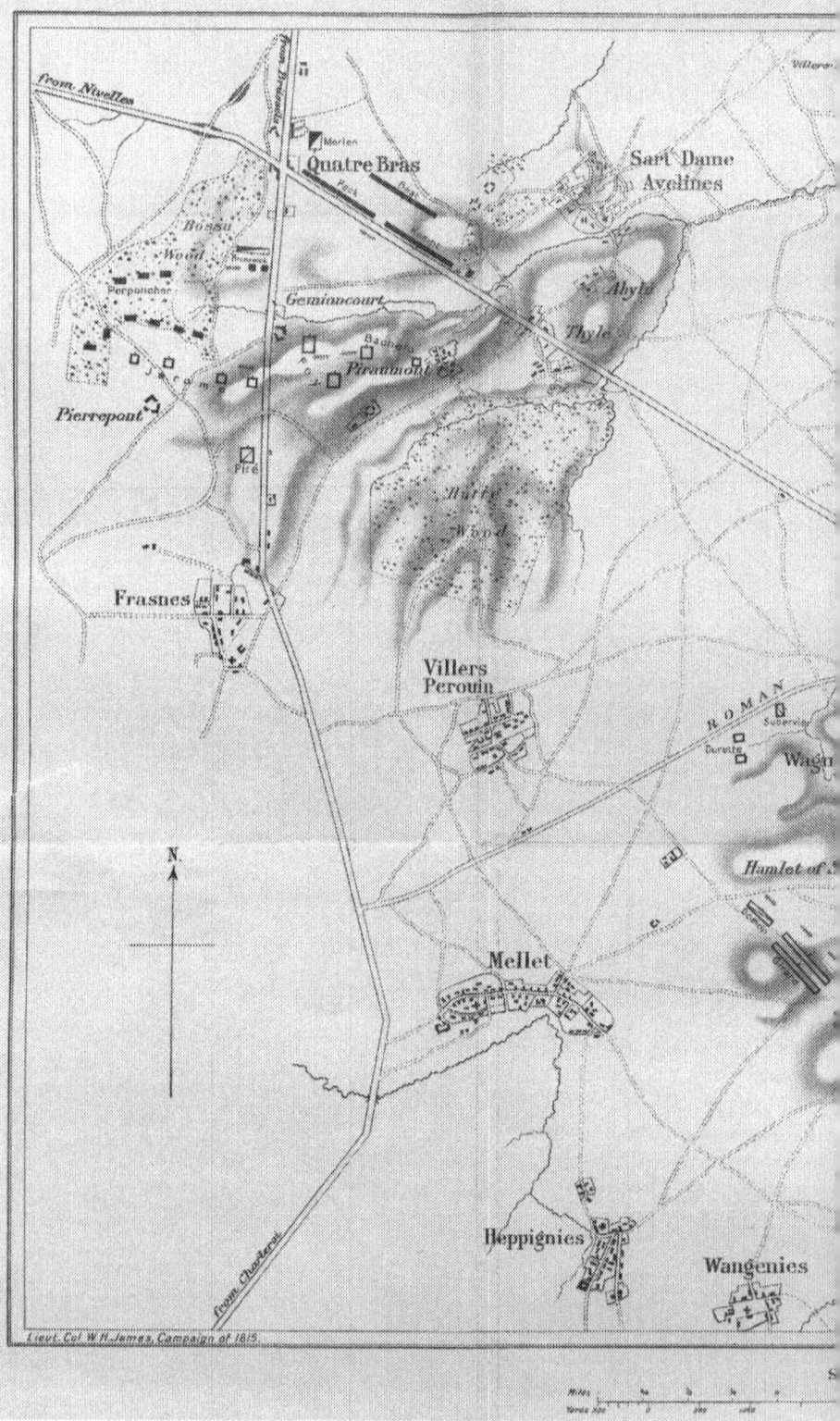

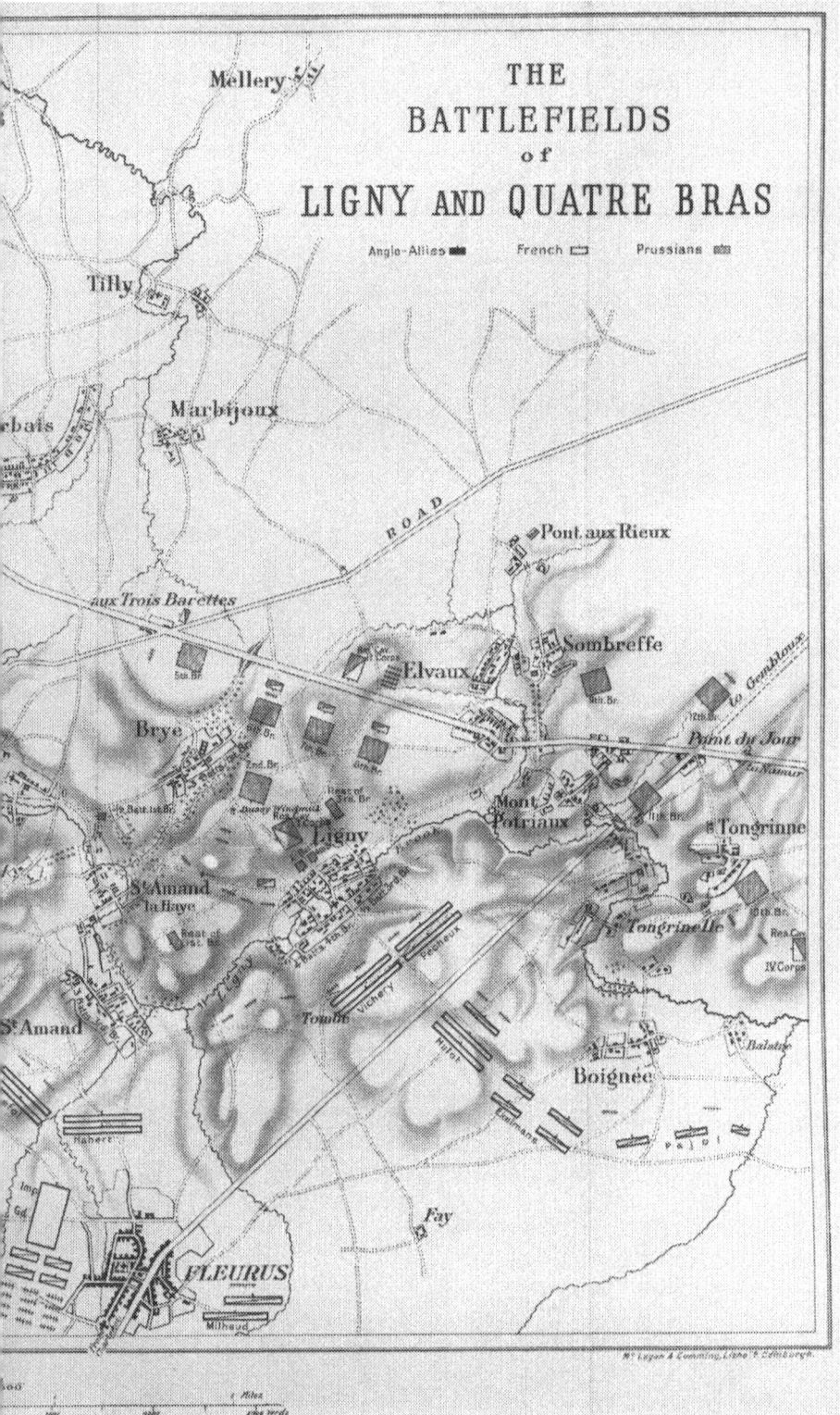

CHAPTER V.

THE WANDERING OF D'ERLON—WELLINGTON'S "DISPOSITION."

It is universally admitted that the wandering to and fro of the 1st Corps between the battlefields of Ligny and Quatre Bras resulted in both battles being comparatively indecisive. It is plain that this marching and counter-marching must have been due to instructions given to the 1st Corps either by Ney or Napoleon. Let us then briefly consider what were the orders issued with regard to it during the 16th June, and thus endeavour to fasten on the right man the responsibility for the muddle which had so disastrous an effect on the issue of the campaign.

It is scarcely too much to say that had d'Erlon been able to assist either Napoleon or Ney, the result would have been a severe reverse either to Blucher or to Wellington. It would doubtless have been better had the 1st Corps been used to help the Emperor, as the result of striking the right wing of the Prussians with a force of 20,000 men at the same time as their centre was pierced at

Ligny, must have been a crushing defeat—such a defeat, in fact, as would have been little short of disaster. Great loss in killed, wounded, and prisoners would have been inflicted on Blucher's men, and his army must have retreated on Gembloux, covered by Thielmann, with a view to joining Bülow. This would have effectually separated it from Wellington. The Prussians too would have been far more demoralised than they were after Ligny, and would, in all probability, have fallen back on Liége, leaving Napoleon free to deal with the Anglo-Allied army.

On the other hand, Wellington's defeat would certainly have ensued had d'Erlon supported Ney. This would have caused him to retire to Waterloo. Owing to the delay which had taken place in concentrating his force, it is by no means certain that he would have been able to collect his army there in time to prevent the French pushing him back and reaching Brussels. Thus the original plan of Napoleon would have been carried out, the Allies would have been driven widely apart, and certainly one of them, the Prussians, would have been very severely defeated.

We may fairly assume, therefore, that for d'Erlon to have been used to aid Napoleon would have been in consonance with the General Idea of the latter.

Nor was there any reason why the Emperor should not have taken him from Ney for the purpose. The commanders of both wings were distinctly told that either might be diminished if Napoleon thought it desirable; but so long as either wing commander

THE ORDERS TO D'ERLON 153

was acting independently, Napoleon would send his orders to that wing through him. If d'Erlon were wanted, therefore, Napoleon would requisition him through Ney.[1]

What, then, were the instructions sent to d'Erlon during the 16th, and by whom were they sent? First of all, it must be remembered that Ney himself was without any until fairly late in the day (10 A.M.), and that Napoleon, relying on the reports of the 15th from both wings and also on his own assumption, certainly did not expect any great opposition either about Fleurus or Quatre Bras. He was so sure that he had anticipated the Allied commanders that he did not believe either would succeed in bringing any considerable force against him. D'Erlon belonged properly to the left wing, and unless therefore the Emperor saw some good reason to change his plans, in which case he might by direct order draw the 1st Corps towards him, the latter would belong to and remain with Ney for the advance on Brussels, which Napoleon evidently contemplated for the afternoon or evening after he had brushed aside the insignificant forces he thought were opposed to him.

The definite instructions to Ney for his task during the day are clear enough both in Soult's and in the Emperor's communications. These are contained in Soult's second and Napoleon's first letter to Ney. In neither is there one word about d'Erlon being used except with Ney, to whom indeed he was necessary if the advance on Brussels was to be

[1] See *ante*, instructions to Ney, pp. 107-9.

carried out. The only detachment to be made was the division to be sent to Marbais. This, with Girard's division at Wangenies, would have given Napoleon a considerable force (about 8000 men) to use against the Prussian right flank.[1] The next order sent also to Ney was for him to unite the corps of Reille and d'Erlon with that of Kellermann, and with these he was to beat and destroy any force of the enemy which might present itself. This is in Soult's third letter to Ney. In this no mention is made of any divisions to be detached for any purpose whatever. As this came after Napoleon's letter and Soult's second letter had been sent to Ney, had the latter interpreted it literally he must have drawn in the division of Girard and stopped d'Erlon sending a division to Marbais! It is an example of bad staff work, because the last order is plainly contradictory to those previously sent. But this is not the only contradiction in the

[1] This was the force Napoleon subsequently stated he expected. See 'Mémoires,' vol. v. p. 139. I have previously on p. 81 drawn attention to the fact that Girard's division was ordered by Napoleon himself against the Prussians on the 15th, and that, although he knew this (see p. 110, his instructions to Grouchy), he in his instructions to Ney speaks of the eight divisions the latter was in command of, and only ordered one to be detached to Marbais. The Emperor meant to use Girard, and yet ordered another to be detached; plainly, therefore, Ney would only have six divisions, not eight. The exact wording of the 'Mémoires' is as follows. After stating that the Emperor, when he learned Ney had not attacked, fearing that the English and Prussians had united about Fleurus, "he [the Emperor] reiterated the order to advance beyond Quatre Bras, and as soon as he had taken up his position there he was to detach a column of 8000 infantry, with Lefebvre-Desnoëtte's cavalry and 28 guns, to move by the *chaussée* from Quatre Bras to Namur, which it was to leave at the village of Marbais to attack the height of Brye in rear of the enemy." There is no trace of this order in existence so far as I know.

CONTRADICTORY ORDERS

orders of that day. Soult's second letter to Ney, sent off a little before but which arrived a little later than the orders taken by Flahaut, state that his Majesty wishes, if it be not unsuitable, that a division with cavalry should be at Genappe, and another division about Marbais, to cover the country between Sombreffe and Trois Bras. He was also to place near these divisions Lefebvre's cavalry as well as the 1st Regiment of Hussars which Pajol had sent on the previous day from Charleroi. Now it is perfectly clear that cavalry could not be at the same time near the division at Genappe and also near the division at Marbais—a striking example of the slipshod way in which the French orders were issued. Moreover, in his own letter Napoleon orders Lefebvre to be kept back, covered by the cavalry of d'Erlon and Reille, yet Soult tells Ney to place him in what was practically the front line. It is difficult to conceive anything more contradictory and confusing than these divergent sets of orders.[1]

The first order in which there is any hint of Ney supporting the Emperor is in the letter which Soult sent off at two o'clock. In this Ney was told, after having attacked and pushed back vigorously the enemy in front of him, to return and help in enveloping the corps between Sombreffe and Brye. The next order sent to Ney at 3.15 says nothing about the Marshal attacking anybody in front of him, but that he was to manœuvre so as to envelop

[1] Napoleon made a similar muddle in 1806 in his orders of the 29th December to Bernadotte, which are in absolute contradiction to those he issued on the 1st January 1807.

Blucher's right and fall on his rear. It is plain, therefore, that

   (1) Napoleon at first had no notion that he had any considerable force of either Prussians or Anglo-Allied troops to deal with.

   (2) He thought he could move to Brussels that day.

   (3) Originally he only wanted "a division" at Marbais to support Grouchy at Sombreffe, or, alternatively, to aid Ney at "Trois Bras" if it became necessary, and that he, apparently, had forgotten all about Girard, who was already on the spot.

   (4) Later on, at two o'clock, when Napoleon thinks he has only "a corps" to deal with, Ney is to defeat what is in front of him and then return to help the Emperor.

   (5) By 3.15 Napoleon appreciates that the Prussians are stronger than he thought, and therefore Ney is to disregard the position at Quatre Bras and return at once to help the Emperor with his whole force, which order, be it remarked, was issued without the slightest knowledge of what Ney had in front of him!

Plainly, therefore, up till two o'clock the Emperor thought he had sufficient force on his right wing to deal with all he had in front of him; judging from the letters sent by Soult to Ney, no direct instructions had been sent to d'Erlon at that time, or otherwise they would surely have been mentioned by Soult in his letter.

But it is contended that orders were sent direct to

THE ORDERS TO D'ERLON 157

d'Erlon; that the latter received them shortly after four, when the half of his column had passed the Roman road; that the messenger in question left Fleurus a quarter of an hour after the officer who took the 3.15 order of Soult to Ney, but having come by the shorter road reached d'Erlon an hour before the bearer of Soult's order. Houssaye takes as his chief witness for this order the commander of the artillery of the 1st Corps, General de Salle. He admits that de Salle reconstituted the letter from memory, but does not say how long after the event. Houssaye also gives what he describes as the testimonies of fifteen other witnesses to confirm this order. Analysed they all amount to this, that various people state their belief that such an order was given, but belief that an order was given is no evidence that it was issued.

What is the evidence against it? Far weightier than the "beliefs" that have been brought forward in its favour. D'Erlon denied that he ever received any such order, Napoleon does not admit he issued it; and surely if the giver and the receiver of the supposed order repudiate it, one may be permitted to doubt its existence. But more than this, Napoleon plainly throughout the day sent orders to Ney, and those we have quoted, while showing clearly that he wished Ney to help him at Ligny, do not describe definitely how it is to be done, but leave it to Ney's discretion. On the other hand, it must be admitted that Napoleon had laid down that he might diminish one or other of the wings if he thought it necessary; but up to the issuing of the 3.15 order by Soult, it is plain that he thought both Reille and d'Erlon were with the Marshal, and we are now asked to believe, a quarter of an hour after the Chief of the Staff had sent the order in question to Ney, that the Emperor sent a pencilled note *direct* to d'Erlon ordering the latter to come to his aid. This seems improbable. Moreover, if the Emperor knew that d'Erlon had received an order to come in the direction of Ligny, it is incredible that when Vandamme saw a column of troops advancing against his flank, and reported this to Napoleon, that the latter should not at once have guessed it was the 1st Corps, and have sent orders by the aide-de-camp General Dejean, whom he sent to see what the column was, to say how it should join in the attack. The supposed order was as follows. See Houssaye, p. 206, footnote.

> "Count d'Erlon, the enemy is tumbling blindly into the trap! Take the whole of your force to the heights of Ligny and fall on St Amand. Count d'Erlon, you will save France and cover yourself with glory!"

It is admitted this is a reconstruction from memory by de Salle. For any force directed in accordance with what de Salle says was Napoleon's order could not have come otherwise than on to the left flank of Vandamme. But if Ney had first driven off the English he would naturally have fallen back by the Namur road, as that was the shortest line to strike the Prussians at Sombreffe. Had he done this, Napoleon would hardly have seen him until his troops were close up to Brye, and hence when d'Erlon's troops arrived he could not think who they were.

WHY D'ERLON CAME BACK

It follows, therefore, that Napoleon sent no direct order to d'Erlon.

Why, then, did the 1st Corps move in the direction it undoubtedly did? The proper solution of this problem is without doubt that given by d'Erlon himself, who states that Ney gave him orders to come to Frasnes and Quatre Bras, where he was to receive further orders. Riding on in advance of his corps, he wished to find out what was going on at Quatre Bras; he stopped just beyond Frasnes to talk with the Generals of the Guard (*i.e.*, Lefebvre and Kellermann), and here he was joined by La Bédoyère, who showed him a pencil note which he was taking to Marshal Ney, and which ordered the latter to direct d'Erlon's corps to Ligny.[1] La Bédoyère told d'Erlon that he had already turned his corps in the required direction, and explained to him where he could find it. D'Erlon at once took this route, and sent General Del Cambre, his chief staff officer, to Ney to tell him where he had gone.

Now either Del Cambre took the pencilled note, or else, which is more probable, the bearer accompanied him to Ney. Had the Marshal received any absolute command from the Emperor, either to himself or to d'Erlon, would he have at once disobeyed it and sent to order d'Erlon back to him? The letter in question therefore was, there is scarcely any doubt, a mere duplicate, possibly somewhat differently worded, of the 3.15 P.M. order to Ney, just as Napoleon's first letter to him was an amplification of Soult's second

---

[1] The bearer of this pencil note has been much disputed, but is quite immaterial.

letter. The Emperor sent it for the same reason—because his aides-de-camp went faster, and probably he told Ney to send the corps *if he could spare it*. If the order was not permissive but definite, how was it Ney ordered the 1st Corps back? and if d'Erlon knew that the Emperor wanted him, why did he return at Ney's bidding? Napoleon was not a man lightly to be disobeyed. Ney in his report to the Emperor, 16th June, 10 P.M., says a misunderstanding on the part of Count d'Erlon deprived him of a great victory. Napoleon, replying on the 17th, remarks [1]:—

> "The Emperor has observed with regret that you did not keep your divisions together yesterday, but that they acted without concert (*elles ont agi isolément*); thus you have suffered loss.
> "If the corps of Counts d'Erlon and Reille had been together, not an Englishman of the body which attacked us would have escaped. If Count d'Erlon had executed the movement on St Amand which the Emperor ordered, the Prussian army would have been totally destroyed, and we should have made perhaps 30,000 prisoners."

These lines are much more consonant with the pencilled note having been of a permissive character for d'Erlon to be sent back if he could be spared, rather than with any peremptory order for the 1st Corps to come to the Emperor, with or without Ney's knowledge and consent.

Ney knowing this, and feeling the urgent necessity for the 1st Corps as the Anglo-Allied force increased,

---

[1] 'Documents Inédits,' p. 45, and Pollio's 'Waterloo,' &c., p. 226.

sent back Del Cambre with a peremptory order for d'Erlon to rejoin him; this the latter did, leaving the leading division, Durutte's and Jacquinot's cavalry, on the French left flank. But Durutte did nothing. Given discretion by d'Erlon, he appears to have thought it was the better part of valour, and notwithstanding the urging of his subordinates and possibly an order from Napoleon, he limited his action to a mere demonstration.[1] Properly employed, he might possibly have turned the Prussian defeat into disaster. He could certainly have stopped their retreat on Tilly.[2]

Reviewing the foregoing arguments, it is plain that the cause of d'Erlon's wanderings was the mistaken zeal of the aide-de-camp, who turned off the whole of the 1st Corps in the direction in which he believed the Emperor wanted it without previously finding out whether Ney could spare it. Next came the mistake of d'Erlon himself in not aiding Vandamme with

---

[1] See 'Journal des Sciences Militaires,' 1863, vol. i. p. 393 *et seq.*

[2] There is an alternative explanation. Bearing in mind Napoleon's statement that he ordered 8000 men, &c. (see *ante*, p. 65), to be detached by Ney against the Prussians, is it not possible that, wanting the division which d'Erlon was to send to Marbais, and thinking it would have reached some point between the Brussels *chaussée* and that point, Napoleon sent an aide-de-camp off to find it and order it on to the heights about Brye? This division, with Girard's division, would have made about the number in question. To have taken the whole corps of d'Erlon away from Ney, unless the latter felt he could spare it, would have been to leave him with three divisions only to deal with the Anglo-Allied army. As to what proportion of this was concentrated, Napoleon did not know, and it is not like him to have left so small a force to stem the tide of what might have been a very serious attack against the Left Wing and on his own left flank and communications. As Napoleon says in his 'Commentaires,' p. 142, "The manœuvres of this column (d'Erlon's) seem inexplicable." Unless the original order is found, they always will remain so.

Durutte and possibly another division, or, at any
rate, in not sending to see whether Napoleon wanted
him. Then d'Erlon's failure to give Durutte definite
orders. Lastly, Napoleon himself failed to act with
decision and give to the 1st Corps definite orders
to stop and help him, although he sent an aide-de-
camp to find out what the troops were coming up
on Vandamme's flank.

We have seen, *ante*, p. 120, that before Wellington
rode over to see Blucher, he had sent him a statement
of what he believed the positions of the various units
were at the time of writing.

This letter was based on a statement signed by
De Lacy Evans, an aide-de-camp of Major-General
Sir W. Ponsonby, and purports to be "a disposition
written out for the information of the Commander of
the Forces by Colonel Sir W. De Lancey." The
statement in question is to be found in the 'Supplementary Despatches,' vol. x. p. 496, where it is
printed without any comment or clue as to its origin
or value.

The annexed table gives (1) the orders issued about
6 or 7 P.M. on the 15th; (2) "after-orders" of 10 P.M.;
(3) the subsequent orders issued early in the morning
of the 16th; (4) the actual position of the troops in
the forenoon of the 16th; (5) the Duke's letter to
Blucher; (6) the "Disposition"; (7) the troops which
arrived at Quatre Bras by the morning of the 17th.
From it three things are clearly shown—viz., that

1. The positions of the troops as furnished to the
   Duke of Wellington by his Staff are grossly
   inaccurate.

Units.	First or "Collection" Order of 15th June.	Station when Order issued.	After-Orders, 10 P.M., 15th June
Dörnberg's Cavalry Brigade and Cumberland Hussars	To march to Vilvorde this night	About Malines	Move on Mont St Jean[3]
English Cavalry	Collect at Ninhove this night[2]	Grammont, Ninhove, and along Dender	Move on Enghien
1st Infantry Division	Enghien and neighbourhood[2]	Enghien	Move on Braine-le-Comte
2nd Infantry Division	Ath[2]	Ath, with 1st Brigade King's German Legion, and 2nd British Brigade; 3rd Hanoverian Brigade at Lens	Move on Enghien
3rd Infantry Division	Braine-le-Comte[2]	Soignies, Braine-le-Comte, and towards Enghien	Move on Nivelles
4th Infantry Division	Grammont, except troops beyond Scheldt there at Audenarde	Oudenarde, 6th Hanoverian Brigade at Nieuport	Move on Enghien
5th Infantry Division and 4th Hanoverian Brigade of 6th Division[1]	...[2]	Brussels and neighbourhood	Move on Mont St Jean[3]
10th Brigade[1]	To march to Brussels	Ghent	...
Brunswick Corps	Road between Brussels and Vilvorde — ready to march in the morning[2]	Brussels and neighbourhood	Move on Mont St Jean[3]
Nassau Troops	Louvain Road—ready to march in the morning[2]	On Louvain road, near Brussels	Move on Mont St Jean[3]
2nd and 3rd Dutch-Belgian Divisions	Nivelles. If this attacked call up 3rd British Division, but not till certain attack on Prussian right and English left	2nd, Nivelles; 3rd, Rœulx, and towards Binche	...
1st Dutch-Belgian Division and Dutch-Indian Brigade	Sotteghem—ready march at daylight	Sotteghem, the Dutch-Indian Brigade at Alost	...
Reserve Artillery	Ready to move at daylight	Brussels	...

[1] This division was formed of the 10th British and 4th Hanoverian Brigades. The Brussels on the 17th, halted till the 18th, when it marched to Waterloo. This brigade had
[2] Ready to move at a moment's notice.   [3] To the
[4] No information procurable, but there can be no doubt from the position recorded in
[5] The 4th Hanoverian Brigade probably on road from Brussels towards Waterloo behin
[6] A portion seems to have arrived at Quatre Bras during the night of the 16th.

...ubsequent Orders.	Actual Position, Forenoon of 16th June.	Duke's Letter to Blucher.	"Disposition," 7 A.M., 16th June.	Troops at Quatre Bras, Morning of 17th June.
...4	Probably between Brussels and Waterloo	Beyond Waterloo, marching to Genappe and Quatre Bras	Beyond Waterloo, marching to Genappe and Quatre Bras	Quatre Bras.
...inue move on Braine-le-...mte	Marching on Quatre Bras. Some reached that night	Nivelles at noon .	Braine-le-Comte, marching to Nivelles and Quatre Bras	Quatre Bras.
...inue on to ...aine-le-Comte ...mediately	Reached Braine-le-Comte 9 A.M.; halt till twelve, and then on to Quatre Bras	Nivelles . .	Do.	Quatre Bras.
...e to Braine-le-...mte on 16th, ...bsequently ordered to march ...Quatre Bras	Only received orders 10 A.M. on this day. Reached Enghien 2 P.M. Braine-le-Comte midnight	Braine-le-Comte .	Do.	...
...4	Arrived Nivelles noon; Quatre Bras between five and six	Nivelles . .	Nivelles, marching to Quatre Bras	Quatre Bras.
...4	Probably about 20 to 30 miles from Enghien	...	Oudenarde, marching on Braine-le-Comte	...
...4	Waterloo 10 A.M.; Quatre Bras about 3 P.M.5	Marching on Genappe, where it will arrive at noon	Beyond Waterloo, marching to Genappe	Quatre Bras.
...	Assche afternoon of 16th	...	...	...
...4	Road to Quatre Bras—arrived there about 4 P.M.	Marching on Genappe, where it will arrive at noon	Beyond Waterloo, marching to Genappe	Quatre Bras.
...4	Following 5th Division and Hanoverian Brigade of 6th Division	Do.	Do.	Quatre Bras.
...4	2nd, at Quatre Bras; 3rd, at Nivelles	Nivelles and Quatre Bras	Nivelles and Quatre Bras	Quatre Bras.
...4	...4	...	Sotteghem, marching to Enghien	...
...red to Quatre ...as on 16th	Brussels 6 . . .	...	...	Mostly at Brussels, or marching down to Waterloo.

... Brigade was at Ghent. It was ordered to Brussels, reached Assche on the afternoon of the 16th, moved to ... recently been completed. The 81st Regiment remained in Brussels guarding treasure.
...ction of the road from Nivelles with that from Namur—*i.e.*, Mont St Jean.
...ext column that the whole army was ordered to its left.
...th Division.

WELLINGTON'S "DISPOSITION" 163

2. Orders had been given, and that the Commander-in-Chief believed them to have been sent, for the continuation of the march towards Quatre Bras.
3. The Duke consulted some member of his Staff before writing the letter, and was led to believe the movement had been continuously carried on. For it is plain from the table that the Duke's letter represents things in even a more favourable light than the disposition, and this view he could only have expressed after asking some one whom he thought would know the exact position of the troops at the time.

It has pleased some foreign writers to attack the honour of the great Englishman, and to say that he deliberately, and of malice aforethought, wrote this letter to deceive Blucher, so that he might fight at Ligny to cover the concentration of the Anglo-Allied army. The position the Duke of Wellington then held in Europe puts him above such silly slander, to which, moreover, his whole career gives the lie; while a little calm consideration, of which the calumniators seem quite incapable, might have led them to see that had the Duke not believed his troops were coming up he would not have hung on there as he did, but would in all probability have fallen back to Nivelles, which would have been a more favourable point for him to concentrate his army at, and one not too distant for him still to have acted in conjunction with the Prussian force. The chief of the detractors is Professor Delbrück, who in his 'Life of Gneisenau' makes the statement, which he reiterated in a subsequent publication, that Blucher was only induced to fight at Ligny on the strength of assurances made by Wellington which the latter knew to be false, the object being to give the Anglo-Allies time to assemble. This statement is amply contradicted by existing documents, and it is absolutely incredible, with these in existence, how such a statement could ever have been made. It is unfortunate that the Prussians were beaten, but that was not the fault of Wellington any more than it was his fault that proper instructions were not sent to Bülow; that Zieten did not keep him properly informed as to the course of the French attack; that one corps of the Prussian Army was so placed as to render it practically of no use to the other two at Ligny; that the position chosen there was a very bad one, because all movements made in it were open to the enemy's view; or that after the battle one-tenth of the Prussian army ran away. Professor Delbrück, who is the chief offender, has been challenged to produce documentary evidence in support of his statement with regard to Wellington's conduct. He has not done so, he cannot do so, and he knows he cannot do so. The opinion of dispassionate men on the issue can only be that it is a gross and baseless calumny.[1]

[1] Pflugk-Hartung has carefully discussed the question of Wellington's supposed promise (see *op. cit.*, pp. 160-64), and quite acknowledges its conditional character. Lettow-Vorbeck takes the other view. As Houssaye remarks, after giving his reasons for believing Wellington only said he would come if he could, "Let him" (*Libre à lui*). See Houssaye, footnote, p. 157.

THE WANT OF NEWS

There is the letter which was based on information given to the Duke. This contains no such assurance, and there is the undisputed evidence that he only promised to come if he overthrew the French in front of him (see *ante*, p. 121). How was it possible for any man to do more? Moreover, it must be remembered that by hanging on to Quatre Bras he diverted d'Erlon's and Reille's corps, whereas had he not done so one of these at least would have attacked the Prussian army in its right rear with disastrous effect.

That Wellington was not able to concentrate his army as rapidly as he had hoped was entirely the fault of those who were supposed to keep him informed of the French movements, but who utterly failed to do so.

After Zieten sent off his despatch about 8.30 A.M. no further information was sent to Wellington. This despatch took over six hours to reach Brussels. Had it been sent with ordinary care it would certainly have arrived at not later than one o'clock. At 11.30 Zieten might have sent off another report, which should have arrived not later than 3.30, containing such details as would have absolutely shown Wellington that the main attack was against Charleroi. Had not the absence of the Prince of Orange from Braine-le-Comte been the cause of the detention there of Dörnberg's despatch, the latter would have reached Wellington certainly by 2.30 or 3 P.M. He would thus have known from Zieten that the Emperor was leading his troops against Charleroi, and this would have been confirmed by Dörnberg's report that the French troops had been withdrawn from the front of

Mons. The latter in itself was too vague without the confirmatory intelligence from Zieten for Wellington to take decisive measures on. Zieten when falling back to Fleurus should have sent a third messenger to Wellington.

Had Prince Bernhard sent an officer to Brussels with the information that the French were at Frasnes, the news would have reached Wellington by 8 P.M., possibly a little before, and this would have been of the utmost utility to him.

Dörnberg also seems to have failed him. Wellington asked on the 29th April for Lieut.-Colonel Colquhoun Grant, 11th Regiment, as head of the Intelligence Department. This officer, who had obtained a great reputation in the Peninsular War, was employed by the Duke in French territory. On the 15th June he sent in a report to Dörnberg, saying that attack was imminent. This report Dörnberg returned to Grant, "saying that so far from convincing him that Napoleon was advancing for battle, it assured him of the contrary. Grant instantly conveyed his letter direct to the Duke, but it only reached him on the field of Waterloo."[1] Dörnberg's belief that no attack was im-

[1] This is an extract from a letter from Lieut.-General Sir William Napier to H.R.H. the Duke of Cambridge, dated 1st September 1857, which is quoted in a footnote on pp. 227, 228 of the 'Memoir of Baron Larrey,' written by Sir Charles M'Grigor, son of Sir James M'Grigor, the celebrated head of the British Army Medical Department. Sir James's wife was a sister of Colquhoun Grant. Sir William Napier, no mean judge, and who saw the latter himself, says (*op. cit.*) it was endorsed by the Duke, "Received from Grant, June the 18th, eleven o'clock." Napier's letter to the Duke of Cambridge finishes by saying, "never was intelligence more important, more exact, or more complete procured for a general in such grave circumstances." Unfortunately it did not reach its destination till too late.

THE FAULTS OF SUBORDINATES

minent explains why he contented himself with the one and only report he sent in that day.

Why did not van Merlen send out patrols to watch his left? He too might have sent in valuable information as to the progress of the French Left Wing, but he did nothing.

The stars in their courses fought against the Duke, and he was fated on 15th June to be as ill-served as ever commander was by the outposts supposed to guard him and warn him of the enemy's approach. Thus was he kept in ignorance for half a day of the movements of the enemy on his front, knowledge of which was essential to enable him to take the steps necessary to meet them.

It is absurd to blame the Duke for not ordering the concentration of his army on Quatre Bras earlier than he did. Till late at night he had no information which would have justified any such definite action. But by his "after orders" he ordered the bulk of his army to the junction of the Namur and Nivelles *chaussées*, while he kept a force on his right in case Napoleon pushed his main attack more in that direction. That he subsequently kept the latter detached from his main army on the day of Waterloo is the only point on which his strategy may be impugned with any show of fairness.

CHAPTER VI.

THE EVENTS OF THE 17TH JUNE—THE RETREAT TO WATERLOO — THE FRENCH ADVANCE TO GEMBLOUX—THE PRUSSIANS UNITE AT WAVRE.

ON the morning of the 17th June, although Napoleon had not obtained full measure of success for his plans, he had on the whole made a considerable stride towards accomplishing them. He had defeated the Prussians and driven them from the field, even if he had not crushed them as he would have done but for d'Erlon's vacillation. Ney, though he had been beaten in his attack on the Anglo-Allies, was still able to hold the ground he had occupied on the 15th. Evidently Wellington had been unable to pursue his advantage, and it was a fair deduction, therefore, for Napoleon to assume that it would take him some time longer to unite his whole army. Blucher had been driven back, in what direction was not certain, but at least he had left the neighbourhood of the battlefield. Which, therefore, was it best to do—follow up and crush the Prussians while holding back the English, or *vice versâ?* If Blucher had fallen back towards Liége, but a comparatively small force would be required to follow and hold him, while the Emperor turned his main body against Wellington. It was manifestly best to show the latter as he had shown Blucher, that he was irresistible on the battlefield.

There were, further, two special reasons why it was desirable to defeat the English commander. The Emperor knew perfectly well that the latter was regarded by the whole of Europe as the best man to pit against himself. For he alone of all European generals had, for six years, won an unbroken series of tactical victories over the French.[1] Moreover, his army, composed as it was of different nationalities, would be easy to rend asunder if severely defeated; especially considering that it numbered many men in its ranks who had actually been French soldiers, and more whose sympathies were known rather to be on the side of the Emperor's cause than that of the Allies who had forced them into the field. Having defeated the Prussians and Blucher, he had now to show that he could defeat the great English General and the troops he led.

As a question, therefore, both of military and political expediency, Wellington's army was the target to aim at on the 17th. But to do this in safety it was necessary to know the exact direction taken by the Prussian troops, for on this would depend the amount of force Napoleon must leave behind to watch and hinder them from aiding the Anglo-Allies. His plan of operations involved the use of a centre and two

---

[1] See Clausewitz, 'Der Feldzug von 1815 in Frankreich,' p. 76 *et seq.* "But the English troops were led by Wellington, who had often defeated the French marshals."

wings, and he had himself laid down that he would, if necessary, diminish the strength of one or other wing in accordance with circumstances. He had used the bulk of his troops against the Prussians in his fight, now he wished to do so against their Allies.

But where were the Prussians?

After the battle of the previous day there had been no question of following them up, as the French troops were too exhausted; and although some of Blucher's troops retired in disorder, yet the rear-guard which Grolmann formed had showed so firm a countenance that it had been thought undesirable to push on farther, and thus, although the whole French army was kept on the battlefield, where even the Guards bivouacked, no attempt was made to keep in touch with the enemy.[1]

The position altogether was a somewhat difficult one. As Napoleon surmised, the whole of the Prussian army had not been present on the battlefield, though probably ordered up, and hence the advent of fresh troops was quite possible; it was better, therefore, to hold on to the position during the night, but not to make any further movement which might have led to fresh fighting. But there was no reason why cavalry patrols should not have watched the

[1] The Chasseur Brigade only of the Guard returned to Fleurus to protect the Emperor. It has been suggested that the weather had something to do with the failure to observe the Prussians. This was not the case: the thunderstorm which broke just before the attack on Ligny was a very local one, of brief duration. The 15th June was fine and very hot. The 16th much the same, except the brief shower at Ligny, which did not touch Quatre Bras or affect the troops marching to it. The 17th was fine till about 2 P.M., when there was a very severe storm, which lasted, with brief intervals of less intensity, till the morning of the 18th.

Prussians. The Emperor knew no details of the fighting at Quatre Bras till late in the night, as Ney had failed to send him reports during the day. One thing was certain, the left wing had been held, for no attempt had been made to carry out the Emperor's orders to move against the Prussian rear after defeating the Anglo-Allied army.

Ney's first report was sent off at 10 P.M., and could not have reached the Imperial headquarters much before midnight. The report in question was to the effect that Ney had attacked the English with vigour, but that owing to the misunderstanding on the part of d'Erlon he failed to gain a great victory, though he had captured a gun and a colour.[1] Flahaut, who, as we have seen, had taken Napoleon's orders to Ney and appears to have then stopped with him, arrived at Fleurus at about seven in the morning and reported to the Emperor the details of the battle of Quatre Bras.[2] At the same time a report from Pajol on the right wing arrived from Balatre at 4 A.M. The information in it was important, and confirmed Napoleon in the view that he doubtless already held, for it stated that he was following the enemy, who was in full retreat towards Liége and Namur, and that he had made many prisoners. The Emperor wished them to retire in this direction, and, without waiting to ascertain what had happened on the left flank of the Right Wing, he assumed the whole of Blucher's troops had gone back on the

---

[1] See Houssaye, footnote, pp. 223-24. This is given in extenso in Pollio, p. 226.

[2] See Houssaye, footnote, p. 225.

Prussian communications, which he believed went through Namur.

Grouchy, as the commander of the right wing, had come in for orders about eight o'clock, and was told by the Emperor to wait and accompany him to yesterday's field of battle. At the same time Soult wrote to Ney saying that he believed he told him what had happened, although Flahaut, who had just returned, said that the Marshal was still in uncertainty as to the events of the previous day. Ney was informed that Pajol was pursuing the defeated Prussians on the road to Namur, and also that several thousand prisoners and thirty guns had been taken. The Emperor was then going to the mill at Brye. It was hardly possible that the English army would do anything against Ney; if it did, the Emperor would march directly against it by the Namur-Quatre Bras road while Ney attacked it in front,—this would lead to its total destruction. Ney was to tell the Emperor exactly what was happening in front of him and the exact positions of his divisions. The Emperor had seen with regret that he had not kept his troops together and thus suffered undue loss. If d'Erlon and Reille had acted together not an Englishman of the corps which had attacked him would have escaped. If d'Erlon had executed the movement on St Amand which the Emperor had ordered, the Prussian army would have been totally destroyed and 30,000 prisoners made. The Emperor desired that Ney should take post at Quatre Bras as ordered; if that was impossible he was to report at once to the Emperor, giving details, and then the Emperor would act as he had said. The 17th was to be used to complete the plan of the Emperor and make good the ammunition expended.[1]

It will be observed from these orders that Napoleon does not seem to be quite so sure of the situation as he was the previous day. Ney is only told to occupy the position at Quatre Bras in accordance with previous orders. If it was impossible, he was to let the Emperor know at once. The 17th June would be occupied in completing these operations. There is thus no further allusion to the rapid advance on Brussels, which was certainly abandoned for the day.

What was in the Emperor's mind? Plainly he felt it possible that the whole Anglo-Allied army, or the greater portion of it, was in front of Ney, while some little doubt arose as to where the Prussians really were. For a time the Emperor did nothing, but a little before nine drove out to the battlefield, taking Grouchy, who had come in for orders, with him. Here, in accordance with his usual custom, he spent some time going over the field, visiting the various bivouacs, and while waiting for the return of a reconnoitring party sent towards Quatre Bras spent the interval talking on war, politics, and various other subjects, with his generals.[2]

Grouchy, on leaving Fleurus, had asked the

[1] 'Documents Inédits,' p. 45. It may be observed that in this letter Soult speaks of the "seven" divisions Ney has under him, thus at last recognising that Girard's, which the Emperor had appropriated on the 15th, was no longer with the 2nd Corps.

[2] See 'Waterloo,' by Prince Edouard de la Tour d'Auvergne, p. 214.

Emperor for instructions, and received the curt response, "I will give you orders when it suits me."

When the patrol which had gone along the Quatre Bras road returned about eleven o'clock, the Emperor determined on his plans and then wrote to Ney, telling him to attack the enemy at Quatre Bras and push them from their position, adding that a corps which had just been ordered to take position at Marbais, consisting of a corps of infantry and the Imperial Guard, would support his operations. The Emperor himself was also going to Marbais. The corps of infantry was the 6th Corps, less Teste's division, followed by the whole of the Guard. Then the Emperor said to Grouchy, that while he was marching against the English he was to pursue the Prussians, taking with him the 3rd and 4th Corps, the 21st Division (Teste's), and the cavalry corps of Pajol, Exelmans, and Milhaud. Hardly had Grouchy gone off to execute these orders than the Emperor wrote and told him to send Domon's cavalry division from Vandamme's corps and Milhaud's cuirassier corps to Marbais, and shortly afterwards wrote again to him as follows:—

You are to go to Gembloux with the cavalry corps of Pajol and Exelmans, the light cavalry of the 4th Corps, Teste's division, and the 3rd and 4th Corps. You will reconnoitre in the direction of Namur and Maestricht, and you will pursue the enemy. I am taking my headquarters to Quatre Bras, where the English still were this morning. Communication between us will be straight along the *chaussée* to Namur. If the enemy has vacated Namur, write to the general commanding the 2nd Military Division at Charlemont to occupy this place with a few battalions of National Guard and some batteries which he will form at Charlemont.

It is important to find out what the enemy wishes to do. Either they are separating themselves from the English, or they desire to unite to cover Brussels and Liége, and try the effect of another battle. In any case, keep your two corps of infantry united in a square league of ground, with several lines of retreat. Post intermediate detachments of cavalry to communicate with headquarters.

The change in the Emperor's view of the situation, which now clearly was one of uncertainty as to the direction taken by the Prussians, was due to a fresh report sent in by General Berton, who commanded a brigade consisting of the 14th and 17th Dragoons in the 10th Cavalry Division, who had learned when near the Orneau that the Prussian army was retiring on Wavre, and that there was a considerable force at Gembloux.[1] He reported this to Exelmans, and received the order to move on Gembloux, where he arrived at nine o'clock in the morning. Exelmans followed to the same place with the whole of his corps, and forwarded Berton's information to Grouchy's headquarters. It appears to have been noted there, and then sent on to the Emperor. Probably it reached him just after Grouchy had left. Hence the written order to the latter, who then made his arrangements for moving in the direction ordered by Napoleon, who plainly was uncertain what proportion of the Prussian army

[1] Berton has left a book called 'Précis des Batailles de Fleurus et Waterloo.' On p. 47 he gives these statements.

was at Gembloux and what along the Namur road, where Pajol had early in the morning captured both prisoners and guns. But no one at the French headquarters, notwithstanding Berton's report, had any idea that practically the whole of the Prussian army was at that time moving to Wavre.

We have seen that after Blucher had been upset in a cavalry charge Gneisenau took command, and had ordered the retreat on Tilly for the I. and II. Corps, while the III. Corps was to retire to Gembloux —*i.e.*, towards the IV. Corps, which had been ordered to Ardenelle. Both the I. and II. Corps were considerably disorganised, and many fugitives tried to follow the Roman road towards Liége, but officers were stationed along it and succeeded in turning the bulk of the troops in the proper direction. Grolmann also ordered an officer to push to the head of the troops marching in disorder through Mellery, where the army headquarters were established for the night. At daybreak he reached the head, and with the help of two other officers managed to stop the troops at the roads leading into the wood there, and instructions were shortly afterwards issued by Grolmann that the I. Corps was to go into bivouac at Bierges; the II. Corps in front of Wavre by St Anne; the III. at La Bavette; the IV. at Dion-le-Mont; guns requiring repair were to be sent to Maestricht. These orders were issued in the early morning of the 17th.[1] Sohr's

---

[1] See Lettow-Vorbeck, pp. 343, 344. It is perfectly evident, as Lettow-Vorbeck states, that the decision to retire on Wavre was come to by the Prussian headquarter staff (Armee-Commando)—*i.e.*, Blucher, Gneisenau,

THE RETREAT TO WAVRE

cavalry brigade was left behind near Tilly and Gentinnes to watch the movement of the enemy, and with this force was left Count Groeben of the General Staff to observe and report the French movements. As their beloved old Field-Marshal rode past the troops on the march, their joyful cheers showed how glad they were to know that the report of his capture was false; and Blucher took the glad expressions of his men not only as the proof of their affection for him, but as an earnest that all who had remained with the columns were in good fettle and eager to be led once more against the foe.

Thielmann reported to Bülow early on the morning of the 17th that he was at Gembloux, and asked for instructions, telling the latter he had heard nothing from Blucher, who he believed had retired towards St Trond. Some time after this he received orders to retire to La Bavette, probably about ten; and Bülow was told a little later to fall back on Dion-le-Mont.

Bülow then wrote to Thielmann saying that he was moving off at once, and requesting him to report when he proposed to do so. He also instructed him to be careful to avoid serious rear-guard fighting, as it was better to wait until the whole of the Prussian army was once more united.

Grolmann, together. This is confirmed by the Duke of Wellington. See Stanhope's 'Notes on Conversations with the Duke of Wellington,' p. 110. The Duke there distinctly stated that Hardinge, the British Commissioner at the Prussian headquarters, told him that Blucher had informed him on the 17th that there had been considerable discussion the previous night, and that Blucher and Grolmann carried the day—to remain in connection with the English army. The decision was come to about 2 A.M. on the 17th (see Lettow-Vorbeck, p. 344).

There does not appear any reason to suppose that, so far as Gneisenau is concerned, he had any intention, when the Prussians fell back on Tilly, of assisting the Duke of Wellington. The line of communications from Namur to Liége had been changed for that by the Roman road since the movement to Sombreffe took place, and he now determined to use the still safer road through Louvain, Tirlemont, and Maestricht, to the Rhine. Instructions were therefore issued early on the 17th to this effect, and the siege train was ordered to Maestricht. The primary reason of the retreat to Tilly was, that owing to the direction of the French attack it was impossible for the I. and II. Corps to retreat up the Roman road. By falling back to Wavre it was still possible for them to gain the more northern line of communication which it was intended to use, while the III. and IV. Corps, moving somewhat eccentrically, could also rejoin at the same place—thus the army would be kept together. Wellington might or might not be helped according to circumstances. But there is no doubt that Blucher most certainly, and Grolmann almost as certainly, wished to act in concert with the Anglo-Allies, and sufficient recognition has never been given to either of these officers for their share in the success of the combined operations.[1] Gneisenau was not so desirous of aiding the Duke, but his scruples were overcome by Blucher and Grolmann.

---

[1] See Lettow-Vorbeck, pp. 371 and 527, in a letter to Knesebeck. In this he states he will do so with Bülow's corps and demonstrate (*figuriren*) with the others! As Lettow-Vorbeck remarks, p. 372, " What was the object of demonstrating ?"

He appears to have been one of those men who are constantly engaged in explaining how badly they have been treated. He disliked not having the supreme command, which his own opinion of his abilities made him think was his due. He appears to have impressed this opinion pretty continuously on all his friends. Blucher died soon after the war, and even if he had lived longer, he was not one to sound his own trumpet; he has, therefore, never been justly treated either for 1813, 1814, or 1815. He may not have been the theoretical strategist that Gneisenau was, but he was a man of far greater determination and of a far greater military insight; and the success of the Prussian arms from 1813 to 1815 was very largely due to his untiring energy and to his willingness to undertake responsibility, feeling, as he did, that war could not be successfully carried on unless risks were sometimes taken. Never was this more clearly shown than on these three days from the 16th to the 18th June.

The Prussian army, therefore, retired to Wavre, opening a fresh line of communications as above indicated.[1] Zieten's corps marched by Gentinnes, Villeroux, Mont St Guibert, reached Wavre about 11.30 A.M. and, crossing the Dyle there, went into bivouac round Bierges. Pirch marched his corps after the I. and halted on the right bank of the Dyle between Aisemont and St Anne, leaving the 7th Brigade at Mont St Guibert to support Sohr's cavalry. Thielmann remained stationary until two o'clock, and then moved by Corbais, crossed the Dyle at Wavre

[1] See Damitz, vol. i. p. 210.

at 8 P.M., and went into bivouac at La Bavette. The 9th Brigade and 2nd Cavalry Brigade of the III. Corps, which formed the rear-guard of the latter, did not come up till 6 A.M. on the 18th, and then the infantry was left on the right bank of the Dyle. Bülow retired with the IV. Corps by Walhain and Corroy, and reached Dion-le-Mont with a considerable portion of his forces in the afternoon, but made no report to Blucher till 10 P.M., as he was waiting for the 13th Brigade, which had not arrived up to that hour.

During the day Count Groeben, who had been attached to Sohr's cavalry,[1] whose duty was to watch the movements of the French, sent in several reports, the outcome of which was that only a portion of the French army was following up the Prussians, the greater part moving after Wellington, and from time to time fire was heard in the direction which the Anglo-Allied army was taking. Thus, on the night of the 17th, the Prussian army was concentrated round Wavre, doubtless somewhat fatigued by the continuous marches, and, so far as the I. and II. Corps were concerned, by the fighting on the 16th; but there was no lack of desire either on the part of the gallant man who commanded it or of the troops which formed it to come again to handi-strokes with their opponent. The recollection of seven years of oppression and indignity was fresh in their memories, and all were eager to be led once more against the arch-oppressor.

The retreat of Zieten's and Pirch's corps quite

[1] A patrol ascertained that Wellington was retiring. See 'English Historical Review,' July 1888, p. 541.

PRUSSIAN RETREAT UNMOLESTED 181

escaped the observation of the French, nor does it ever seem to have struck anybody, from Napoleon downwards, that these corps were moving in the direction they actually retired by. On the right, Pajol's vedettes observed the retreat of Thielmann's corps, and reported it about 2.30 A.M. Pajol therefore sent the 4th and 5th Hussars of Soult's brigade, all he had for the moment available, in the direction of Namur; but here he was merely following the runaways who had gone in this direction, not any organised Prussian force. Between five and six he came up with them, captured a battery and some waggons, and sent out patrols in various directions, but could find no further trace of the enemy, and about mid-day he turned in a northerly direction towards St Denis, hearing that the Prussians were retiring to Louvain. He was now joined by Teste's division, which had been sent him by the Emperor, and with this and Soult's brigade, now complete, he had three regiments of cavalry, eight battalions of infantry, and sixteen guns available.

Berton with his dragoon brigade had also observed Thielmann's retreat from Sombreffe, but unfortunately followed up Pajol instead of keeping close to the retiring enemy. After going a short distance, he learned from peasants that the Prussians were falling back to Gembloux, and this information he sent on to Exelmans, who instructed him to move to that place. He reached it about nine o'clock, and saw on the opposite side of the Orneau a considerable force of the Prussians. When Exelmans arrived with the remainder of his division shortly afterwards, he estimated them at 20,000 men. But he sent no further information as to the position of the enemy to Grouchy. Thus neither the latter nor the Emperor knew anything more than that there were Prussians at Gembloux, and did not know whether they had retired therefrom, or what their force was. Exelmans also failed to let Pajol know what he had discovered.[1] Grouchy had meantime ordered Vandamme to concentrate the 3rd Corps at Point-du-Jour and march to Gembloux. From Ligny, Gérard was ordered to follow Vandamme, and thus he had to wait while the 3rd Corps defiled in front of him to gain the head of the column, and did not reach the point of departure until three o'clock, about which time Grouchy arrived there. Here an aide-de-camp he had sent for news to Exelmans rejoined him, bringing a letter from this general saying that there was a large mass of the Prussians on the left bank of the Orneau, and that he would follow them as soon as they marched off. Moving onwards with his troops, Grouchy reached Gembloux with the head of Vandamme's column about six o'clock; Gérard arrived there at seven. Grouchy found the Prussians had retreated. They had indeed marched off at two o'clock, and at three Exelmans had occupied the village. He afterwards moved on to Sauvenières,

---

[1] Exelmans appears to have informed Grouchy about 8 A.M. that he was going to Gembloux in pursuit of the Prussians, but to have sent no details as to what he found there; nor did he do so until about one o'clock. This report reached Grouchy only at four. See Houssaye, p. 246, footnote 3. It was then of no value, as all the arrangements were made. Nor did Exelmans, notwithstanding the force he had with him, do anything more than observe the Prussians.

and at six o'clock he sent on Bonnemains' brigade to Sart-à-Walhain, and the 15th Dragoons to Perwez. The first of these two detachments found the village of Tourinnes occupied by the Prussian rear-guard, and Bonnemains fell back and bivouacked at Ernage. A little later he learned that the Prussians had fallen back from Tourinnes towards Wavre. Similar information was brought in by the 15th Dragoons, and this information was sent on to Grouchy, but did not reach him till late in the night. He had, however, heard from Pajol at six o'clock that the Prussians were moving on Louvain, and he also received various reports, according to some of which the enemy was retiring on Liége or Maestricht, though the majority showed they were falling back on Wavre.

From all these observations one thing was quite certain, that the enemy was not going to Namur, as had been thought to be the case in the morning, and, on the whole, it seemed likely that the Prussians were moving in a northerly direction, and were in all probability trying to reach Wavre. At ten o'clock, therefore, Grouchy wrote to Napoleon that the Prussians were retiring in two columns from Sauvenières—one on Wavre, the other on Perwez. It seemed, therefore, that one part was going to join Wellington, that the main army was retiring to Liége, and that another column with artillery had retreated to Namur. He had ordered Exelmans to push out parties to Sart-à-Walhain and Perwez. If their reports showed that the main body of the Prussians was retiring to Wavre, he was going to follow them so as to keep them apart from Wellington and prevent them reaching Brussels; if, however, they were marching to Perwez, he would follow them in that direction.

Notwithstanding this report to the Emperor, the orders he issued to his subordinate commanders bore a quite different complexion; they were sent out at the same time as the report to the Emperor, but in them Exelmans and Vandamme were to move to Sart-à-Walhain, Pajol to Grand Leez. Gérard was to follow the 3rd Corps to Sart-à-Walhain, and to send his cavalry to Grand Leez as the enemy was retiring to Perwez. Thus, to his subordinates no mention is made of the idea that any portion of the Prussians was falling back on Wavre, and it is fair to conclude that Grouchy thought any body going in this direction was a comparatively small one.

During the 16th connection had been kept up between the two Allied armies by means of detachments along the Namur-Quatre Bras road. In the evening, when it began to be seen that a retreat would be necessary, a Prussian officer was sent to tell Wellington, but he was severely wounded near Piraumont, probably by some of Bachelu's men who held the Hutte wood, which ran close up to the *chaussée*. He sent to Müffling to tell him he had information to give him, but refused to give it to anybody but a senior officer, and hence the news did not reach Wellington. Another officer was sent after the former to go to Wellington to give him information as to the "then state of the fight."[1] This officer succeeded in reaching Quatre Bras, and told the Duke that the Prussian army was still holding on to the villages

---

[1] See Ollech, pp. 138, 139.

in the position which had been taken up, but that the losses were increasing, and as there was no hope of support by Bülow it was impossible to expect any great result, although the battlefield would probably be held till nightfall. Thus, at the close of day, Wellington believed the Prussians were still in possession of the field, and he returned to pass the night at Genappe. Early the next morning the Duke rode out to Quatre Bras again, where he now had the 1st, 3rd, and 5th British Divisions, the Brunswick Corps, the 2nd Dutch-Belgian Division, the 1st, 2nd, 3rd, 4th, 5th (except one regiment), and 6th Cavalry Brigades—a total of 45,000 men.

Having no news of Blucher, he sent a troop of the 10th Hussars with his aide-de-camp Lieutenant-Colonel Sir Alexander Gordon to ascertain the situation. The Namur road was found to be in possession of the French, and Colonel Gordon, therefore, in consequence of information obtained from a peasant who said the Prussians had retired towards Tilly, moved off in that direction. On arriving there he came up with Zieten's rear-guard, and learned that the Prussians had fallen back from Ligny and were then retiring to Wavre. This information reached Wellington about 7.30 A.M., and about nine o'clock a Prussian officer sent by Blucher also reached the Duke, bearing the information that it was intended to concentrate the whole Prussian army at Wavre, and asked him whether he was determined in conjunction with it to attack the Emperor. Wellington's reply was: "I still hold to the original intention of a united offensive against the

French army, but I must now get back to the position at Mount St Jean, where I will accept battle with Napoleon if I am supported by one Prussian corps.[1] After the battle I hope, in conjunction with the Prince, to assume the offensive. Without Prussian support on the 18th I shall be obliged to fall back to Brussels." The orders issued for the retreat were as follows:—

17th June, 1815,
QUATRE BRAS, 9 A.M.

The 1st Division to keep piquets only in the wood on the right of the high road, and to be collected on the road to Nivelles, in rear of the wood.

The 2nd Division to march from Nivelles to Waterloo at ten o'clock.

The 3rd Division to collect upon the left of the position, holding by its piquets the ground it now occupies.

The 4th Brigade, 4th Division, now at Nivelles, to march from Nivelles upon Waterloo at ten o'clock.

The brigades of the 4th Division on the road from Braine-le-Comte, or at Braine-le-Comte, to collect and halt this day at Braine-le-Comte.

All the baggage on the road from Braine-le-Comte to Nivelles to be sent back to Braine-le-Comte, and to be sent from thence to Hal and Bruxelles.

The 5th Division to collect upon the right of the position in three lines, and the 95th Regiment to hold the gardens.

The 6th Division to be collected in columns of battalions,

---

[1] There seems to be some doubt as to whether Wellington asked for one or two corps. Siborne, p. 159, says two; so does Gneisenau in his letter to Knesebeck—see Lettow-Vorbeck, p. 527. Müffling, 'Passages,' &c., p. 241, says, "even with one corps only." Hofmann states, p. 135, that one of Müffling's aides-de-camp went to Wavre early on the 17th to ascertain if Blucher would aid Wellington if he stood at Quatre Bras. Blucher answered this was impossible, but on the 18th he would support him with two corps. Probably Wellington asked for one and Blucher offered two.

showing their heads only on the heights on the left of the position of Quatre Bras.

The Brunswick Corps to be collected in the wood on the Nivelles road, holding the skirts with their piquets only.

The 2nd Division of the troops of the Netherlands to march from their present ground on Waterloo at ten o'clock (then marching). The march to be in columns of half-companies, at quarter distance.

The 3rd Division of the troops of the Netherlands to march from Nivelles at ten o'clock.

The spare musket ammunition to be transported behind Genappe, as well as the reserve artillery. The waggons of the reserve artillery to be parked in the Forest de Soignes.

The British cavalry to be formed at one o'clock in three lines in rear of the position at Quatre Bras, to cover the movement of the infantry to the rear and the retreat of the rear-guard.[1]

The 1st and 5th British, and 2nd Dutch-Belgian Divisions, and the Brunswick Corps, retired through Genappe, their retreat being covered by a rear-guard formed by Alten's division, supplemented by four battalions from the Reserve and Uxbridge's cavalry. The infantry of the rear-guard retreated by Baisy and Ways-la-Hutte, cutting into the main road after crossing the Dyle. The cavalry retired in three columns *viâ* Baisy-Thy-Genappe, and a ford above the latter village. The 4th and 6th Brigades formed the left, which went by Thy; the right, of the 3rd Brigade, less one regiment (23rd Light Dragoons), and one regiment of the 5th Brigade; the centre

[1] These orders are given in the 1852 edition of 'Wellington Despatches.' They are stated by Sir De Lacy Evans to have been made by him from the Duke's original draft instructions.

being made up of the remaining brigades and regiments present.

Ney remained inactive during the forenoon, and the first attempt made against the Anglo-Allied force was by Napoleon moving up with Lobau and the Guards together with Domon's light cavalry, Milhaud's cuirassiers, and Subervie's cavalry division.[1] About two miles from Quatre Bras the cavalry scouts of the French force were driven back by the English patrols, and the Emperor formed his troops for battle. It was about 1.30, and nothing had been heard of Ney, nor was any sound of firing heard in his direction. Napoleon, therefore, determined to push on with the cavalry and clear up the situation.[2]

The Emperor had almost arrived at Quatre Bras when he found the British cavalry and artillery ready to meet him with guns pointing down the Namur road. The weather had become very overcast, and as the British artillery opened fire a thunderstorm broke in all its vigour and the rain fell in torrents. The order was given for the rear-guard cavalry to retreat. The infantry had marched off some four hours previously, and had by this time crossed the Dyle, and was moving into the position chosen by

---

[1] Ney's inactivity may possibly be explained by his waiting for orders, and by these, when received, laying stress on the necessity for uniting his forces and refitting.

[2] Houssaye says, p. 264, following the statement of Gourgaud and Napoleon, that the latter learned of the retreat of the Anglo-Allies by capturing "une vivandière Anglaise." But the English army had not then nor ever has had *vivandières* attached to it. Who the lady was it is impossible to tell, or what she was doing two miles in advance of her army, and I am somewhat inclined to doubt her existence.

Wellington, which had been surveyed earlier in the year with a view to its forming a battlefield.[1] The retreat was effected in good order, our cavalry skirmishers keeping back the French until the Dyle was passed.[2] Here a skirmish took place between the 7th British Hussars and the 2nd Lancers who were leading the French advance, and a smart fight ensued between the two rival cavalries. Lord Uxbridge, who was present at it, withdrew the hussars through their supporting regiment the 23rd Dragoons, and brought forward the 1st Life Guards against the advancing French. The ground was favourable for the charge, sloping down gently towards Genappe, and the heavy men on big horses coming in full career down it, rode over and dispersed their lighter opponents, and drove them through the street to the other side of the village.

Previous to leaving Quatre Bras, Wellington issued orders for a portion of his army to hold the road through Hal to Brussels. The brigades of the 4th Division at Braine-le-Comte were to retire at daylight on the 18th to Hal. Prince Frederick of Orange was to move from Enghien in the evening and take up a position in front of Hal, occupying Braine-le-Chateau with two battalions. Erstoff's brigade was also to retire to Hal, and act under Prince Frederick.

---

[1] See 'History of the Corps of Royal Engineers,' by Major-General Porter, vol. i. p. 380.

[2] According to Houssaye the English were driven back from Quatre Bras in confusion. See *op. cit.*, p. 266. The best reply to this is that the total loss of our cavalry in killed, wounded, and missing was 92, of whom 46 belonged to the 7th Hussars, and these most certainly fell in the fighting at Genappe.

The Prince was to defend the position taken up as long as possible.

General Colville was told to remain at Hal, and that the army would probably continue in this position in front of Waterloo the next day.

When Napoleon, following up the Anglo-Allies, arrived on the field in front of Belle Alliance, a deployment of cavalry which he ordered drew down on it such a fire of artillery as convinced him that Wellington's entire force lay before him, and that they had not drawn off, as he feared, through the forest of Soignes. At night his troops were disposed as follows: the 1st Corps in front, between Plancenoit and Mon Plaisir, the Reserve Cavalry behind it. The 2nd and 6th Corps and Kellermann's cavalry had got no farther than Genappe. The Guards bivouacked about Glabais, except the 1st of the 1st Chasseurs with the Emperor at Caillou.

The slowness of the march was largely due to the weather. The troops on the *chaussée* could move very well on the paved portion, but the soil in this part of the country is of such a nature that the heavy rain transformed it at once into a quagmire, in which the horses sank over their hocks and sometimes up to their knees. Hence while Wellington was able to withdraw his infantry from Quatre Bras to Waterloo (eight miles) with practically no difficulty, because they could march on a broad front using the fields, yet Napoleon's troops were compelled to move much more slowly, as the road formed the only practical path for them. The same cause delayed Grouchy's march somewhat. From Ligny

SITUATION AT NIGHT, 17TH JUNE

to Gembloux is but five miles, yet it took his men, moving along by-roads, five hours to complete the distance. Grouchy doubtless displayed a somewhat lack of energy in halting his troops at Gembloux, but it would be unfair not to recognise that the march was conducted under very difficult circumstances, and the atrocious weather no doubt influenced the Marshal in keeping his men round the village.

Thus, on the night of the 17th, Napoleon had divided his forces.[1] The main portion was, it is true, gathered together opposite his English opponent; but his right, owing to a want of care in keeping touch with the Prussians after the battle of Ligny, had been sent after them in a direction which, in fact, was nearly at right angles to their actual line of retreat. In front of Waterloo lay the Anglo-Allied army ready to receive the French attack the next day, but with a considerable detachment (some 18,000 men) at Hal and Tubize, nine and eleven miles respectively from what was to be the deciding battle of the war.[2] At Wavre was assembled the whole Prussian force under its gallant leader, sore in body but fresh and undaunted in his mind, ready to lead it to help his ally in a combined stroke against the Emperor.

---

[1] The position was similar to that which obtained on the 13th June 1807. On this date he sent 60,000 men after l'Estocq, who formed the right wing of the Prusso-Russian army, and thus diminished very largely the force he had at the battle of Friedland on the 14th June. The detachment was unnecessarily large, for the Prussians did not number 20,000.

[2] Napoleon was so anxious to fight Wellington that at one o'clock on the 18th he left the farm of Caillou and went round the outposts to see if the Anglo-Allies were still there. He is reported to have said: "Enfin je vais me mésurer avec ce Wellington." He was indeed, with a result fatal to himself and the cause of the empire.

CHAPTER VII.

THE EVENTS OF THE 18TH—THE BATTLE OF WATERLOO—THE ACTION AT WAVRE.

(See Plan.)

WE have seen that Napoleon, Soult, Grouchy, and all the French Staff thought on the morning of the 17th the Prussians were retreating towards the Meuse. Even when Milhaud reported at 9 P.M. that his flanking patrols on the march from Maubeuge to Quatre Bras had noticed a column of Prussian artillery retiring by Tilly towards Wavre, Napoleon does not seem to have changed his views. The result of the cavalry explorations during the afternoon of the 17th had, it is true, brought home to Grouchy the possibility of a portion of the Prussians having retired in the direction of Wavre, but he still thought that some had gone to Namur, and that the greater part was going through Perwez towards Liége, and this idea lasted through the night and part of the next morning.[1]

---

[1] It is clear from his subsequent conduct that he never believed the united force of the Prussians had gone to Wavre, for in his letter to Napoleon of 10 P.M., 17th June, he states he will follow whichever of the two bodies was the larger—*i.e.*, that going to Wavre or that going to Perwez.

GROUCHY'S DOUBTS

The hours fixed by Grouchy for the departure of his troops were not what might have been expected from a commander following on the tracks of a retreating force and charged with the duty of keeping it in sight and holding it. Vandamme, who had passed the night at Gembloux, was told to move off at six o'clock and march on Sart-à-Walhain,[1] covered by Exelmans' cavalry, which was to lead the advance. Gérard, who was somewhat in rear of Gembloux, was to march at 8 A.M. and follow Vandamme, sending his cavalry towards Grand Leez as the enemy was retiring on Perwez. Pajol was also to march on the same point from Mazy, where he passed the night. During the night Grouchy received fresh intelligence which made him think the Prussians were retiring on Wavre: but he did not alter his instructions to any of his generals. He was torn between two opinions. Were the enemy falling back to Wavre in one body, or were part of them going to Perwez? The new information, indeed, indicated the former intention, yet he still obstinately clung to the idea that the main part was retreating eastward, and did not alter his orders to Pajol and the cavalry of the 3rd Corps to go to Grand Leez, which was of no possible utility unless the Prussians were gone to Perwez—*i.e.*, were retiring by the Roman road to Liége.

Unfortunately for Napoleon, in the face of fairly clear contrary evidence, he still thought the Prussian main body was retiring towards the Rhine.

[1] There has been considerable confusion between Walhain and Sart-à-Walhain. Walhain was the more important of the two villages, but on some of the maps of the period one only appears to have been marked. Sart-à-Walhain is called Sart-lez-Walhain on modern maps.

At six o'clock he reported to the Emperor as follows :—

> SIRE,—All my reports and information show that the enemy is retiring on Brussels, to concentrate there, or fight a battle after uniting with Wellington. The first and second of Blucher's Army Corps seem to have gone, the first to Corbais, the second to Chaumont. They apparently left Tourinnes at 8.30 last evening, and marched all night; fortunately it was so bad that they will not have gone far. I am starting for Walhain, whence I shall go to Corbais and Wavre.[1]

Although Grouchy thus seems to have grasped the situation to some extent, he allowed the troops to carry out the orders previously issued.

This report reached Napoleon some time after 10 A.M., at which hour he had written to Grouchy in reply to his report of 10 P.M. of the 17th (see *ante*, p. 183), saying that in addition to the two columns the Marshal mentioned as retiring through Sauvenière and Sart-à-Walhain a third column was reported as having passed by Gery and Gentinnes towards Wavre. This information had been brought in by Milhaud at 9 P.M. on the 17th, his cavalry patrols having seen the Prussians retiring from Tilly on Wavre, and confirmed by Jerome before the despatch went off.[2] Grouchy was further told :—

---

[1] This report is in archives of the French War Office, as also is Soult's reply, sent off at 10 A.M.

[2] See Foy, p. 278, who says that he was supping with Jerome at the inn at Genappe, where a waiter told them Wellington had been there the night before, and one of his Staff had stated the Duke had gone to a position in front of the Forest of Soignes to wait for the Emperor, and that the Prussians would advance from Wavre, whither they had gone to join him.

GROUCHY TO MOVE ON WAVRE

His Majesty desires you will direct your movements on Wavre, so as to get nearer to us, and thus connect our operations and keep up communication between us, pushing before you the Prussian force which has taken this direction, and which may have halted at Wavre, which you ought to reach as soon as possible.

You will follow those columns of the enemy which have gone to your right by detachments of light troops. . . .

Let me know immediately your dispositions and the direction you are marching, as well as any news you have of the enemy, and do not neglect to keep up communication with us; the Emperor desires to have very frequent information from you.

This despatch only reached Grouchy about 3.45 P.M., when he was well committed to his advance on Wavre, and served to confirm him in his view that he was acting in accordance with the Emperor's wishes.

Plainly the latter anticipated no attempt on the part of the Prussians to aid Wellington. For, as he said to his brother at Caillou in the morning before sending off the above letter, "the junction of the Prussians with the English is impossible for the next two days after such a battle as Ligny, and followed as they are by a considerable body of troops." [1] Thus Napoleon thought he had the Anglo-Allies only to deal with, and had no wish for Grouchy to join him.

The hours of march ordered by Grouchy were late, they were made later by the fact that owing to the

[1] See Foy, p. 278.

time taken to distribute provisions the troops did not move off at the hours named. Thus his movement became a walk after the Prussians rather than a pursuit. Vandamme did not leave Gembloux till after seven o'clock; Gérard had to wait until Vandamme passed through the village. It is true Napoleon had ordered Grouchy to keep his troops well together. But this did not necessarily involve moving them all by one road. Yet he preferred to do so, and thus retarded the march.

Grouchy joined the head of his force about ten o'clock, as it was nearing Walhain, and from this place he sent off at 11 A.M. the following despatch to Napoleon:—

> SIRE,—I do not lose a moment in informing you the reports I have gathered here. I regard them as reliable. . . .
>
> The 1st, 2nd, and 3rd Corps of Blucher are marching in the direction of Brussels. Two of these corps passed by Sart-à-Walhain, or a little to the right of it; they moved in three columns about on a level. They took six hours to pass. The one which marched in sight of Sart-à-Walhain may be assumed as having at least 30,000 men and 50 to 60 guns.
>
> A body of troops, coming from Liége, has joined those which fought at Fleurus (as the accompanying requisition proves). Some of the Prussians who are in front of me are going towards the Plain of la Chyse, situated on the Louvain road and about two and a half leagues from that town.
>
> It would seem that their intention is to mass there, either to fight the troops pursuing them, or to re-unite with Wellington, the project announced by their officers,

THE REPORT FROM SART-À-WALHAIN

who, with their usual boasting, pretend they only left the field of battle of the 16th so as to bring about their reunion with the English army near Brussels.

To-night I shall be massed at Wavre, and so shall be between Wellington, whom I presume is retreating before your Majesty, and the Prussian army.

I have need of further instructions as to what your Majesty desires me to do. The country between Wavre and the Plain of la Chyse is difficult, much cut up and marshy.

By the Wivorde road I shall arrive easily at Brussels before those who have halted at la Chyse, if it should be that the Prussians have halted there.

Deign, Sire, to send me your orders; they could reach me before I commence to move to-morrow. Most of the information which this letter contains was furnished to me by the owner of the house where I stopped to write to your Majesty; this officer has served in the French Army, is decorated, and appears entirely devoted to our interests. I annex them to these few lines.[1]

By this it would seem that Blucher was not joining Wellington, and therefore, by marching to Wavre, Grouchy could interpose between the two Allied commanders. This opinion was supported by the report of a patrol sent to Mousty, which had seen no Prussians there, and served to confirm Grouchy in the view he had already taken.[2] He does not seem to have thought for a moment that Wellington

---

[1] See 'Mémoires du Maréchal Grouchy,' vol. iv. p. 71. This letter is written in a somewhat confused manner. The house where Grouchy stopped belonged to Hollert the notary, who had never served as a combatant officer. The "officer" in question does not appear to have been present at the interview.

[2] See 'Mémoires du Maréchal Grouchy,' vol. iv. pp. 141, 142.

would stand to fight Napoleon, although the Emperor had told him he meant to fight the Anglo-Allies.

After the report had left, the sound of guns from the battlefield of Waterloo reached Walhain, and was heard by Grouchy and his staff. Among those present, besides Grouchy, were General Valazé commanding the engineers, General Baltus commanding the artillery of the 4th Corps, besides Gérard and his chief-of-the-staff Colonel Lorière. The sound of fire became more intense, and Gérard expressed his opinion that they ought to march towards it. The notary (Hollert) in whose house Gérard was breakfasting, said that it came from the border of the forest of Soignes, distance $3\frac{1}{2}$ leagues.[1] Some discussion took place: Baltus objected that the roads would be difficult, and that

---

[1] This would mean fourteen kilometres, or about nine miles, if the ordinary *lieue de poste* of 4000 kilometres was meant. But the expression league in those days was a very vague one. As a practical fact, the distance from Walhain by Mousty to Plancenoit is about $13\frac{1}{2}$ miles, to the forest of Soignes $15\frac{1}{2}$ miles. Quinet, 'Histoire de la Campagne de 1815,' p. 298, gives five hours seven minutes as the time taken by a single pedestrian to walk from Walhain to Plancenoit, which seems a very long time. But considering the weather, the badness of the road, and the narrowness of the bridges, which would have necessitated marching on a narrow front, it is not probable that a quicker pace than two miles an hour would have been possible. If Grouchy had ordered his troops at once to Waterloo, they would not have arrived till seven o'clock. For it would have been at least 12.30 before the order would have reached the heads of the columns, as the new direction would not have been taken the moment the first gun was heard. This, moreover, is assuming Grouchy met with no resistance. But at three o'clock the IV. Corps was at St Lambert. Grouchy's march would have been observed and hindered by the II. and III. Corps, and would have been observed from the first by the Prussian flankers. To have set off for Waterloo at mid-day would, therefore, have been no assistance to Napoleon.

the artillery waggons could not pass by them; Valazé said that with his companies of sappers he would smooth all difficulties; Gérard added, "At any rate I would get there with the limbers;" a guide whom Valazé had secured said that it would be easy to march as desired. Grouchy, however, considered it his duty to follow on the heels of the Prussians, in accordance with the orders of the Emperor. While the discussion was going on an aide-de-camp of Exelmans' returned from the front and said that a strong Prussian rear-guard was in position before Wavre, and that there was every indication that the Prussians had passed by the bridges there during the night and morning to join the English army, and that Exelmans thought he ought to cross over at Ottignies to the left bank of the Dyle.[1] But Grouchy, strong in his views as to the direction taken by the retreating Prussians, and in his belief that he was doing as the Emperor wished, which it will be seen from the Emperor's despatch of 10 A.M. was really the case, adhered to the opinion he had formed, and the troops continued their march on Wavre.

By midnight on the 17th Blucher had determined on the steps to be taken to assist Wellington. Wellington's note, sent off from Quatre Bras when he learned that the Prussians had retired to Wavre, had informed Blucher that he was falling back to

[1] There were bridges over the Dyle at Mousty (called Moustier on some maps), Ottignies, and higher up at Limelette, Limal, and the mill of Bierges. Of these the best were those at Mousty and Ottignies. There was a good stone bridge at Wavre and two others of timber.

the chosen position at Waterloo, and would fight there if aided by one Prussian corps. This message arrived at Wavre somewhere about noon. At 9.30 P.M. Müffling wrote that the Duke had taken up a position with his right on Braine-l'Alleud and his left on La Haye. This letter reached Blucher about 11.30 P.M., who at once replied as follows:—

HEADQUARTERS, WAVRE,
17th June 1815.

I beg to inform your Excellency that in consequence of your report to me that the Duke of Wellington will accept battle in the position from Braine-l'Alleud to La Haye, my troops will be put in motion as follows: Bülow's corps will advance at daybreak from Dion-le-Mont through Wavre to attack the enemy's right flank; the II. Corps will follow on immediately after the IV.; the I. and III. Corps will hold themselves in readiness to follow in the same direction. The exhaustion of the troops, some of whom have not yet arrived, makes it impossible to advance earlier. I ask your Excellency to let me know in good time when and how the Duke may be attacked, so that I may take my measures accordingly.[1]   BLUCHER.

The following orders were then issued to Bülow. He was to march at daybreak through Wavre on Chapelle St Lambert, there to take up a position under cover if the French were not strongly engaged with Wellington—if they were, then he was at once to advance as rapidly as possible and attack the

---

[1] See Lettow-Vorbeck, p. 365. This letter was received by the Duke before 3 A.M. on the 18th, as his letters to Sir Charles Stuart and the Duke de Berri, dated at that hour, show. From Waterloo to Wavre was about 12 miles.

BLUCHER'S ORDERS TO HIS ARMY

enemy's right flank. The II. Army Corps was to be in immediate support of Bülow. The I. and III. Corps were also to hold themselves in readiness to follow if needed. Bülow was to send a detachment for the purpose of observation to Mont St Guibert, which was to fall back on Wavre if pressed.[1] All baggage and trains not necessary for fighting were to be sent to Louvain.

Orders to the same effect were sent to Pirch, and the two other corps were informed of the measures which had been taken. They were to cook and hold themselves ready to start early in the morning, and all three were to send back their trains not wanted for fighting purposes to Louvain by the right bank of the Dyle, to avoid the confusion which would arise from passing them through Wavre.[2]

The reasons why the orders were not issued before were, first of all, because Blucher did not know until late at night that the IV. Corps had arrived at Dion-le-Mont; secondly, because Zieten had reported on the 17th that he had heard the sound of cannonade in the direction of Braine-l'Alleud, and added in his statement "from the direction of the smoke the English army must be retiring." Gneisenau had ordered Zieten to send on a cavalry detachment towards Braine-l'Alleud to report at once what was happening there, and at 6.30 P.M. Zieten sent in the result of his observations and the measures he

---

[1] The strength of the force actually detached was two battalions of infantry, a cavalry regiment, and two guns. It was afterwards strengthened by two more battalions from Brause's brigade (II. Corps).

[2] See Lettow-Vorbeck, pp. 394, 395.

had taken.¹ There had been also some hesitation on account of the non-arrival of the ammunition trains which had been ordered to Wavre, when the line of communication from Namur was given up, and which only arrived at five o'clock in the afternoon. But during the day (the 17th) the reports sent in from the rear-guard of the I. and II. Corps left no doubt that the greater portion of the French troops had gone after Wellington.

Early in the morning, between 7 and 8 A.M., von Groeben, who had come in from the Prussian outposts, reported that the French were still at Gembloux, he did not think they were more than 15,000 strong, and added that even if they were 30,000, one army corps would suffice to guard the line of the Dyle, and that it was at Mont St Jean that the fate of the campaign was to be decided.² Gneisenau and Grolmann then took him into an adjoining room, and the latter recorded his opinion, with which the former agreed, that only in case the enemy did not appear at Wavre in too great force should the I. Corps follow the II. and IV., and perhaps the III.: the I. Blucher, who gauged the situation more accurately than his staff, wrote to Müffling at 9.30 A.M. the following letter:—

> I ask your Excellency to say to the Duke of Wellington on my behalf that, ill as I am, I shall nevertheless put myself at the head of my troops to at once attack the

---

¹ See Lettow-Vorbeck, p. 374. Unfortunately Lettow-Vorbeck gives no details as to what these were, though apparently the report is still in existence in the military archives in Berlin. See also footnote, p. 180.
² See Ollech, p. 189.

right wing of the enemy as soon as Napoleon undertakes anything against the Duke. If the day should pass without the enemy attacking, it is my opinion that we should together attack the French army to-morrow.[1]

I charge your Excellency to inform the Duke of this my firm intention, and that I believe it to be the best and most in accordance with our present situation.

(Signed) BLUCHER.

This very decided line of action was perhaps not quite in accordance with the more philosophic temperaments of his Chief of the Staff and Quartermaster-General, but eminently more practical, more in accordance with the requirements of the case, and certainly more loyal to Wellington. This letter was dictated by Blucher himself to Nostitz, and when the latter showed it to Gneisenau before transmission to Müffling, the latter caused the following postscript to be added:—

General Gneisenau agrees to the contents of this letter, but asks your Excellency to be quite certain whether the Duke really has the firm intention to fight in his position, or whether he merely intends to demonstrate, which would be very fatal to our army.

Your Excellency will have the goodness to let me know the Duke's intentions, and it is of the highest importance to know exactly what the Duke will do in order to arrange our movements.

Blucher had no fears on this score, and he left Wavre at eleven o'clock to join Bülow.[2]

[1] Blucher, with characteristic energy, is stated to have said he would rather be tied on his horse than miss going to the battle.

[2] See Ollech, p. 189. The fact of the matter is, Gneisenau being of a somewhat peevish and carping disposition himself, could only see in

It may here be observed that Wellington had taken post in front of Mont St Jean, relying on Blucher's

Wellington similar characteristics. To say that he was angry because Wellington had not supported him at Ligny, and that he therefore distrusted the Duke, is ridiculous. He knew perfectly well that Wellington's promise of support had only been conditional, and that whether the Anglo-Allied army came to his aid or not he had from the first meant to fight a battle at Ligny, because he hoped to defeat the French and get the glory of doing so unaided. He had previously told Müffling, when the latter received the appointment of Prussian Commissioner at the English headquarters, "to be much on" his "guard with the Duke of Wellington, for that by his relations with India, and his transactions with the deceitful Nabobs, this distinguished general had so accustomed himself to duplicity that he had at last become such a master in the art as even to outwit the Nabobs themselves." See 'Passages,' &c., p. 212.

A more gratuitous insult to the Duke, of whom Gneisenau knew absolutely nothing, was never uttered; and it seems laughable to us who know from his record that the Duke of Wellington was the soul of honour, that a man who was scarcely acquainted with him should have held or pretended to hold such an opinion. But Gneisenau was not a man of nice disposition : he was jealous of Blucher, thinking himself the man who ought to have had supreme command (see a letter from Hardenberg to him, Lettow-Vorbeck, p. 140). His relationship with Blucher was purely official in character, as he did not like the old Field-Marshal's methods of expression, which savoured more of the camp than of the court. He was always in his opinion an injured man. But I cannot help thinking that a candid perusal of the history of the period will show that Gneisenau owed more to the determination of Blucher than Blucher did to the organising powers of Gneisenau. If the latter had had his way, the battle of Waterloo would never have been fought to a decisive finish. These expressions of distrust towards Wellington were the outcome of nothing more than a disagreeable disposition, and possibly based on a total misconception of the situation of the 16th June. Grolmann, in his letter to the King of Prussia, probably written on the 17th June from Wavre, states that Napoleon had on the 16th June 120,000 men in the field, of whom 10,000 only were used against the Anglo-Allies. We know that Ney began the fight with fifty per cent more than this, and that towards the end he had over 20,000. Wellington might have swept 10,000 out of the way, a larger force he could not deal with, especially as a considerable portion of the troops under him did not fight. We have seen that it was very greatly the Prussian fault Wellington had not ordered his troops to concentrate earlier on the 15th. Thus Grolmann, and therefore Gneisenau, quite underestimated the French

support, as Gneisenau well knew; yet when the gallant old Marshal determined to support Wellington, and

numbers Wellington met with. But even if he did not come to Ligny, they had no reason to assume that he was a treacherous scoundrel. Yet we see in this letter to Müffling Gneisenau insinuated as much.

It is, indeed, rather difficult to understand Gneisenau's attitude at this juncture. In a letter written by him from Wavre at mid-day on the 17th June, when he knew nothing of the details of the fighting at Quatre Bras, he speaks of Wellington as having been compelled to retreat from that place. We know this retreat was entirely due to the Prussians having retired from Ligny. No doubt the Prussian Chief of the Staff was a sorely tried man. By his own muddle the IV. Corps had not arrived to take part in the fight. A good many of the Prussian troops had proved unsatisfactory, for a number amounting to about 10,000 men—see Plotho, p. 96 of Appendix —had fled from the colours after the battle, and the cavalry had behaved badly. In the same letter he appears to have thought that Napoleon would turn off towards Liége, and then move up the Rhine to attack the Russian columns in flank, a really marvellous assumption in the situation! Gneisenau knew that Napoleon had only 120,000 men, and yet thought that he would execute a flank march in the face of the Prussians and the Anglo-Allies who had double his numbers,—his judgment was wandering when he considered for a moment such a ridiculous idea. Even his latest advocate, Lettow-Vorbeck, has to admit this (see *op. cit.*, p. 372). With regard to the postscript, there is this much to be said for Gneisenau, that its exact wording was not his but that of Blucher's aide-de-camp, Nostitz, whom he asked to attach this postscript to the letter he had written at Blucher's dictation. See 'Das Tagebuch des Generals der Kavallerie, Grafen v. Nostitz,' p. 37.

One thing is quite clear from Nostitz's diary, that it was Blucher, not Gneisenau, who daily determined on the course of action. It was the custom of Blucher to listen to a clear exposition of the various courses open and the means available for carrying them out, and then, after asking questions as to various points, Blucher, says Nostitz, invariably selected "the bold, the daring, and—from its results—the decisive." See Nostitz, p. 55. Müffling (see 'Passages,' &c., p. 95) states that a similar course was pursued when he filled the office of Quartermaster-General in 1813-14. He adds, "The Field-Marshal *never* made difficulties when the talk was of advancing and attacking." With this completely accords Hardinge's statement given in the Earl of Stanhope's 'Notes of Conversations with the Duke of Wellington,' p. 110, in which it is recorded by Hardinge, the British Commissioner with Blucher, that Gneisenau wanted to retreat on Liége, but that Blucher, supported by Grolmann, determined to remain in communication with the Anglo-Allies.

sent to say he would do so, Gneisenau adds a postscript which would have justified the Duke in abandoning his position, as it made the chance of support so very problematical. However, the loyal Englishman trusted the loyal Prussian, to the advantage of their common cause, and his reliance was not misplaced.

But Gneisenau and the Headquarter Staff of the Prussian army had yet to have their say in the matter, and the arrangements they made were as bad as it was possibe to make them.

If it was sincerely desired to support the Anglo-Allies, common-sense would have suggested that the corps nearest to them should have been sent to their assistance. These were the I. and III., at Bierges and La Bavette, distant only about eight and nine miles from Waterloo. Now it is quite true that the former had lost most severely on the 15th and 16th, but it could quite well have been used for the direct support of Wellington, for which only a small force was required. The III. Corps had not suffered much at Ligny,[1] and might have been employed for the flank attack on Napoleon. It could have been supported by the II. Corps from Aisemont and St Anne crossing the Dyle at Bierges and Limale, and all these corps could have moved at daybreak, the I. Corps by St Lambert on Frischermont, the III.

---

[1] At Ligny this corps lost only 7 officers killed and 53 wounded, which proves this. See Plotho, Appendix, p. 109 *et seq*. Evidence shows that the Prussian army was none the worse for the runaways, and that those with the colours were full of fight.

GNEISENAU'S BAD ARRANGEMENTS 207

by Froidmont and Ohain, the II. by Bierges and Limale on Lasne or Couture St Germain, while Bülow might have been left to cover Wavre, which his troops were already in a position to do.[1] It is, of course, true that they had not fought, and therefore it is possible the sentimental idea prevailed that it would be well to give them the honour of taking part in what was felt would be the deciding stroke of the campaign; but questions of sentiment of this kind are misplaced in war when they tend to the harm of the cause they are supposed to aid. The IV. Corps was, moreover, the most distant of all from the decisive field of action, and yet was told off to play the chief part on it! Besides which, the troops composing it had been marching almost without ceasing for the past two days, in which they had gone over fifty miles, and now were called on to do twelve more before they could come into action!

Worse even than the general idea of the supporting movement, was the method in which it was planned out.

Bülow was indeed to march at daybreak, but he was to move through the narrow streets of Wavre, while he could perfectly well have been sent round the town. The II. Corps was to follow the IV. This rendered it practically certain that it would

---

[1] It will be remembered that he had to send a detachment to Mont St Guibert, and it would have been better therefore that his corps should have remained to support it and defend Wavre, rather than that this duty should have been placed on the III. Corps.

not reach the battlefield in time to be of any use. The line of march of the I. Corps was so arranged that it crossed that of the IV. and II. Corps. Moreover, it received no instructions to move till mid-day; had it started at 3 A.M. it would have reached Wellington by nine o'clock, it did not do so till six. If the III. and II. Corps had been employed as suggested above, the former might have arrived about ten, the latter about eleven or twelve. Thus it is perfectly plain that either the General Staff and its chief Gneisenau did not know their business, or that the latter deliberately delayed the march of the Prussian army which his gallant leader had promised to bring with him to Wellington's aid. It is a matter of indifference to me which solution is accepted to account for the extraordinary arrangements made on this day, of which I firmly believe Blucher to have been absolutely and entirely ignorant. Into details of this kind it was not his province to enter. Had he known them, I feel sure they would at once have been altered. Wellington expected the Prussians at mid-day or shortly after; they first came into action at half-past four.

The position on which the Battle of Waterloo was fought consists in its main features of two opposing ridges, one on which the French were drawn up, the other that held by the Anglo-Allies. The intervening valley slopes gently down from either side, and is well adapted for the movement of all arms. It was entirely without enclosures, except at Hougomont, La Haye Sainte, the farms of Papelotte and La

THE WATERLOO POSITION

Haye, with the hamlet of Smohain. The soil was tenacious in character, and being covered with standing corn soddened by the rain, rendered movement difficult.[1] One of the reasons alleged for Napoleon's delay in beginning the action is that he waited for the ground to harden sufficiently for the artillery to manœuvre, and doubtless this had something to do with the late hour at which the battle commenced.

The Anglo-Allied army was placed along a line which is roughly that of the road from Wavre to Braine-l'Alleud. It was for a great part of its length a hollow one, and thus afforded shelter; while on the east of the Brussels *chaussée* a straggling hedge on a slight bank on both sides gave cover from view, and some obstacle. The second line and reserves were fairly safe on the reverse slope of the ridge along which it ran. Its right was guarded by the advanced post of Hougomont, by holding the village of Merbraine in rear and the village of Braine-l'Alleud more to the west, and by massing troops on this part of the position. The left rested on no obstacle, but was protected by occupation of Papelotte, La Haye, the adjacent hamlet of Smohain, and the chateau of Frischermont. This flank was, moreover, secured by the fact that the Prussians in advancing would come to its support. The centre of the Allies' line was strengthened by the farm of La Haye Sainte, an advanced post capable of good defence.

[1] It resembles in character the black-cotton soil of India, and when thoroughly wetted is almost impassable off the roads.

Between the French and Allied position a secondary ridge exists to the east of the *chaussée* (marked *a b* on the plan), which was of importance as forming an artillery position for the French. The Anglo-Allied line was somewhat broken to the west of La Haye Sainte by the projecting flat spur (*c*), which hid a good portion of the valley from view and allowed the French cavalry to remain unseen within 400 yards of the position; but on the whole it was strong and suitable. The front measured about 4250 yards, and to hold this there were just 50,000 infantry, or 12 men to the yard.[1]

The chateau and farm of Hougomont (see sketch No. 1) formed a strong advanced post, covered to a great extent from artillery fire by the wood and orchard surrounding it. The garden was bounded by a strong wall on its south and east sides, in front of which, on the south side, was a thick hedge forming a considerable obstacle. The rest of the enclosures, other than those formed by the main buildings, consisted of stout hedges which, in the case of those enclosing the orchard, had ditches outside them. The main buildings, the garden wall, and the northern hedge of the orchard were prepared for defence, the first two with a double tier of fire. The eastern wall was flanked by the northern hedge, which was therefore of considerable value to the defenders. The defences of this post

---

[1] The front is taken as being from Smohain to the western edge of Hougomont, not to Braine-l'Alleud, as the troops there were brought into the main position during the battle.

SKETCH No. 1.

THE CHATEAU OF HOUGOMONT.

Taken chiefly from Kennedy's 'Notes on the Battle of Waterloo.'

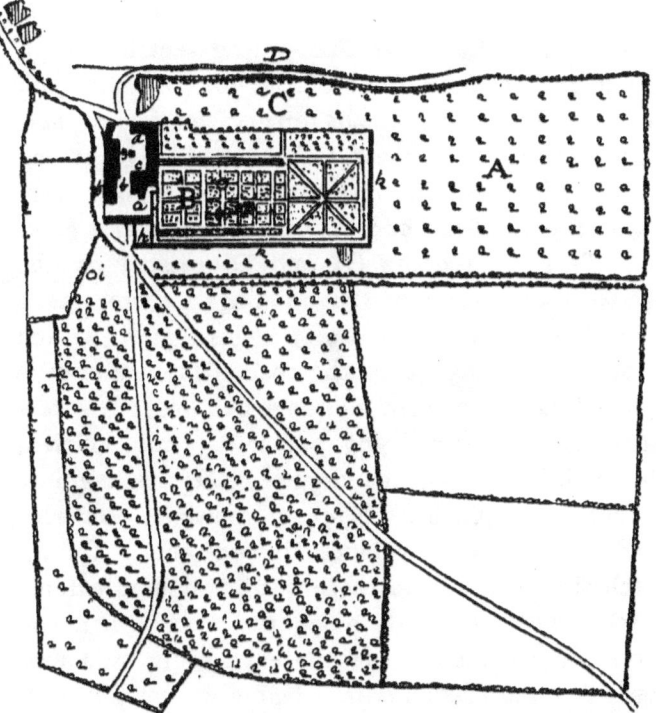

A, Great orchard. B, Kitchen-garden. C, Small orchard. D, Hollow road.
a, Chapel. *b*, Chateau. *c*, Farm buildings. *d*, Cowshed. *e*, Gardener's house. *f* and *g*, Barns. *h*, Small garden. *i*, Haystack. *k, k*, Wall loopholed by British troops.

were completed by holding the avenue which leads into the Nivelles *chaussée,* and the Braine-l'Alleud road beyond; the Nivelles road itself being blocked by an abattis. Access was obtained to the buildings through a gate which opened on to the avenue above alluded to, and the troops told off to hold the orchard could retreat into the chateau through a gate at the south-west corner (near h in the sketch).

The farm of La Haye Sainte (see sketch No. 2), situated 250 yards in front of the Wavre road, consisted of a courtyard about forty yards square, surrounded on the north, west, and south sides by strong masonry buildings, and on the east by a good wall, towards the southern end of which there was a great gate. Two large doors (H and G) existed on the south-west extremity of the buildings; there was a door (M) in the northern wall; a great gate (K) and a door (L) opening on to the road. The walls were loopholed, but the want of tools and materials prevented the buildings being put in a really efficient state of defence, and the doorway (H) leading into the barn had been broken up for firewood, rendering it difficult to efficiently block this entrance. On the French side of the farm there was an orchard extending for about 230 yards along the road, which was surrounded by a hedge on the east, south, and west sides. A small garden with a hedge was at the back.

On the opposite side of the road to La Haye Sainte, and in line with the rear of the farm, was a gravel-pit, which afforded an additional position

SKETCH No. 2.

GROUND-PLAN OF THE FARM OF LA HAYE SAINTE.

(Not drawn to scale.)

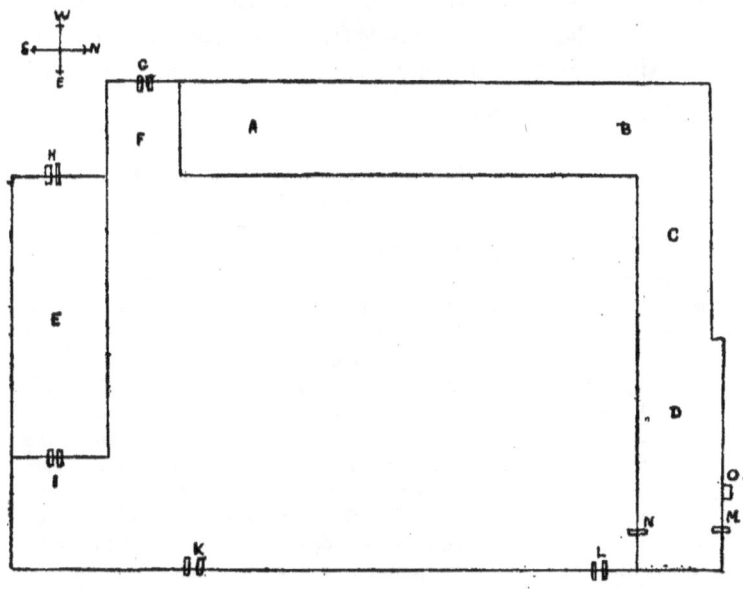

→ THE GREAT ROAD—CHARLEROI TO THE ALLIED POSITION. →

A, B, C, D, Dwelling-house, stables, and cow-house, of which D is the dwelling-house.
E, A barn.
F, A passage.
G, A great gate.
H, A great gate.
I, A door.
K, A great gate.
L, M, N, Doors.
O, A well, being a square building, with loopholes flanking the door and wall.

The interior measure of the yard, from the building C, D to the building E, is 40 yards, and 45 yards from the building A, B to the wall K, L.
The buildings are very strongly roofed and built. The passage F has the same roofing as the houses.

From Kennedy's 'Notes on the Battle of Waterloo.'

in front of the main line flanking the *chaussée* and eastern edge of the orchard and farm. The rear of the pit was covered by a hedge which extended about 150 yards from the *chaussée* and nearly at right angles to it. The road itself was blocked by an abattis in prolongation of the south wall of the farm, and by another at the edge of the pit.[1]

[1] It seems remarkable that no attempt was made to strengthen the line of battle, which might easily have been done. The position had been surveyed some time before, and Wellington had a plan given to him on the 17th; but he "did not wish to have any ground entrenched beforehand which might give any clue to his intentions." The only company of sappers and miners available was at Hal. It was sent for late on the 17th to come to Braine-l'Alleud, which the Duke wished to have prepared for its defence. It lost its way marching through the woods in the dark and wet, and only arrived at Waterloo at 9 A.M. on the 18th. Sufficient tools do not appear to have been available for any extensive work, but there can be little doubt that with a little more care on the part of the Staff, the hamlets in front of the left flank and the farm of La Haye Sainte might have been properly strengthened. Sir John Burgoyne, who visited the battlefield in 1816, points out that the position might have been made much stronger. "Two companies of sappers and 3000 men might, on the night of the 17th, . . . have thrown up such a line as would have afforded great cover to our infantry and guns, have brought them more to the ridge of the hill, and would have considerably checked and broken the advances of cavalry" (see 'Life and Letters of Sir John Burgoyne,' pp. 328, 329; also 'History of the Corps of Royal Engineers,' pp. 378, 379). Sir H. Clinton, who commanded the 2nd Division, states in a memorandum he made at the time, which is now in his family, that "about 11 A.M. the Light Brigade and German Legion were ordered to furnish working parties to throw up breastworks to cover our guns; but when they arrived the officer with the intrenching tools was not present, and before these works were begun the enemy had commenced his attack." That the tools were not available would appear to have been largely the fault of the Headquarter Staff, another proof of the bad way in which its duties were carried out. Each battalion had five spades, five shovels, five pickaxes, five fellingaxes. See 'General Orders of the Duke of Wellington,' 2nd edition, p. 422.

WELLINGTON'S FORCE

The number of troops at Wellington's disposal was as under [1]:—

	Infantry.	Cavalry.	Guns.
British	15,200	5,800	78
King's German Legion	3,300	2,000	18
Hanoverians	10,300	500	12
Brunswickers	4,600	900	16
Nassauers	2,900	...	...
Dutch-Belgians	13,400	3,200	32 [2]
	49,700	12,400	156

The French forces are somewhat difficult to determine accurately.

It would appear that the Emperor had with him on the battlefield the numbers given below [3]:—

	Infantry.	Cavalry.	Guns.
Guard	14,000	3,500	122
1st Corps	17,400	1,600	46
2nd Corps	14,000	1,900	38
6th Corps	7,200	...	24
3rd Cavalry Corps	...	2,600	12
4th Cavalry Corps	...	3,200	12
3rd Cavalry Division	...	900	6
5th Cavalry Division	...	1,200	6
	52,600	14,900	266

[1] These numbers are taken from Siborne. After carefully comparing them with those given on p. 486, vol. xii., 'Wellington Despatches,' de Bas, and other sources, I am inclined to think the actual strength present was about 1000 more.

[2] Charras states Prince Bernhard had only three guns, five of Bijleveld's battery having been "disorganised" at Quatre Bras. Siborne contradicts this statement, and says the guns were not lost. Internal evidence of the fight would seem to show that Bijleveld's battery had only seven guns in action with Bijlandt's brigade, the other being with Stievenart's battery behind Papelotte. See de Bas, p. 655.

[3] These numbers are taken chiefly from Houssaye.

The value, however, of the opposing forces was very different. Kennedy estimates that of the Allies at 41,000. For, as he justly remarks, part of the Dutch-Belgians did not fight, and the remainder, with the Hanoverians, Brunswickers, and Nassauers, who were raw troops, were not worth more than 11,000, and there were only 30,000 British and King's German Legion on the field.[1]

The Prussian forces present at the battle were Bülow's corps, the 5th Brigade (Pirch's[2] corps), the 1st Brigade, and Röder's cavalry of Zieten's corps—in all some 36,000 men.[3]

On the left of the line held by the Allies was Vivian's cavalry brigade (A),[4] with Gardiner's battery of horse artillery. The 10th Hussars of this brigade had a squadron in Smohain, its front covered by vedettes.

Next to Vivian's came Vandeleur's brigade (B). In front of them, holding the advanced posts from the chateau of Frischermont, the cluster of houses at Smohain, the farms of La Haye and Papelotte, was Prince Bernhard of Saxe-Weimar's Nassau Brigade, of Perponcher's division, less one battalion at Hougomont (C, C, C), having about half its force in reserve, with one gun of Bijleveld's and Stievenart's

---

[1] See Kennedy, 'Notes on the Battle of Waterloo,' p. 57.

[2] The cavalry of the II. Corps and the 6th and 8th Brigades came up as the fight terminated, and are usually included in the number present, but they did little of the actual fighting.

[3] These numbers are taken from Lettow-Vorbeck and from Pflugk-Hartung, 'Jahrbücher für die Deutsche Armee und Marine, August and September 1905.'

[4] These letters refer to the plan of battle.

WELLINGTON'S DISPOSITIONS 217

battery on the slope behind. The chateau of Frischermont, with its outbuildings, was well adapted for defence. The farm of Papelotte was also a strong position, but Smohain and La Haye were not so strong. Both Frischermont and Papelotte were held by the Nassauers during the whole of the fighting. Very little seems to have been done in the way of putting these posts in a proper state of defence.

Next to Vandeleur came the Reserve Corps, in the following order of brigades: Vincke's (5th Hanoverian, D), Pack's (9th British, E), and Kempt's (8th British, F), all belonging to the 5th Division. Interpolated between the first two was Best's (4th Hanoverian, G), while Bijlandt's (1st Dutch-Belgian) brigade (H) was placed in front of and between Pack's and Kempt's men. The general line held by these troops extended from the left to the Charleroi *chaussée*, along the Wavre road, and except in the case of Bijlandt's brigade was in rear of it. On the right of Best was placed Rettberg's Hanoverian battery of six guns. Seven Dutch-Belgian guns, of Bijleveld's battery, were placed on the right of Bijlandt's brigade, and Roger's foot battery was in front of Kempt's brigade. During the action the Dutch-Belgian troops moved to the rear, and Kempt then closing to his left gave place for Lambert's 10th English Brigade (J), which arrived about 11 A.M., and which at first was in reserve. The gravel-pit and hedge were held by three companies of the 95th from Kempt's brigade.

On the right of the Charleroi *chaussée* was the

3rd Division (see sketch No. 3). Next the road Ompteda's 2nd King's German Legion Brigade (K), having the 2nd Light Battalion, numbering 400 men, under Major Baring, in La Haye Sainte. Next to Ompteda came Kielmansegge (1st Hanoverian Brigade, L); then, in second line, Kruse (Nassau Contingent, M); followed by Halkett's (5th British) brigade (N). The 1st Division completed the front line to the right. On the hill behind Hougomont was Maitland's brigade (O), next to Halkett's, while Byng's (P), behind Hougomont, acted as a reserve to the troops holding that post, the garrison of which consisted of the four light companies of the Guards, a Nassau battalion from the 2nd Dutch-Belgian Brigade (Prince Bernhard's), and 200 men from Kielmansegge's brigade, about 1500 in all.[1] Mitchell's (4th British) brigade (R) held the avenue from Hougomont to the Nivelles *chaussée* and the hollow road towards Braine-l'Alleud, with four companies of the 51st and the light companies of the other two battalions. The remainder of the 51st (R1) and the 14th (R2) being in support, while the 23rd (R3) was posted behind Byng. On the plateau behind was massed the 2nd Division (S). The Brunswick troops (T) were placed in reserve at Merbraine. Chassé's Dutch-Belgian division held the village of Braine-l'Alleud, to the right-rear of the line, and

---

[1] The light companies of the Grenadiers were in the Great Orchard, under Lord Saltoun, those of Byng's brigade in the hollow road and lane at the north and west of the Great Orchard. The latter were under Colonel Woodford.

SKETCH No. 3.

FORMATION OF THE 3RD DIVISION AT WATERLOO.

Adapted from Kennedy's 'Notes on the Battle of Waterloo.'

(Not drawn to scale.)

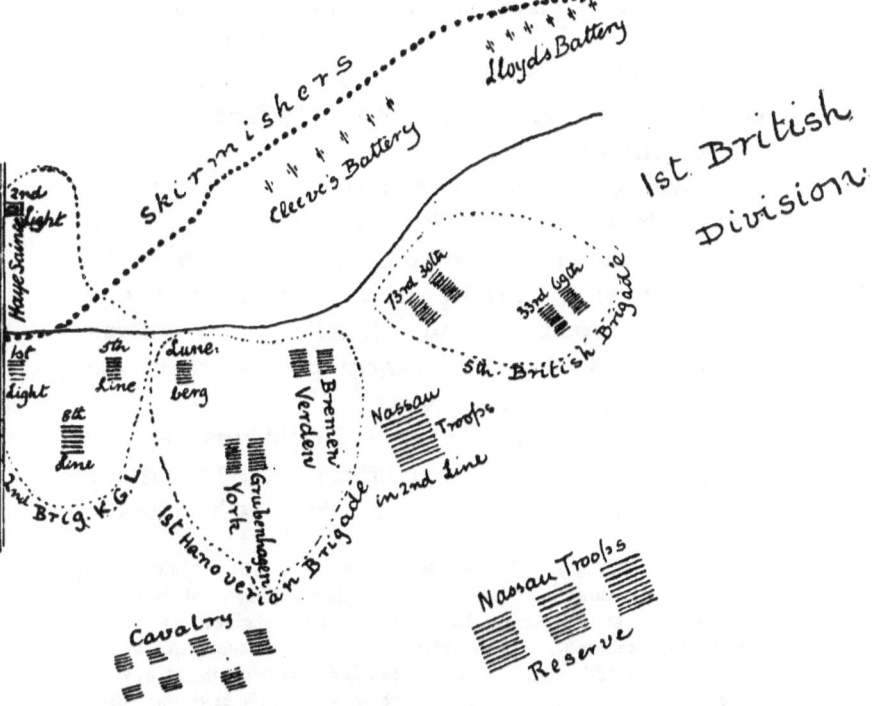

The 3rd British Division consisted of the
    5th British Brigade.   2nd Brigade K.G.L.   1st Hanoverian Brigade.

N.B.—The skirmishers, as drawn by Gen. Kennedy, are plainly too close to the guns; they were down the slope about on a level with Haye Sainte.

THE CAMPAIGN OF 1815

with the force about Hal was intended to secure Wellington's flank in this direction.[1]

To the west of the Charleroi road the artillery was distributed as follows: Ross's battery on the high ground behind La Haye Sainte, having two guns pointing down the *chaussée*; Roger's and Cleeve's batteries were placed in front of Alten's division, one on either side of the spur marked *c*; Kuhlmann's and Sandham's were placed in front of the Guards. Sympher's and Bolton's batteries were in reserve with the 2nd Division, and five horse batteries, exclusive of the one with Vivian's, were with the cavalry brigades.[2] Bean's, Sinclair's, and Braun's batteries were in reserve about Mont St Jean. The two Brunswick batteries (sixteen guns) were with their own troops. With Chassé's Dutch-Belgian division at Braine-l'Alleud were two batteries (sixteen guns) of the same force.

The cavalry on the centre and right was disposed as follows: Grant's[3] (5th) brigade (U) behind the Guards, with a squadron of the 15th Hussars

---

[1] See *ante*, pp. 189-90. In after-life Wellington stated he had information that a French cavalry force was detached in this direction. This Napoleon also said when at St Helena. But there is not the slightest evidence to support this statement, as every cavalry unit can be accounted for on the 16th, 17th, and 18th June. Sir Henry Smith says that on the 17th, when the 10th Brigade was nearing Brussels, there was a rumour to this effect. See 'Autobiography of Sir Henry Smith,' vol. i. pp. 266, 267.

[2] These were, Bull's, Webber-Smith's, Whinyates', Mercer's, and Ramsay's. Although nominally attached to the cavalry, they were used independently where needed.

[3] The 13th Light Dragoons replaced the 2nd Hussars King's German Legion in Grant's brigade, the latter having been left to guard the frontier. This left Arentsschildt with only one regiment, the 3rd Hussars King's German Legion.

WELLINGTON'S DISPOSITIONS

covering Mitchell's flank; Dörnberg's[1] (3rd) and Arentsschildt's (7th) brigade (V and W) were in rear of Alten's division. Right and left of the Charleroi *chaussée* were the Household and Union Brigades (X and Y), under Somerset and Ponsonby, while still farther to the rear was the Dutch-Belgian brigades in reserve (Z, Z, Z). The whole of the cavalry was at the disposal of its commander, the Earl of Uxbridge, to employ as he liked.[2] Lord Uxbridge sent verbal orders to the commanders of the cavalry brigades "to act discretionally under certain limitations." The latter, so far as Vandeleur and Vivian were concerned, were probably not to move from the left flank.

The front of the position was, in accordance with Wellington's usual custom, covered with skirmishers, furnished by the light companies of the brigades united under a field officer.[3]

The French position, like the English, was somewhat concave. On the left it somewhat overlapped the Anglo-Allied, so that artillery could partially enfilade the latter, as indeed it did during the battle.[4]

---

[1] The Cumberland Hussars from the Hanoverian cavalry were attached to this brigade.

[2] See 'Waterloo Letters,' pp. 3, 4, 16.

[3] See 'Supplementary Despatches,' vol. x. p. 262. It will be observed that the army corps were broken up. Probably this was because the Duke did not wish the Prince of Orange should be in such a position as would enable him to make again the mistakes of the 16th. Moreover, only one of the three brigades of Dutch-Belgian troops present was employed in the front line, so that there was no longer any reason whatever why in such a critical battle this inexperienced Prince should take command over more experienced officers.

[4] See *post*, p. 244.

On the right it was brought by the ground into close contact with the advanced posts of Smohain and Frischermont.

In rear of the right centre stood the village of Plancenoit, which, owing to the action fought by Napoleon to defend his right, played an important part in the battle in conjunction with the long spur to the north-east, stretching out towards Frischermont. The chief point in Plancenoit was the church, standing on a knoll with a wall at the foot, which thus formed a strong keep. The ground to the east of the village was difficult for manœuvring, though affording cover to the Prussians in their advance.

The Emperor drew up his troops in the following order. East of the road was d'Erlon's corps, having its flank covered by its cavalry division (Jacquinot's); west of the road were the three divisions available of Reille's corps, with Piré's cavalry on the outer flank; behind d'Erlon was placed Milhaud's 4th Cavalry Corps, while Kellermann's, the 3rd Cavalry Corps, was in rear of Reille.[1] Lobau's corps, the 6th, was in second line in the centre, having Domon's and Subervie's cavalry divisions beside it. The Imperial Guard was in reserve, with its cavalry division, the Light Brigade (Lefebvre-Desnoëttes') on its right, and the Heavy Brigade (Guyot's) on its right behind the 4th and 3rd Cavalry Corps respectively.

[1] D'Erlon's and Reille's infantry were in two lines, in accordance with the usual French practice.

NAPOLEON ORDERS THE ATTACK 223

Orders for the attack were issued by Napoleon at eleven o'clock.[1] They were as follows:—

> When the army is in battle array, about an hour after noon, and when the Emperor gives the order to Marshal Ney, the attack on the village of Mont St Jean at the intersection of the roads will begin. For this purpose the 12-pounder batteries of the 2nd and 6th Corps will be joined to that of the 1st Corps. These twenty-four guns will fire on the troops about Mont St Jean, and Count d'Erlon will commence the attack, pushing forward his left division, and supporting it according to circumstances by the other divisions of the 1st Corps.
>
> The 2nd Corps will advance at the same level as Count d'Erlon to protect him.
>
> The sapper companies of the 1st Corps will be ready at once to barricade the village of Mont St Jean.[2]

These orders show clearly that Napoleon's plan from the first was to penetrate the centre of the Anglo-Allied army—to repeat on it the manœuvre of Ligny.

---

[1] His first orders for the 18th appear to have been issued on the 17th, but are not to be found. But on the 18th, between 4 and 5 A.M., Soult issued the following order:—

"The Emperor orders the army to be ready to attack at 9 A.M. The commandants of army corps will collect their troops, see that the arms are put in order, and that the soldiers prepare their food which is to be eaten so that all may be ready for battle at 9 o'clock in the position pointed out by the Emperor in his orders of yesterday evening, with the artillery and ambulances."

The army was not ready by the hour named, and the ground was too soft to allow the artillery to manœuvre, and hence the attack was delayed for over two hours. That the army was *not* in battle order by *nine* is shown by the order in the text of *eleven*. See also Walter Scott, 'Life of Napoleon,' vol. viii. p. 599.

[2] See 'Correspondance de Napoléon,' vol. xxviii. pp. 292, 293.

The battle is usually considered to be divisible into five phases, tolerably distinct from one another, each phase representing an attack on the Allied line. But it must not be thought that these are absolute divisions, and that between them no fighting took place. The first attack was directed against Hougomont, and was practically continued during the whole battle, though not always with the same ardour. During the early part of it Napoleon was collecting his forces and concentrating his artillery for a stroke against Wellington's left centre. When all was ready, this, the second or main attack, was commenced. It was followed by the third, the great cavalry assault on the Allies' right centre. This was succeeded by a combined infantry and cavalry attack delivered against the same point, accompanied by an infantry attack against Wellington's left. Finally the Imperial Guard was launched against that part of the position from which the cavalry had been driven back. All the attacks, therefore, with the exception of the diversion against Hougomont, were in accordance with the Emperor's original plan of penetrating Wellington's centre.

It does not appear that the Emperor ever wished the attacks on the Anglo-Allied right to be very formidable — that is to say, he had no desire to push them home. They were rather intended to divert Wellington's attention from those other portions of his line to which the French efforts were mainly directed. No mention is made of Napoleon's intention to advance against the chateau in his orders, and the movement seems to have been an afterthought, the instructions for it being given to Reille verbally. But commenced at first with one division only (Jerome's), covered by the artillery of Reille's corps (less the 12-pounder battery) and the guns of Piré's cavalry division, the attacks on this outpost eventually absorbed the greater part of the 1st Corps with its cavalry and some artillery from the Guard Corps.

Bearing this fact in mind, it is more convenient in describing the battle to deal with the various attacks on Hougomont as a separate phase, it being understood that the series of actions now to be described commenced at 11.30 and went on to the end of the battle.[1]

At 11.30 the attack commenced by Jerome's division advancing to attack the chateau.

The guns of Reille's corps were arranged in front of his left to bring a fire to bear on the western side of the chateau. This being protected by the trees in the woods and avenues, but small effect was produced. Jerome's men found little difficulty in pushing back the Hanoverian and Nassau skirmishers in the wood; but they were completely stopped at the southern garden wall which they had no means of scaling, and the fire from which was so severe as to completely check their advance. They were finally driven back by the fire of Bull's howitzers[2] from the high ground in rear, sup-

---

[1] See 'Vie militaire du Général Foy,' p. 280.

[2] These guns, 24-pounder howitzers, used shrapnel shell with time-fuzes. The time-fuze of that date was fairly easily driven into the shell, and thus acted as a percussion-fuze; there is no doubt in my mind that these

plemented by a charge of the light companies of the Guards.

A fresh advance was made by the French, and this time a portion of Jerome's division, passing round the west side of the chateau, attempted to force their way in by the gate of the north-western extremity of the building. A few succeeded in making their way into the building, but there were killed, and the attack was driven back. Part of the division, however, pushed across the Braine-l'Alleud road, and the skirmishers brought a severe fire on Smith's battery, placed here to check Piré's guns, the fire of which somewhat affected the English line in this direction. Here again a counter-attack by four companies of the Coldstream Guards forced them back. Colonel Woodford then occupied the enclosures between Hougomont and the Nivelles road with a portion of his men, and with the rest reinforced the garrison of the chateau. The French efforts against the garden succeeded no better. Part of Foy's division compelled the light companies of the Grenadiers to retire behind the northern hedge; but the cross fire to which the French were exposed from the eastern garden wall, and from the troops they had pushed back before them in front, was so severe that they could not maintain their position.[1]

shells did so act when they struck the trees, and to this fact is largely to be attributed their great effect. For it is quite certain that Bull's fire alone sufficed to drive the French back out of the wood.

[1] "My division was employed on the eastern border of the Hougomont wood, sometimes it advanced, at others it was pushed back.... From time to time I detached battalions to support or replace those of Jerome's division." See Foy, p. 280.

THE ATTACKS ON HOUGOMONT

Lord Saltoun then led the light companies forward together, reinforced by two other companies of the 3rd Guards which Wellington sent down from the hill behind, and drove back the French once more.

The attack was again renewed. Jerome's division advanced once more, supported by Foy's, the latter moving up the eastern border of the wood; and about 2.45 P.M. the buildings were set on fire by the fire of the howitzers which Napoleon brought up from the Guard for this purpose, making with the artillery of Reille's corps some fifty-eight guns in action against the Allies' right. But the main lines of defence—namely, the south and east garden walls and the northern hedge—were never carried by the French; and, although it was necessary to employ the whole of Byng's brigade of Guards successively in the defence of the post, while Duplat's brigade was subsequently brought up to support it, the French obtained no real success against the Anglo-Allied right flank. The tide of battle thus ebbed and flowed to and fro around Hougomont, while Napoleon was directing his main efforts elsewhere. But it cannot be said that the result to the French in this part of the field was in any way commensurate with the loss suffered by Reille's corps. The general outcome of the fighting being that the English maintained their ground and paralysed, with a relatively small force, a large proportion of the Emperor's army, of which he might have made valuable use in other directions.

Having, as he hoped, diverted the attention of Wellington by the assault on Hougomont, Napoleon turned his attention to his opponent's left centre. The Emperor proposed to advance in echelon from the left of d'Erlon's corps, force the Anglo-Allied centre, seize the village of Mont St Jean, and thus grasping the main road to Brussels divide his opponents in two, and cut off the greater part from junction with the Prussians and from the Belgian capital.

Ney was entrusted with the conduct of this portion of the battle. By the Emperor's orders the heavy batteries from the 2nd and 6th Corps and two foot batteries from the Guard were joined to the artillery of the 1st Corps, and the whole, making in all seventy-eight guns, were assembled together in one large battery on the spur $a\ b$, so as to bring under fire the Allies' line from the left of Alten's division to Vandeleur's cavalry brigade. The massing of these guns over the tenacious soil and through the standing crops was a work of some time, and it was one o'clock before they were ready to commence firing. The artillery preparation was continued for half an hour, and at half-past one the infantry was ordered to advance.

The formation made use of has been very much disputed, but the French authors of the best authority unite in saying that the various divisions were, with one exception, drawn up in huge masses, consisting of the eight or nine battalions of which they were formed, deployed, and placed in a column one behind the other, with only five paces interval between them. The one exception was the division of Allix.[1] Its two brigades were formed in a similar manner,

[1] Commanded by Quiot, the leader of the 1st Brigade.

but side by side instead of behind one another. This was done because, being on the left of the four divisions, it was ordered to send one (Quiot's brigade) against the south and west of La Haye Sainte, while the other (Bourgeois') was to attack the eastern side of the same post. The divisions were to advance in echelon from the left at a distance of 400 paces apart,—Donzelot's on the right of Bourgeois' brigade, Marcognet's next, and Durutte's on the right,—and in the formation described they were led by Ney to the assault, each column having a front of about a hundred and sixty to two hundred files.

Quiot's brigade was the first to come into collision with the enemy, and it drove the Germans out of the orchard of La Haye Sainte, though unable to make any impression on the farm itself, which does not seem to have been previously brought under artillery fire. But the French soon extended round the farm and captured the garden in the rear. To support the left of the attack, Travers' brigade from Milhaud's division of cuirassiers had been ordered to the front by the Emperor, and as Quiot's men swept round the western flank of the farm, they followed behind, and somewhat to the left. To reinforce Baring at his post the Lüneberg Field Battalion was detached from Kielmansegge's brigade, and advanced down the slope towards La Haye Sainte. It was composed of young troops, scarcely suitable for a counter-attack. Thrown into some disorder by the French fire from the garden, and by their own skirmishers falling back on them, they commenced to retire, when they were charged by the cuirassiers and driven back with great loss.

Elated with their victory, the horsemen swept up the slope to charge the infantry and guns they saw before them. But their triumph was a short one: Lord Uxbridge had seen the advance of the French columns against the Allied centre and 'left, and knowing the weakness of this portion of the line felt that it might be necessary to use the heavy cavalry brigades to repel the assault. He therefore ordered Ponsonby rather more to the left, towards the point against which the French infantry columns were advancing, while he himself, with Somerset's brigade, took post on the ground which lies to the west of the Brussels road. Seeing the French cuirassiers mounting the slope, the King's Dragoon Guards and 1st Life Guards were sent in front line against them, supported by the 2nd Life Guards on the left, the Blues being held in reserve. At the time of the collision the French left was thrown somewhat forward, and thus the 1st Life Guards and two squadrons of the King's Dragoon Guards struck this flank first and drove it back. The right of Travers' brigade pushed on, came on the hollow road near La Haye Sainte, scrambled down into it, and barely reached the farther side when they were met by the rest of the King's Dragoon Guards and the 2nd Life Guards. The shock was decisive— the Frenchmen were repulsed. Part turned and rode back the way they had come, pursued by the King's Dragoon Guards, the 1st Life Guards, and Blues. Part turned away to their right, scrambled

THE HEAVY CAVALRY CHARGE 231

down the steep sides of the road, which threw them into further confusion, and endeavoured to retreat by the paved *chaussée*. Stopped by the barricade, they inclined to their left and fled through the open space left between the gravel-pit and Kempt's brigade, followed by the 2nd Life Guards.[1]

To return to the other divisions. The troops of Bourgeois' brigade advanced at the same time as Quiot's, but on the eastern side of the road. Coming near La Haye Sainte, they felt its fire, and that of the Rifles from the gravel-pit and hedge, while Ross's two guns struck them in front. The fire was so severe that, coupled with the actual obstacle of the pit, they were forced to oblique to their right. This change of direction, and the retardation caused by the fire, delayed them in their advance, and in their new direction against the Anglo-Allied line they found themselves on about the same level as Donzelot's division, and together they advanced against their foe.

Bijlandt's brigade had suffered considerably from the artillery fire of the great French battery. The fighting capacity of the men was not very great, their enthusiasm in the cause they were defending still less, and the near approach of the threatening columns destroyed what little steadiness they ever possessed. Notwithstanding the entreaties of their officers, the whole brigade moved backwards, sweeping with it

---

[1] Some of the cuirassiers fell into the pit, and some no doubt were upset into the hollow road, but no large numbers can have so suffered, as there is no contemporary account of any such occurrence, which seems mainly due to the lively imagination of Victor Hugo.

Bijleveld's battery, until it reached a position of safety, where it re-formed, but took no further part in the struggle.[1]

[1] Bijlandt's brigade was drawn up in two-deep line at first on the south side of the road, but about one o'clock it was moved back to the road itself. Here it received the attack of Bourgeois' brigade on its right, while Donzelot menaced its centre. "The musketry fire of this brigade (*i.e.*, Bijlandt's) was not able to stop the French advance, the numerous losses had caused gaps which upset the ranks; the first line began to waver, and the Netherlands troops made a retrograde movement to the right and left to give space to the second line." (See Van Löben-Sels, p. 278.) This manner of describing the falling back of Bijlandt's brigade is skilful but not accurate. What happened was that it retreated in two masses, one behind Kempt's the other behind Best's men, leaving a gap which Pack stopped by bringing up his brigade to fill it. A little later Best's and Vincke's men closed to their right, Pack and Kempt somewhat to their left, and thus the line was once more made continuous. The 10th Brigade was shortly after brought up to occupy the ground on the right of the 5th Division. Löben-Sels asserts that Bijlandt's brigade re-formed and took its position in the line. How could this be the case when Pack was there? There is not one single British officer engaged in that part of the fight who does not clearly state that the Dutch-Belgian remained in the rear and came on no more.

The table below shows what was the fighting capacity of these troops :—

LIST OF KILLED, WOUNDED, AND MISSING, 16TH TO 18TH JUNE.*

REGIMENT.	† Strength at commencement of campaign.	Killed.	Severely wounded.	Slightly wounded.	Total killed and wounded.	Missing.	Total killed, wounded, and missing.
27th Jagers .	809	15	41	137	193	178	371
7th Line Regiment.	701	20	49	89	140	83	223
5th Militia .	482	73	87	52	212	109	321
7th Militia .	675	20	23	41	83	285	308
8th Militia .	563	17	66	41	124	194	318
	3230	145	266	360	752	849	1541

* This list is taken from Plotho, where it will be found on p. 93 of the Appendix. It is dated Curgies, 1st July 1815, and signed by the Adjutant-General, van der Wijk.

† Taken from de Bas, p. 1332. From this it is plain that out of a strength of 3200 engaged in the fighting on the 16th and 18th June, they lost more missing than killed and wounded, and that the slightly wounded formed half the killed and wounded. Moreover, the missing amounted to one-fourth of the force. The statement that Bijlandt's

BIJLANDT'S BRIGADE RETIRES   233

The retreat of these troops left a dangerous gap in Wellington's line, and against this gap was advancing Bourgeois' brigade and Donzelot's division, and these reached the hedge which grew on the south side of the road. The moment was one of danger, but a danger that was to quickly pass away before the bravery of the British troops under Picton. Deploying Kempt's battalions, which numbered only about 1800 men, he led them to the charge against Bourgeois' men, in which he met his own death. In accordance with his usual practice the line first poured a volley into the advancing column at close range, and then closed with the bayonet. The unwieldy nature of their formation prevented the French from deploying to fire, and they slowly fell back. Their disarray was now augmented by their own horsemen (Travers' brigade) coming on

Dutch-Belgian brigade did not fight properly is clearly proved by these figures. Now Kempt's and Pack's brigades were in the same part of the field at both Quatre Bras and Waterloo as Bijlandt's. The table below gives their losses in the two fights, and the two tables bring out clearly the relative fighting capacities of the troops concerned:—

	Strength at commencement of campaign.	Killed and wounded, Quatre Bras and Waterloo.	Missing, Quatre Bras and Waterloo.
Kempt's Brigade . .	2471	1270	2
Pack's Brigade . .	2173	1287	17

Percentage of loss killed and wounded—
    English { Kempt, 51.4 per cent.
            { Pack, 59.2 per cent.
    Dutch-Belgian, 23.3—*i.e.*, about two-fifths of the English loss.
Percentage of missing—
    English . . less than ½ per cent.
    Dutch-Belgian . 26 per cent, or more than fifty times as much as the English.

In the face of these figures and the evidence of British officers who were present and saw what the 1st Brigade of the 2nd Dutch-Belgian Division did, it is idle to contend that it provided any very serious contribution to the success of the battle.

them, as these fled before the Heavy Brigade, and the charge of the Union Brigade completed their discomfiture. They retreated in great disorder with the loss of a large number of prisoners.[1]

For while the British infantry were advancing to the charge, Ponsonby had been watching his opportunity, and at the right moment launched his cavalry against the French. The Royals struck the right of Bourgeois' brigade, the Inniskillings Donzelot's, while Marcognet's division, having first received a biting fire from Pack's brigade, which had advanced to fill the gap left by Bijlandt, was then smitten by the Scots Greys, who had come through the ranks of their countrymen to get at the foe. The French advance was at an end. Damaged by the artillery fire from Rettberg's, Roger's, and Bijleveld's batteries in their onward course, met by the undaunted front of the opposing infantry, then charged by the cavalry, moving in a formation which rendered deployment hopeless and even marching difficult, they had no chance against their active and mobile foe. Down the slope they had but just mounted they were driven, pursued by the British cavalry, the infantry assisting to gather the harvest of prisoners reaped by the swordsmen.

Durutte's division alone had been more fortunate. It formed the extreme right echelon of the advancing columns, and had first of all to deal with the advanced posts about Papelotte. Leaving two battalions to guard the right flank of the long line of guns, he moved the

[1] Probably about 2000 men and two eagles were taken from d'Erlon's corps as the result of this encounter.

rest of his division against the allied left. Being the last to move, and having the longest way to go, since he was obliged to incline inwards to avoid the fire from Papelotte, Durutte hardly came into close action before the troops on his left had been defeated, and he, therefore, found himself in an isolated position and compelled to retreat. This he did in good order, although charged by Vandeleur's cavalry. During his advance a part of his force had carried the outlying portions of the Anglo-Allied advanced posts in Smohain and La Haye, but they were driven out of it by a counter-attack, and henceforward, during the remainder of the battle, the engagement here was in the main confined to skirmishing action between the opposing forces, and until quite the end of the battle Prince Bernhard held his ground.[1]

At this period of the fight it will thus be seen that the French attack on the English left centre had failed. Quiot's brigade was only partially successful against La Haye Sainte. For having its left menaced by the English cavalry and finding itself isolated by the retreat of the troops on its right, it was compelled to retire across the road, its retreat being covered by Bachelu's division, brought forward to the high ground on the left of the big French battery when d'Erlon's corps had advanced to the

[1] When the Prussian infantry came up to support the left flank of the Anglo-Allied line a portion was directed on the advanced posts. Mistaking the Nassauers for French, on account of their uniform, they poured a heavy fire into them. This was too much for Prince Bernhard's men, and the greater part fell somewhat precipitately back, but were rallied by their commander three-quarters of a mile to the rear. See Starklof, p. 212.

attack. Bourgeois' brigade had suffered most, and the 105th had lost their eagle; the fire from Kempt and the charge of the Royals had largely reduced its numbers, and it could do no more until completely reorganised. In falling back it took up the position which it had formerly held, on the left of the 1st Corps, and was there joined by Quiot when he retired from La Haye Sainte. Donzelot's division had not been handled so severely. It had had no infantry in front of it, owing to the retreat of the Dutch-Belgians, and it only received the fire from a part of Pack's and Kempt's men. It retired in comparatively good order, and took a position on the right of Allix's, falling back after Bourgeois' brigade had been forced from its side. Marcognet's division had felt the full force of Pack's fire, and the Greys in their charge surprised it. It had lost severely, and the eagle of the 45th Regiment had been captured. Completely disorganised, it was for a time incapable of further action.

The British cavalry in their pursuit followed recklessly the retiring Frenchmen in loose and open order, more like a mob of horsemen than disciplined troops. In their progress they swept away two batteries which had endeavoured to follow the French infantry, but which could make little progress in the stiff and tenacious soil. Nothing could stop the horsemen, and they were soon among the guns of the great French battery, cutting down the gunners and stabbing the horses. But they were without support, and the opportunity was too good to be lost by the French cavalry. Jacquinot sent a regiment of lancers in extended order against them, while Farine's brigade

THE UNION BRIGADE CHARGED 237

of cuirassiers from Milhaud's cavalry corps attacked them in front. The British cavalry horses were blown, their men tired, and no longer in any formation. In consequence they speedily suffered defeat from the French, who inflicted great loss upon them, until stopped in the pursuit of their retreating foes by an opportune charge of Vandeleur's brigade. The 12th Light Dragoons first rode over part of Durutte's division, and then, aided by the 16th Light Dragoons on its right, took the lancers in flank and defeated them, not without considerable damage to themselves.[1] Vandeleur did not follow up his advantage too far; but, calling his men together in the valley, brought them back in safety to the position they had previously occupied. Ghigny's brigade was also brought forward by its commander to support Vandeleur. The two regiments composing it, the 4th (Dutch) Light Dragoons and the 8th Belgian Hussars, went to the left of the 4th Brigade, the first-named acting as a support on the left of the 12th Light Dragoons, the second as reserve.

The net result of the fight so far was, that on the French right, d'Erlon's corps had lost about a third of its men, including 2000 prisoners. Two eagles had been captured by the English, and about 15 to 30 guns rendered more or less unserviceable. On the other hand, Bijlandt had been driven back, and a battalion of Kielmansegge's cut up by Travers' cavalry.[2] The

[1] The 11th Light Dragoons were left as a reserve on the slope behind.
[2] Some French accounts speak of standards captured and offered to the Emperor. Only three battalions, Germans, were broken by the French during the whole battle, and only one of them appears to have lost a colour. See *post*, footnote, p. 280.

attacks against Hougomont had been no more successful, and on this side there was no compensation for the losses incurred. For the whole of Jerome's and part of Foy's divisions had been involved in the attack without any advantage being gained.

About one o'clock, just when the preparatory stage of the attack on the Anglo-Allied left was about to commence, Napoleon had seen some troops in motion about St Lambert. To ascertain who they were, whether Prussians under Blucher or French under Grouchy, Napoleon sent a party of cavalry to reconnoitre to the right flank. Soult now sent off the following despatch to Grouchy :—

> You wrote to the Emperor, at six o'clock this morning, that you would march on Sart-à-Walhain ; your intention therefore is to go to Corbais or Wavre. This movement is in accordance with the dispositions of his Majesty, which have been communicated to you. Nevertheless, the Emperor orders me to tell you that you should always bear in mind the necessity of manœuvring in our direction and seeking to get nearer to the army, so that you can join us before any Prussian corps places itself between us. I do not give you any directions ; it is for you to see where we are so that you can make the necessary arrangements, so as to keep in communication, as well as to be always ready to fall on the enemy's troops who might seek to upset our right and crush them.
>
> At this moment the battle is begun on the line of Waterloo, in front of the Forest of Soignes ; the enemy's centre is at Mont St Jean. Manœuvre, therefore, so as to join our right.

The messenger taking the letter was just leaving,

BÜLOW'S ADVANCE OBSERVED 239

when a captured Prussian hussar was brought in who cleared up the mystery.[1] He was the bearer of a note to Müffling, saying that Bülow was advancing against the French right and rear. A postscript, which ran as under, was therefore added to the despatch :—

> A letter has just been taken, to the effect that General Bülow will attack our right flank. We think we see this corps on the heights of St Lambert; do not therefore lose a moment in joining us to crush Bülow, whom you will take *en flagrant délit*.

As a practical fact, however, the troops in question were only the advance-guard of the IV. Corps, the main body of which had been delayed on its march through Wavre. But Napoleon could not know this, and notwithstanding that he was informed that the whole corps, 30,000 men, was advancing against him, he took no steps to hold them, beyond sending Domon's and Subervie's light cavalry to observe their movements. When first seen, Bülow's main body was on the far side of the Lasne, and a small force sent to this point would have effectually

[1] This hussar appears to have belonged to the 2nd Silesian Hussars, and he was captured by Marbot's 7th Hussars, who had been ordered about 11 A.M. from about Frischermont to cover the French right flank, sending patrols to Lasne, Couture, Mousty, and Ottignies. The hussar was captured near Lasne. See Houssaye, p. 325, and Marbot, vol. iii. p. 404. He seems to have been taking the following message to Müffling (see Lettow-Vorbeck, pp. 401, 402): "In case the centre of left flank of Marshal Wellington's is attacked, General Bülow is willing to pass the Lasne with his corps at Lasne, and to form up on the plateau between Haye and Aywiers, so as to advance against the right flank and rear of the enemy." Wellington, however, knew about eleven (see footnote 1, p. 255) that Bülow was advancing.

delayed the Prussians. But it was not till later that Napoleon despatched that portion of the 6th Corps which he had with him, to take up a position and stop them, ordering Durutte at the same time to capture Papelotte and Smohain and Frischermont.[1] The exact time at which this was done is doubtful, but it seems probable that it took place a little before four o'clock, about the time the cavalry attack commenced.

The attacks on the Anglo-Allied left and right employed nearly the whole of the infantry of d'Erlon's and Reille's corps, while Lobau was wanted to guard the French right flank; of this arm, therefore, Napoleon had only the Imperial Guard left. He had then to choose between using it or the cavalry for his fresh endeavours, and he chose the latter.[2] For from the first he had thought of employing his mass of horsemen, who had so often brought him victory, and he had placed at Ney's disposition the cuirassiers and the cavalry of the Guard.[3]

Ney seems to have mistaken a slight rearward motion of the Allied infantry to find shelter behind the crest of the position for the beginning of a retreat, and to have thought the moment come to ensure it by driving home the mass of French horse-

---

[1] It will be remembered that Teste's division of this corps was with Grouchy.

[2] See Houssaye, p. 367.

[3] See Houssaye, p. 367. Houssaye thinks, after reviewing the existing evidence, that although Ney was given these bodies of cavalry he was not to use them without the express order of the Emperor. This seems unlikely. Either Ney had Milhaud and the Guard cavalry at his disposal, or he had not. If he had, it was to use when he thought fit.

THE FRENCH CAVALRY ATTACKS

men. Milhaud's division, supported by Lefebvre-Desnoëttes' light cavalry of the Guard, was told off for the purpose, and these moved across the road into the valley between it and Hougomont. To cover their advance a large number of guns were brought into action on the ground to the left of the road, so as to bring a powerful fire to bear on Alten's division. For this purpose the 12-pounder batteries which had been placed in front of d'Erlon's corps were withdrawn, and moved to a new position on the high ground in front of La Belle Alliance, and these were supplemented by others from the Guard and from the cavalry divisions.

Sterner measures had meanwhile been taken with Hougomont. The guns of Piré and Reille were reinforced by some heavy howitzers from the Guard, and a powerful artillery fire opened against it. At a quarter to three this set the buildings of the chateau on fire, which, after some trouble, was extinguished.

The great cavalry attacks on the Anglo-Allied right centre were now about to commence. As soon as the artillery arrangements to prepare them were complete the French guns opened fire, and a little before four o'clock Milhaud's cuirassiers advanced at a trot (the charging pace of the French heavy cavalry) against the Anglo-Allied centre. Their front, narrowed by the posts of Hougomont and La Haye Sainte, did not measure more than about 600 yards. This, with the numbers available, would allow of about twelve lines of cavalry charging in succession. The formation used by the French was a succession of lines at short distances, so that a series of waves of cavalry were sent against the English and German squares, and like waves beating against the firmly planted rocks on a seashore they were broken and shattered to pieces by them.

At this time the situation of Wellington's troops at this portion of the line of battle was as follows: Beginning with Alten's division, the Lüneberg battalion was greatly reduced in strength, and a portion of the battalions on its left—namely, the 5th line battalion and the 1st light battalion—had also suffered considerably in the previous attacks, and from the fact that they had despatched troops to aid the garrison of La Haye Sainte. With these exceptions, however, the remaining battalions had not suffered very much, except from the artillery fire, from which they were partially sheltered by being withdrawn behind the crest of the ridge on which they stood, and then ordered to lie down. To the right of Alten's division was Maitland's brigade of Guards. Byng's brigade had, with the exception of two companies kept in reserve as a guard to the colours, near the Nivelles road, been sent forward into Hougomont, and a portion of the Brunswick troops had been brought up to fill the vacant space thus made.[1] When they arrived they were disposed as follows: two battalions as above on the right of Maitland's; two battalions right and left of the Nivelles road on the slope, about 400 yards north of Hougomont. The remaining four were used later

[1] It will be remembered that they were originally stationed by Merbraine.

on to fill the gap which occurred in Alten's corps, when owing to the losses in Kielmansegge's and Ompteda's brigades a gap was made at this point of the line, and when this was done two battalions of Kruse's brigade were placed on their left, *i.e.*, next to Kielmansegge's men.

Shortly after the cavalry attack commenced, Clinton's division was brought up to the front. Hew Halkett's (3rd Hanoverian) brigade was placed as a support to the Brunswickers on the right of Maitland's, and Duplat was stationed as a support to Hougomont on the slope behind that post. Adam's brigade was ordered to close the interval between the north-east angle of Hougomont and the Brunswickers. To give a moral support to the latter, which the youth and want of training of the men rendered necessary, the 23rd Regiment was brought from Mitchell's brigade (the 4th British) and placed between the two squares that the Brunswickers had in the front line on Maitland's right. The artillery at this portion of the field was strengthened before and during the cavalry attack until some sixty-two guns were available to keep down the French fire and resist their cavalry charges.[1] The gunners were instructed to work their guns up to the last moment, and then to take refuge in the nearest infantry squares, the limbers moving to the

---

[1] The artillery was made up as follows : Seven British or King's German Legion batteries, forty-two guns ; a Belgian and Brunswick battery, sixteen guns ; four guns of Ross's battery above La Haye Sainte, two guns of this battery being engaged in firing down the road. Possibly another British horse battery was also at this point of the field.

rear out of danger.¹ While the attacks now about to be described were going on, Wellington made up his mind that no attempt would be made to turn his right, and he therefore ordered up Chassé's division of Dutch-Belgians from Braine-l'Alleud, and placed them in second line behind Maitland's brigade, and to its left rear. But he still allowed the troops at Tubize and Hal to remain there.

Before the French advance actually took place, and while the cuirassiers were moving into the valley, Piré's cavalry on the left made a demonstration against the British right, accompanied by some artillery fire somewhat enfilading the line. Grant was therefore ordered, with the 13th Light Dragoons and the 15th Hussars from his brigade, to oppose it; while the 2nd Light Dragoons King's German Legion were detached from Dörnberg's brigade, in the direction of Braine-l'Alleud, to watch the movement. At first, therefore, the only cavalry available west of Alten's division was the 7th Hussars of Grant's, the 1st Light Dragoons King's German Legion, and the 23rd Light Dragoons of Dörnberg's brigade, the Brunswick cavalry, and the 3rd Hussars King's German Legion of Arentsschildt's brigade, six regiments in all, besides three brigades of Dutch-Belgian cavalry.² In addition to these there were the Heavy and Union Brigades, which had suffered considerable losses in their previous charges.

[1] It seems probable that the guns were loaded with a round-shot and a case, and that the last fire was delivered at very close range—under fifty yards. Although the French were frequently in possession of the guns they never spiked any of them.

[2] Ghigny's brigade had returned from the left flank.

THE CAVALRY CHARGES

The first French attack, which was led by Milhaud's cuirassiers, supported by Lefebvre's light cavalry of the Guard, took place a little before four o'clock. It was unsuccessful, no square was broken, and, although made in good order, the cavalry were not ridden home on the infantry. The consequence was that, played upon in the first instance by the artillery and received by the infantry fire from the squares, they opened out, passed by the front line and came upon the squares of the second line, where they were as unsuccessful as in their attempts on the first.[1] This wedging apart, as it were, by the front line of infantry, produced confusion in the already shattered ranks, and when thus disordered they were charged into by the cavalry in the rear, and driven backwards down the slope. Here they formed again and made another attempt to penetrate the Allied infantry, Lefebvre-Desnoëttes' light cavalry leading. On this occasion a part was kept in hand with a view to meeting the Allied cavalry; but the attack was no more fruitful than the first one. Many efforts were made by the French cavalry, but all with equal unsuccess.

Their assaults had, however, served to cover the advance of Allix's division, supported by a part of Donzelot's, against La Haye Sainte, while at the same time the French infantry of Foy's division had

---

[1] The squares were arranged chequerwise in two lines. The ranks were four deep, and kept this formation when deployed into line. See sketch No. 3, which shows the arrangement of Alten's division. The infantry formed four in accordance with the usual practice for squares, and then deployed to the front on the front face of the square, thus retaining the four-deep formation. This was by Wellington's order.

crept up to the eastern boundary of Hougomont to turn the flank of the Guards occupying the northern boundary ditch. But when the French cavalry retired, the infantry acting against La Haye Sainte retired also, and the Guards advancing from their cover drove back the skirmishers from the orchard, which they once more occupied. During the engagement Grant, who had seen from the right the advance of the French cavalry, and judging, therefore, that the demonstration by Piré was only a feint, brought back his cavalry (with the exception of one squadron of the 15th Hussars, left to observe the enemy) to the rear of the threatened right.

The Emperor appears to have thought Ney's first attack premature, but when it was beaten determined to support it with fresh troops. Another French cavalry attack was therefore prepared. The shattered squadrons of Milhaud and Lefebvre-Desnoëttes were reformed, and Kellermann's corps was by the Emperor's orders sent into the fight. While these were getting ready to advance the artillery fire was renewed against the Allied infantry in all its intensity. As before, the French cavalry advanced and passed through the guns against the infantry. As before, they were charged by the Allied cavalry, and as before, they were driven back. In vain was Guyot's heavy cavalry of the Guard brought up to aid the sadly diminished force—no square was penetrated; and decimated by the fire of the guns, shot down in numbers by the fire of the four-deep formation, the gallant French horsemen were, after many efforts, driven down the slope. Their defeat was accentuated by the repeated charges of the English and German cavalry, and sometimes of the Dutch-Belgian, and the two former suffered severely in the fight. On one occasion Grant was able to deliver an effective blow before the French charged home. For with the 13th and 15th Hussars, passing over the end of the plateau where it begins to dip toward Hougomont, he struck the advancing cuirassiers on their left flank and defeated them before they reached the infantry line.

Towards the centre, the French were more successful. La Haye Sainte had been set on fire, which was with difficulty put out, and a strong column of infantry (probably Quiot's brigade) was advancing towards the right centre, covered by the cavalry. Uxbridge charged the infantry with the Household Brigade, but made very little impression on it. Trip's Belgians, on whom he relied for support, refused to follow him, and in retiring put in disorder part of the 3rd Hussars King's German Legion; the latter, however, rallied and advanced against the French, but were driven back with severe loss—and it may be as well at once to dispose of the part played by the Dutch-Belgian cavalry in the battle by saying that, with the exception of occasional and halfhearted support to the British and German cavalry, they contributed very little towards the success of the struggle.[1] The Cumberland Hussars retired from the field altogether.

[1] There were three brigades of Dutch-Belgian cavalry in the field—viz., Trip's (heavy), Merlen's, and Ghigny's.

The evidence with regard to them is quite clear. The Dutch-Belgian as

Two guns were now brought to the knoll to the north of La Haye Sainte to enfilade Kempt's line, but

well as the British and German cavalry was under Lord Uxbridge. He stated, with regard to Trip, "I had the strongest reason to be excessively dissatisfied with a general commanding a brigade of Dutch heavy cavalry. . . . I led them beyond the ridge of the hill a little to the left of Hougomont. There they halted, and finding the impossibility of making them charge I left them" (see 'Waterloo Letters,' p. 12, and p. 11). Sir Horace Seymour was aide-de-camp to Lord Uxbridge—he states, "Lord Anglesey tried all in his power to lead them on; I believe I called his attention to the fact that he was not being followed." Not only did they not go on, but they turned back, and breaking through the 3rd Hussars King's German Legion put it in some confusion. The Germans, however, were soon in order again, and executed the required charge. See Siborne, p. 297. Gawler also saw the Dutch heavy cavalry retiring in confusion. 'Waterloo Letters,' p. 289.

Trip's cavalry may occasionally have followed up the British and German cavalry when it advanced against the enemy, but that it took any real part in the fighting there is no evidence to show, though judging from the smaller number of their missing I should say they behaved better than either Ghigny's or Merlen's. The three brigades suffered some casualties, as any force that did not run off the field necessarily must have done. Wellington's mention of Trip in the despatch goes for nothing—when he wrote it he had not consulted with Lord Uxbridge. It is as reasonable to quote this as a proof of the conduct of the cavalry in question as it would be to bring forward Blucher's proclamation to the Belgians of the 24th June as representing exactly his feelings towards them. High personages, in writing despatches or proclamations, are always prone to make them somewhat flattering in character. For Blucher's proclamation, see Reiche, vol. ii. p. 442.

Merlen's brigade had, as we have seen, behaved badly at Quatre Bras. Van Löben-Sels admits (see *op. cit.*, 223) that "the charge executed by the Netherlands cavalry failed completely." He goes on to say that this was due to the charge being made by isolated half-troops, or at the most troops. Well, even granting this, how was it that the brigade consisting of the 5th Dutch Light Dragoons and 6th Belgian Hussars was entirely useless for the remainder of the day, and that a large proportion of it quitted the field? Merlen's men it was who carried dismay into Brussels early on the 17th, as certainly no other mounted men fled there that day. See 'Circumstantial Details relative to the Battle of Waterloo,' &c. p. 16. "Between five and six we were roused by the loud knocking at the door and cries of 'Les François sont ici.' Starting up, the first sight we beheld was a troop of

FRENCH ATTACK RENEWED

these were silenced by the 95th, yet the French skirmishers pressed round La Haye Sainte, and Alten

Belgic cavalry, covered not with glory but with mud." See also 'A Visit to Flanders,' by James Simpson, Edinburgh. "On Saturday foreign soldiers began to arrive in hundreds at Brussels. Although at least fifteen miles from a Frenchman, the horsemen galloped, . . . the infantry ran. . . . They lay down in crowds on the pavement of the suburbs. . . . Towards the afternoon the wounded English from Quatre Bras began to arrive."

With regard to Ghigny's brigade, the chief claim is that it supported Vandeleur's brigade in its charge against Jacquinot's lancers. Van Löben-Sels, p. 279, says that the 4th Light Dragoons charged French infantry and suffered great loss, and that the 8th Hussars remained in second line. This would appear to have been done on the right of the English cavalry, because Löben-Sels says, p. 280, that as Jacquinot's division made some progress on the left the brigade retired behind Picton's division. Now, it is difficult to imagine that a cavalry brigade could have come to the point and charged without being noticed by either Vivian or Vandeleur. The only allusion to it is that Colonel Sleigh, who was in command of the 11th Light Dragoons, which regiment were in reserve, and therefore could see what was going on, says "there was some Belgian cavalry in rear of our brigade to the left, a few went down with the 12th Dragoons, but I cannot say I observed them take any part in the attack" (see 'Waterloo Letters,' p. 108).

Löben-Sels' narrative is absolutely inaccurate. Vandeleur charged the French cavalry after the Union Brigade had driven back the French infantry, and when Jacquinot's men had been launched against the left flank of the English cavalry. Jacquinot was beaten back by Vandeleur, and certainly made no progress "on the left," as Löben-Sels states.

Löben-Sels, p. 301, also claims for the Dutch-Belgian cavalry that Trip and Ghigny followed the advance of Chassé's infantry when Wellington gave the order for the whole line to advance, and that Merlen's brigade (Merlen had been killed before this) was on the right; but he does not say it did anything. In a footnote on the same page he states Merlen's brigade was ordered by Lord Uxbridge to join on to a British brigade of light dragoons, and that the 6th Hussars, in carrying out this movement, were not followed by the 5th Light Dragoons. No trace of this having been done is to be found, and Vandeleur, who commanded the only brigade which agrees with this description, makes no note of it. Löben-Sels adds that the 5th Dragoons joined Ghigny in the evening. Where were they meantime?

We know from Lord Edward Somerset, 'Waterloo Letters,' p. 20, that towards the end of the battle he did not dare withdraw his brigade, then extended in single file to save them from artillery fire, because if he did so the Dutch would move off. This was Ghigny's brigade behind him. Now,

sent to Ompteda to ask him if possible to deploy a battalion of his brigade and lead it against Quiot's

let us examine the loss of these troops in the fighting on the 16th and 18th, remembering that only Merlen's brigade was engaged on the first date.

Brigade.	Strength at commencement of Campaign.*	Losses.†				
		Killed.	Severely wounded.	Slightly wounded.	Total killed and wounded.	Missing.
Trip .	1237	76	98	76	244	71
Ghigny	1086	65	133	161	369	184
Merlen	1082	21	86	60	167	132

* From de Bas.   † From Plotho.

It will be seen from this table that, as in the case of the Dutch-Belgian infantry, there is again a large proportion of missing.

The strength and losses of the British cavalry were as under :—

Strength.	Killed.	Wounded.	Missing.
5913	561	1047	407

The percentages of losses in British and Dutch-Belgian were as follow :—

	Killed.	Wounded.	Missing.
Dutch-Belgian . . .	4.7	18	11.17
English . . .	9.5	18	7

The proportion of wounded to killed was :—
    In the Dutch-Belgians . . . . . nearly 4 to 1
    In the English . . . . . . nearly 2 to 1

It is, of course, to be remembered that of the missing, in the case of cavalry, a good many are due to the men having lost their horses; but even allowing for this, there is a striking difference in the proportions. A similar discrepancy is shown in the ratios of wounded to killed. Many of the Dutch-Belgian "slightly wounded" must have been very "slightly." No further comment on these statistics is necessary.

Kennedy, see 'Notes on the Battle of Waterloo,' p. 119, says: "To understand these great cavalry attacks it is necessary to bear in mind the extraordinary fact that the large bodies of Dutch-Belgian cavalry and the Cumberland Hussars, that stood in reserve behind the 1st and 3rd Divisions of infantry, took no part in the action." Now, Kennedy was most emphatically in a position to state accurately what he saw, and there is plainly no doubt in his mind as to what did happen. The great deeds of Dutch-Belgian cavalry are a figment of the imagination.

column. Ompteda, knowing that the French attack was seconded by cavalry, and that to lead his sorely tried troops in line down into the valley was to court sudden and sure disaster, sent to explain his views to the Commander of his division. But the Prince of Orange came up, and when Ompteda repeated his opinion to him, the Prince again gave the order with considerable vehemence, and Ompteda led down the 5th Battalion to the charge. They pressed back the French skirmishers. But as soon as the latter cleared the ground, Travers' cuirassiers came down on the right flank of the Germans and drove them back with great slaughter. Ompteda went, as he knew, to his death, and thus was a gallant soldier sacrificed to the presumptuous ignorance of a military stripling.[1]

Arentsschildt observing the cuirassiers' attack, sent the 3rd Hussars King's German Legion against the flank, and these drove the Frenchmen back. But the latter were supported by fresh cavalry, who compelled the hussars to retreat, but in turn were forced back by the rifle fire of the 95th.

The defence of La Haye Sainte was drawing to a close. Baring's men were considerably diminished in numbers, their ammunition was failing, and, although Baring sent repeatedly for a fresh supply, none was

[1] The 5th Battalion entered on the campaign 379 strong; it lost at Waterloo 154 men. See 'Memoirs of Baron Ompteda,' p. 311. The Prince, in reply to Ompteda who pointed out the actual situation of the French cavalry, said, in a sharp and peremptory manner, with the fatal self-sufficiency of military ignorance, "I must still repeat my order to attack in line with the bayonet, and I will listen to no further arguments."

obtained.[1] The brigade furnishing the garrison (Ompteda's) had suffered very severe loss, and could scarcely be looked upon as a fighting body. About six o'clock Ney led forward the 13th Light Infantry and some sappers and broke into the farm. The gallant defenders, having no longer any means of resistance, fell back; but only a small portion were able to reach the main position in safety.

Alten's division had suffered very severely in the struggle. La Haye Sainte was in the possession of the French, thus giving them a point from which fresh attacks could be made against the Allied centre, and cover by which to approach it. Occupying the garden and knoll behind, they were able to bring a severe infantry fire to bear on Kielmansegge's already diminished forces, and in rear of these there was nothing but the attenuated line of the Household Brigade.

On the Allied right the struggle was still going on about Hougomont, but here it was unfavourable for the French. For two-thirds of Reille's corps was held at bay by Byng's brigade of Guards, a few details from other regiments, Duplat's troops in reserve on the slope behind the chateau, with the 4th British Brigade on the right flank, and the four Brunswick battalions of troops. Just after the first cavalry attack on the Allied squares, Adam's brigade had been

---

[1] It is usually said that the cart containing the ammunition had been upset on the Brussels road. It is highly probable also that these men were armed with a rifle of different calibre to the Baker rifle of the 95th. For many of the German riflemen of this epoch were foresters who took their own rifles into the field with them.

moved forward in squares into a position somewhat in advance of the north-east corner of Hougomont, and with its left a little thrown forward. This advanced position, though dangerous,[1] gave a very efficient flank fire on the French horsemen as they advanced to the main position of the line, and served greatly to break them. As the cavalry attacks drew to a close about 6.30 P.M., Wellington withdrew this brigade from its advanced position towards the main ridge behind, where it formed on the right of Maitland's right.[2]

The strong line of French skirmishers extended right along the Anglo-Allied up to and beyond Maitland's brigade. The fire they brought to bear on the left of these troops and on the right of Colin Halkett's, formed by the 30th and 73rd regiments, was very heavy, and the attack on the latter was intensified by some French guns brought up to close range. A battalion of the Grenadiers was therefore sent forward to drive off the skirmishers. This it did, and then returned to its position in line.

Little impression had been made on the Allied left, where Prince Bernhard still held the greater part of Papelotte and Frischermont, although Donzelot's skirmishers had occupied Smohain and La Haye.

We have seen that Blucher had ordered the II.

---

[1] They were under the fire of both artilleries, and some of the shrapnel from the British burst over their heads, and caused casualties.

[2] Adam's brigade was apparently placed between the Brunswickers and Maitland's Guards, room having been made for it by the Grenadiers closing to the left, where they formed four deep. See 'Waterloo Letters,' p. 254.

and IV. Corps to the battlefield, and before noon it was quite decided that the I. Corps should move towards Ohain on the right of the II. Corps, and that Thielmann only should be left to cover the rear. Bülow's advance-guard consisted of the 15th Brigade together with the 6th Hussars and a 12-pounder battery. It marched off at daybreak, and was followed by the 16th Brigade, the 13th Brigade, the Reserve Artillery, the Reserve Cavalry, under Prince William, the 14th Brigade forming the rear-guard. At six o'clock the advance-guard had marched through Wavre, when a fire broke out which had to be extinguished before the main body could follow; this and the bad roads so delayed the march that the bulk of the corps did not reach St Lambert until one o'clock, the 14th Brigade not until three, although the advance-guard had arrived there about ten o'clock and found that the enemy had sent no troops to oppose it.[1] From St Lambert to Lasne the road was steep and bad, the Lasne had to be crossed and the severe slope on the far side climbed, and it was only about four o'clock that the Paris Wood was reached by the 15th and 16th Brigades.[2] The vanguard, consisting of two battalions and a cavalry regiment, arrived here about one o'clock, but took up position under cover till towards three. Some of the cavalry appears to have reached the

[1] Bülow had sent two flanking patrols, one towards Maransart, which was found occupied by the enemy; the other towards Ceroux, with instructions to gain touch with the detachment left at Mont St Guibert. These both reported that the enemy was making no advance by the Lasne valley against the Prussian left flank.

[2] On some maps called the Frischermont Wood.

neighbourhood of Papelotte before the battle began, and to have informed Wellington that the Prussian army was coming up, and led to the hope that the Prussians would arrive on the field between one and two o'clock.[1] The Frischermont wood formed an important supporting point for the advance-guard, which it was necessary to hold to cover the advance of the rest of the corps from St Lambert, yet nothing was done, and Bülow's corps remained halted at St Lambert.

Major von Lützow, an officer of the headquarter staff, had been sent on to observe the progress of the fight, and had been for some time in the Frischermont wood, waiting in vain, notwithstanding his repeated messages, for it to be occupied by the Prussians. Leaving the vanguard to watch the situation he himself rode back and found Blucher and Gneisenau at St Lambert. Lützow urged his view that the wood should be at once held, but no decision was come to. At this moment General Grolmann came up from Wavre, where he had remained to give Thielmann the necessary instructions for his conduct.[2] Grolmann, without hesitation, cried

[1] See Sir Feltham Harvey's Letter, published in the 'Nineteenth Century' in March 1903. He was one of Wellington's aides-de-camp at Waterloo. A squadron of the 10th Hussars under Major T. W. Taylor was on piquet to the east of Papelotte, and received the Prussian officer who brought the news that Bülow was advancing and was "three-quarters of a league" distant. Lieutenant Lindsay took this message to the Duke. See 'Waterloo Letters,' p. 169. The time was probably about 11 A.M.

[2] It seems to me that Grolmann must have met Lützow on his return to the front—*i.e.*, some distance ahead of where Blucher and Gneisenau were. It is impossible to imagine Grolmann would have given this order in the presence of Blucher. In all probability Grolmann had found

"Forward! forward!" to the leading troops; "in the name of the Field-Marshal I order you at once to advance over the defile."[1] Inspirited by the determined manner of the Quartermaster-General, the column moved forward, and Blucher seeing the troops going on at once fell in with the idea and urged the troops forward with repeated appeals, "Lads, I know it is hard, but we must get on. I've promised my friend Wellington, and you won't let me break my word, will you?"

The advance-guard at once seized the wood, which they were able to do unresisted, for Domon's cavalry merely watched the border and made no attempt to find out what was going on inside. Here they remained hidden, so as to secure the passage of the defile in rear to the 15th and 16th Brigades with the corps artillery and cavalry. As the troops began to arrive the infantry was posted in close formation in the wood, the artillery on the road, and the Reserve Cavalry in rear, the whole being under cover. About 4.30 P.M. Blucher, impatient of delay and full of loyal desire to support Wellington as quickly as possible, ordered these troops to advance to the attack.

The 13th and 14th Brigades had not quite come up

Gneisenau full of hesitation, had then ridden on himself, met Lützow, heard his report, and at once gave the order which produced such happy results. Blucher would then have found the troops going on, which was exactly what suited this really Grand Old Man, and he at once fell in with the idea.

[1] See 'Leben und Wirken des Generals, &c., Carl v. Grolmann,' by General Conrady, part ii., p. 308. The same statement is made in Hofmann's 'Zur Geschichte des Feldzuges von 1815,' &c., 2nd edition, p. 116.

THE PRUSSIANS BEGIN TO ATTACK 257

when at 4.45 the 15th Brigade, emerging from the wood, sent two battalions to connect with the Nassau troops on the left of Wellington's line. The 16th Brigade moved on the left of the 15th, on the extreme left the Reserve Cavalry. At 5.30 P.M. the 13th Brigade arrived, and at six o'clock the 14th Brigade reached the rear of the 16th. The IV. Corps was then complete. The 16th and 14th Brigades were directed on Plancenoit, the 15th being ordered to link on to the advanced post of Papelotte. But as the long spur along which they advanced somewhat divided these brigades, a portion of the 13th was brought to fill up the gap between them, which was also covered by the Reserve Cavalry of the IV. Corps and part of the Reserve Artillery.

A slight engagement took place between the French cavalry and the advancing Prussians, the former being driven back. Then, seeing the 6th Corps, which had been formed up with its two divisions in one line at right angles to the French front, the 15th Brigade inclined to its right, and thus it happened that the 15th and 13th Brigades attacked Lobau, while the 16th, supported later by the 14th, assaulted Plancenoit.

Meanwhile, towards the middle of the Anglo-Allied army, the capture of La Haye Sainte had put the French in a favourable position, affording as it did cover for a further advance against the Allies' centre, which was now much weakened by the fight.

Conscious of the vital nature of the struggle, for unless he could defeat the Anglo-Allies the cause of the Empire was lost, Napoleon ordered a fresh effort

R

to be made against Wellington to drive him from the position he was holding with such tenacity.¹

Durutte was sent against Smohain and to support the left of Lobau's corps; Marcognet was ordered to attack the English left, Allix and Donzelot's divisions were to advance against the shattered line from the cover of La Haye Sainte. Guns were ordered up to support this infantry, and two were even pushed to the knoll at the cross-roads north of the farm. Their action here was very severe on the already attenuated battalions of Ompteda and Kielmansegge, and on the 27th, formed by Lambert in square and placed in the angle of the roads by Kempt's left. But, fortunately, the riflemen of the 95th on the east side of the *chaussée* soon silenced them. Other guns were pushed up on to the projecting spur (*c*), and they brought a terrible fire to bear upon the already exhausted British artillery.² On the left Jerome and Foy were once more sent forward against Hougomont, Bachelu's division was ordered to support the assault against the Anglo-Allied right centre about to be executed by the Imperial Guard, while the remains of the French cavalry were told off to aid the attack.

The attack against Hougomont failed. But in the centre the French advance from La Haye Sainte drove back the shattered German troops which held

---

[1] When Ney sent to the Emperor for more infantry, he is said to have replied, "Où voulez-vous que j'en prenne, voulez-vous que j'en fasse?"

[2] Mercer describes this incident very graphically. See his 'Journal of the Waterloo Campaign,' vol. i. p. 325. At this time a considerable number of the batteries to the east of the Brussels *chaussée* were reduced almost to silence, owing to casualties among the detachments and want of ammunition.

CRITICAL POSITION IN THE CENTRE

this part of the field, and caused a dangerous gap in Alten's division, to fill which the Duke brought forward in person the remaining battalions of the Brunswick corps, while the British cavalry, extended in a thin line behind Kielmansegge's and Ompteda's troops, prevented the latter sorely tried men from retiring. At first the French drove back Kielmansegge's battalions, but, reanimated by their leaders and renewed in confidence by the presence of the Commander-in-Chief and his action in bringing up the reserves, together with the opportune advent of Vivian and Vandeleur's light cavalry brigades to this part of the field, they turned upon the foe and drove him back.[1] Marcognet's division made little progress against the Allies' left centre, and Durutte's advance was stopped by the action of the Prussians, whose advance was now beginning to tell on the French right wing.

Napoleon now determined to make a last endeavour for victory, and for this purpose called on his Imperial Guard.[2] Unfortunately for him their attack, instead of being made under cover from the position gained by the capture of La Haye Sainte, was directed across the open ground against Wellington's right centre.

The eight battalions of the Young Guard had already been sent to Plancenoit to aid Lobau in defending the army against the flank attack of the Prussians, and two battalions of the Old Guard, the 1st of the 2nd

[1] Vivian moved off to do so of his own initiative, but Vandeleur declined to do so without orders. But Uxbridge, riding to the left-wing cavalry to bring it to the centre, met Vivian and then sent for Vandeleur.

[2] The Old Guard had been present at many battles, but had taken an active part in few. Never was this body of veteran troops so much used as in the Waterloo campaign, a fact which shows the nature of the crisis.

Grenadiers and the 1st of the 2nd Chasseurs, had been detached to aid them. This left fourteen battalions of

SKETCH No. 4.
THE ATTACK OF THE FRENCH GUARD.

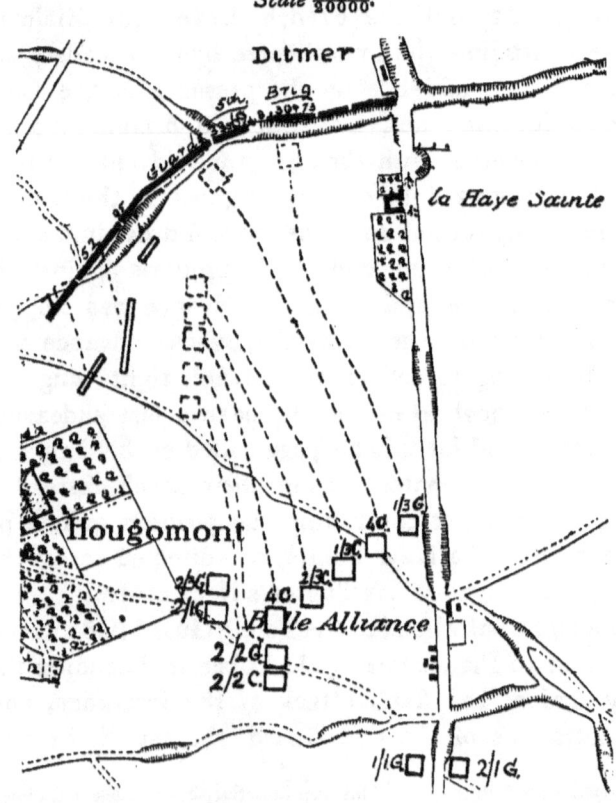

the Old Guard at the disposition of the Emperor. The 1st Grenadiers had its two battalions, as shown on Sketch No. IV.; the 1st Chasseurs were on duty as

THE IMPERIAL GUARD ATTACKS 261

personal guard to the Emperor, and were left at Caillou. Thus eleven battalions were available. But of these the remaining two battalions of the 4th Grenadiers and 4th Chasseurs were so weak that they were united into one for the attack about to be delivered.[1]

On the west of the Brussels road the 1st of the 3rd Grenadiers, the 4th Grenadiers, the 1st of the 3rd Chasseurs, the 2nd of the 3rd Chasseurs, and the 4th Chasseurs, were arranged as shown in the sketch, two guns moving in each of the intervals between the battalions. The five columns of attack thus formed moved in echelon at about deploying intervals, but the distances between the columns were very small.[2] Some way to the left, apparently near Hougomont,

---

[1] This account is based on the following authorities: Houssaye, '1815'; 'L'infanterie de la Garde à Waterloo,' by the Vicomte d'Avout, in the January and February numbers of the 'Carnet de la Sabretache' for 1905; General Petit's account of the Waterloo Campaign, 'English Historical Review,' 1903, p. 321 *et seq.*; Hamilton's 'Origin and History of the First or Grenadier Guards'; Batty's 'Historical Sketch of the Campaign of 1815'; Macready's article in 'The United Service Magazine,' March 1845; 'The Waterloo Letters'; Cotton's 'Voice from Waterloo'; several regimental histories; Siborne, de Bas, Löben-Sels, and others.

[2] It seems probable that the formation used was double column of companies on the centre at half-company distance. Petit, who commanded the Grenadiers of the Old Guard, says squares. See 'The English Historical Review,' April 1903, p. 321. The question of the Guard attack is very ably dealt with in the 'Carnet de la Sabretache,' Jan. and Feb. 1905. It is possible that they were formed in squares before they moved off, but that they moved to the attack in this unheard-of formation is highly improbable. They would have re-formed column before advancing, and then would have been in double column of companies at half-company distance. Possibly during the march the rear companies may have closed up to "close column." The reports of officers of the 52nd, who state that the French formed up their left sections so as to reply to the 52nd's fire, confirm this view. See Leake's 'Lord Seaton's Regiment at Waterloo,' vol. i. p. 45; 'Waterloo Letters,' pp. 273, 284.

was the 2nd of the 3rd Grenadiers formed in square, to which Napoleon betook himself during the movement. This battalion was subsequently joined by the 2nd of the 1st Chasseurs, but neither took part in the attack. The 2nd of the 2nd Grenadiers and the 2nd of the 2nd Chasseurs were told off to support the main assault, and were directed somewhat to the west of the chief attacking force. The total number of battalions employed against the Anglo-Allied line was eleven battalions formed into nine battalions, seven in the main attack, two in the supporting attack, and the total strength of the whole was some 4500 men.[1]

[1] After deducting losses at Ligny, and allowing for a five per cent diminution owing to the ordinary causes which operate in war, and assuming the 1st and 2nd battalions of each of the regiments were of equal strength, the numbers of these battalions were as follows: the 1st of the 3rd Grenadiers, 575; the 4th Grenadiers (two battalions), 700; the 3rd Chasseurs (two battalions), 1180; the 4th Chasseurs, 950. These formed the main attack total strength—viz., 3405. The front of each of the columns would be about 70 men, far too few to deal with the lines they were led against. The supporting battalions—viz., the 2nd of the 2nd Grenadiers and the 2nd of the 2nd Chasseurs—were about 585 and 595 respectively. Total of the whole attacking force, 4525. The isolated attacks of the Grenadiers were bound to be beaten by the much larger front of infantry they attacked, while the Chasseurs and those behind them were subject to such an infantry fire in front and flanks that no troops could resist it. The approximate strength of the opposing troops were as follows: the 1st of the 3rd Grenadiers, 580 men, with a front of 70, attacked 500 of Halkett's brigade and about 300 Brunswickers in line—*i.e.*, 800 muskets to 210. The 4th Grenadiers, 700 strong, front 70, were opposed by 1100 Guards and 400 of Halkett's—*i.e.*, 1500 muskets to 210. The Chasseur column, 3310 strong, with a similar front, received a frontal fire of 1860 muskets from the Grenadiers, 95th, and the right wing of Halkett's brigade, while the 52nd struck them in flank with the fire of 950 men. Attacks such as these were predestined to failure, and form a conclusive proof of the advantage of the line over the column. The Chasseur column consisted of fifteen lines of men three deep,—an unwieldy mass quite incapable of deployment, and which suffered terribly from the flanking fire of the 52nd.

THE FRENCH GRENADIERS ATTACK 263

Ney led the leading battalion, the 1st of the 3rd Grenadiers, against the left of Colin Halkett's 5th Brigade, where were the 30th and 73rd Regiments, which acted together as one battalion on account of their losses, with the Brunswick battalions on their left. The 4th Grenadiers attacked the left centre of Maitland's Brigade, while the 3rd and 4th Chasseurs moved more to the west against his right.

The attacking troops had been subject during their forward march to a considerable artillery fire from the batteries already in position, to which was added further force by Krahmer's battery from Chassé's Dutch-Belgian Division, which had now been brought up to support the front line of the Anglo-Allied right centre.[1] The artillery fire had caused great havoc in the French ranks, and now, when on the point of crossing bayonets with their English foe, they were received by a volley from the four-deep line which barred their way, which in the case of the English Guards was followed by independent firing, rendered more intense by the men of the third and fourth ranks loading for those of the first and second and changing muskets with them. In vain the columns tried to deploy. The narrow front of the leading companies, only about seventy men, could give but a

[1] They had been ordered up from Braine-l'Alleud about 3 P.M., and had been kept in reserve behind the right centre, where they had suffered somewhat from the artillery fire directed at the front line. See Chassé's report in de Bas, p. 1205. The battery was placed in the middle of the 5th Brigade, where there was a gap, owing to the 33rd and 69th Regiments, forming its right, being four deep and resting on the Grenadiers, while the 73rd and 30th being in the same formation, narrowed the front held, and thus made the interval filled by the Dutch-Belgian guns.

small return compared with the heavy fire the longer line poured into them. They paused, hesitated, and when Maitland and Halkett led their men forward to the charge, the French fell back down the hill.[1]

In the meantime Colborne, who commanded the 52nd, had seen the preparations for attack, and had determined to meet it with a counter-blow, which was destined to produce a decisive effect. The 3rd and 4th Chasseurs, advancing against Maitland's right, were supported by the 2nd of the 2nd Grenadiers and the 2nd of the 2nd Chasseurs, the two latter being somewhat behind the two former. Maitland brought forward his left against the Chasseurs' right, while Colborne, moving the 52nd down to the north-east end of Hougomont and some little distance from it, wheeled up his right until the regiment, which was a strong one and formed four deep, occupied a line parallel to that over which the French were to advance.[2]

Colborne now brought a terrible fire to bear upon

---

[1] Halkett's brigade halted after a short advance and then came under a severe artillery fire. It was therefore ordered somewhat more to the rear. But in the retirement a panic ensued, and the men lost all formation. However, the officers were soon able to restore order, and the brigade was led back to its former position.

The Grenadiers had followed the Guard some way down the slope, when Maitland perceived the Chasseurs advancing against him. He therefore ordered a return to the position originally held. Some confusion arose owing to part of the men thinking the order to form square had been given; but the ranks were soon re-formed, and Maitland's brigade was ready to receive the new attack directed against its right.

[2] The 52nd was the strongest battalion on the field, numbering 1000 men. It had been manœuvred in two wings (half battalions), and now Colborne brought the left wing behind the right wing, thus making a four-deep line. See 'Lord Seaton's Regiment at Waterloo,' vol. i. p. 39.

LA GARDE RECULE! 265

the flank of the latter portion of the Imperial Guard, and drove it back.

About this time the first portion of the Imperial Guard, which had pushed on more rapidly than the rear portion, had been met and defeated by Maitland and Halkett, and as they poured back towards the *chaussée* they carried with them Allix and Donzelot's men. The attack was supported by Detmer's brigade of Chassé's division, led by the divisional commander himself, who brought it up in the interval made by Maitland's movement between his brigade and Halkett's, but by the time it reached the front the French were already moving down the hill.[1]

---

[1] It is claimed by the Dutch-Belgians that Chassé's division was used in the final phase of the battle for two purposes (see Löben-Sels, p. 298, &c.) Part of Detmer's brigade was employed to fill the gap caused by the dispersal of three battalions in the front line, and that Chassé himself led his division, and especially Detmer's brigade, against the enemy with the bayonet. That Krahmer's battery came up close to the 1st British Brigade to support the guns in the front line, the fire of which had become feeble from the want of ammunition.

Krahmer's battery was undoubtedly of the greatest value; it was well served, and produced great effect on the advancing Guard. But that Detmer's brigade had anything to do with the final repulse of the latter, or that he ever closed with the bayonet, or did anything more than follow up after the French had been defeated, there is no evidence to show. To begin with, if three battalions were used to fill the gap (quite imaginary) there would only have been three Militia battalions to charge, for the time was too brief to have allowed the deployed battalions to have been gathered in once more beneath Detmer's command. The evidence is quite clear that the right of the 5th Brigade rested on the left of Maitland's Brigade, and the only gap which ever existed there was when Maitland wheeled forward his left wing. It was through this interval that Chassé came.

General Chassé in his report differs from Löben-Sels, and says that d'Aubremé was kept in reserve and that Detmer's was led in close column against the French Guard (see de Bas, p. 1205, Chassé's Report to the Prince of Orange). Lord Hill in his report to Wellington, dated 20th June, praises Krahmer's battery, and mentioned the steady conduct of the

Not content with the decisive stroke he had already dealt the enemy, Colborne advanced with the 52nd, followed later by the other battalions of Adam's brigade and the Osnabrück battalion of Hew Halkett's Germans across the field of Waterloo, until they reached a point where Napoleon's last remaining reserve (four battalions of the Guard)

3rd Division of the troops of the Netherlands under the command of Major-General Chassé, which was moved up in support of Adam's brigade to repulse the attack of the Imperial Guard. Chassé not thinking that he had received sufficient acknowledgment, wrote to Hill on the question, and Hill replied to him that in his report he had not failed to inform Wellington that his (Chassé's) division had advanced to repel the attack of the French Guard. Lord Hill's letter is a very cautious non-committal communication, and can certainly not be quoted in favour of Detmer's having taken an active part in the repulse of the Guard. It is perfectly compatible with the accounts of English officers who saw Detmer's brigade advance—viz., that it took place as the French Guard were retiring (see Major Macready, 30th Regiment, in 'United Service Journal,' part i., 1845).

Löben-Sels makes no mention of d'Aubremé's brigade, which with Detmer's constituted Chassé's division, and for a very good reason: this brigade was on the point of running away, and was only restrained by the English cavalry in rear preventing it, and by Wellington saying, "Tell them the French are running." Not even the most zealous advocate of Dutch-Belgian pretension can claim that d'Aubremé's men contributed anything important towards the victory. There is no doubt, then, on the whole, that the description given by Siborne is an accurate one, and it seems to me that the action of Chassé's division was as follows: The whole was brought up as he suggests. D'Aubremé's brigade was left in reserve. Chassé did lead Detmer's brigade to the front, and it did support the movement made by the Guards and Halkett's brigades, but did not come into anything like the active collision that these two English brigades did. It would be ridiculous to impugn Chassé's bravery, and his example appears to have inspired Detmer's men to a considerable extent. But this was the only brigade of Dutch-Belgian troops that did behave as did the other brigades of English and Germans on the field of battle. The attempt, therefore, to suggest that Detmer's brigade defeated the French Guard has no foundation, and does not really appear to have been claimed for them by General Chassé in his original report on the

THE COUNTER-ATTACK

stood, and three of these battalions were defeated by the 52nd.[1] The fourth was attacked and driven back by Halkett's men, and General Cambronne captured.

As soon as the Imperial Guard fell back Wellington ordered a general advance. Vivian and Vandeleur were sent against the French along the eastern side of

---

subject. See de Bas, p. 1205: "I marched with the 1st Brigade, commanded by Colonel Detmer, in close column against the enemy, and I had the pleasure of seeing the French Guard falling back before the brigade." A little later in the report he adds: "At the moment that the Grenadiers of the Guard were attacked and repulsed by Colonel Speelman with a part of the 1st Brigade." This, it will be seen, is not incompatible with the French Guard having retired before the movement of Detmer's approached them. The officers of the 30th Regiment, however, are quite clear this was the case. They state that after the French Grenadiers had retired, and after the 5th Brigade had fallen back behind a hedge, "a heavy column of Dutch infantry (the first we had seen) passed drumming and shouting like mad, with their chakos on the top of their bayonets, near enough to our right for us to see and laugh at them," *i.e.*, through the interval made by the advance of the 30th and 73rd and by the wheel to the right of the 33rd and 69th Regiments. The last two had made this movement to fire on the 4th Grenadiers attacking the English Guards. This is the evidence on both sides. If Lord Hill and the Duke of Wellington, who were both present at this time, make no mention of this Dutch attack, if English officers who saw it say that it was not an attack but only a support to the attack after the French retreated, it seems difficult to believe that the part Detmer's brigade took was of a serious utility to the Allied cause. Both Maitland's and Halkett's men, after firing, advanced to the charge, but the French Guard did not stay to meet it. Detmer's men were then seen advancing with their "chakos" on their bayonets, scarcely the attitude they would have assumed if the bayonets were to be used for fighting purposes. The losses of these two brigades are illuminating :—

	Killed.	Severely wounded.	Slightly wounded.	Total.	Missing.
Detmer's	27	52	85	164	197
d'Aubremé's	24	49	54	127	145

[1] Halkett sent back his brigade-major to bring up the rest of his brigade, but this officer was killed before the message was delivered.

Hougomont, and completed the disorder into which they had fallen, and the whole Allied right wing advancing across the field drove the French headlong before them down towards the road which leads to Genappe. This rearward movement took place shortly before the Prussian attack forced back the Emperor's right.

A little after six Zieten's advance-guard, consisting of the 1st Infantry Brigade and the Reserve Cavalry, had reached Ohain.[1] Reiche, the chief of the staff of the I. Army Corps, rode on to see how the battle was going, and met Müffling, who explained to him the situation, and that Wellington anxiously awaited the arrival of the Prussians. He therefore rode back to Zieten. The latter had already formed a vanguard of Steinmetz's two batteries and his cavalry regiment, to which was attached one from the Reserve Cavalry. These troops had been met by Reiche on the road, and he ordered them forward at a trot. He then went back and found Zieten, and the latter pushed on his 1st Brigade, followed by the Reserve Cavalry, as rapidly as possible, ordering the remainder to come on as quickly as they could. But while these troops were advancing a report came back that Wellington's army was retiring, and this brought the advance to a standstill, and immediately after an order arrived from Blucher that the I. Corps was to support him in his attack on Plancenoit. Reiche, who had once

---

[1] According to Pflugk-Hartung, 'Jahrbücher f. d. Deutsche Armee,' &c., August and September 1905, the strength of the I. Corps which fought at Waterloo was 5500 infantry, 1100 cavalry, and 22 guns.

more gone to the front, now returned and found the troops halting. Zieten arrived and determined to obey the order sent him. Fortunately Müffling persuaded him to change his destination, and once more the Prussians moved to Wellington's assistance. But the vacillation had lost time, and the foremost troops only reached the left of Wellington's line about seven. The artillery was at once brought into action against Durutte's right, which was attacking Smohain, and drove it back. The infantry, coming up later, expelled the French from this village, Frischermont, La Haye, and Papelotte. Unfortunately the advancing Prussians mistook the retiring Nassauers for French troops, and brought a severe fire to bear on them, and they, notwithstanding the efforts of their officers, abandoned their posts in large numbers, but were rallied about three-quarters of a mile back, and advanced again to the front.[1]

Zieten's guns were now joined by the horse battery from the Reserve Cavalry and by the battery of Prince Bernhard's troops, which had previously fallen back but now came up again, the whole forming a mass of thirty pieces, enfilading Durutte's division which filled up the gap between Marcognet's division and Lobau's corps. The fight between the newly-arrived Prussians and the French was for a time somewhat uncertain, but finally Marcognet's division, having been beaten back by the Anglo-Allied left which followed up the retreating French in accordance with Wellington's order, uncovered Durutte's flank;

[1] Starklof, p. 212. The Prince says a quarter of an hour back. This would mean 1250 toises, which amount to nearly three-quarters of a mile.

the Prussians then advanced against him, and he was compelled to retreat, the Reserve Cavalry under Röder supporting the movement.

The attacks on Plancenoit had meanwhile been carried on with great intensity. When Bülow first neared the village, the 16th Brigade was formed into columns of attack, supported by the 14th Brigade, and pushed into the village as far as the churchyard, driving Lobau's men before them.[1] Napoleon, seeing the necessity of strengthening Lobau, detached Duhesme with the Young Guard (eight battalions), and some guns. The Prussians were driven back, and a second attempt made by the 14th Brigade met with no better fortune, as it was defeated by two battalions of the Old Guard (the 1st of the 2nd Grenadiers and the 1st of the 2nd Chasseurs), sent forward by the Emperor for the purpose. But a third assault, when supported by the 5th Brigade from the II. Corps, which had come up in the meanwhile, was successful, and Plancenoit fell into the hands of the Prussians, the French falling back towards the *chaussée*, where they joined the stream of fugitives from the front. For in the meantime Lobau had been driven back by the 15th and 13th Brigades, while the advance of Steinmetz, coupled with the forward movement of the Anglo-Allied left, had compelled the retreat of d'Erlon's corps in disorder.

The defeat on the French right flank was now as

---

[1] Shortly after the attack commenced Blucher learned from Thielmann that he was attacked by superior forces. "Let him do his best to hold the enemy," was the reply; "even the destruction of the corps would be more than compensated for by victory here."

complete as was that of the left wing. The double success of the Allies was decisive, and their continued advance turned the French defeat into a rout. The Prussians had received as a point of direction La Belle Alliance, and, driving the French before them, their whole force united round this farm, and to the south of it.

The Anglo-Allied troops bivouacked for the night on the field of battle, the Prussians, by a mutual understanding between the two commanders, carrying on the pursuit. The I. Prussian Corps was ordered to assemble at Maison du Roi, and the 6th, 7th, and 8th Brigades of the II. Corps, which had come up in support of the IV. Corps, received orders to go after Grouchy.

The IV. Corps, with the 5th Brigade, pursued the French as far as Genappe. Two regiments of Röder's cavalry, and portions of the 15th Regiment from the 16th Brigade, and the 1st Pomeranian Regiment from the 14th Brigade, pushed on beyond. Fatigued as they were with marching and fighting, these rapidly fell away, and at last Gneisenau is said to have put the only remaining drummer on horseback, to give the frightened French the idea that the infantry was still following them. The cavalry continued the pursuit to Frasnes, where they halted. The French army, as an army, had ceased to exist, and re-crossed the frontier as a mere armed band, dragging with it Girard's division in its disorder, which had been ordered up from Ligny to Quatre Bras, to secure the line of communications.

Napoleon himself barely escaped capture, and his

travelling carriage fell into the hands of the Prussians. He waited but a moment at Quatre Bras to dictate orders to Grouchy to retire, indicating Laon as a rallying-point for his scattered forces, and then continued his flight towards the frontier. Charleroi was reached about daybreak, and here, after a short halt, the Emperor entered a carriage and continued his journey towards the French capital.

The struggle on the field of Waterloo had indeed been an arduous one, but the results gained were not incommensurate. Two eagles, 150 guns, and 7000 prisoners remained in the hands of the conquerors, while the French killed and wounded amounted certainly to more than 30,000. The total loss of the Anglo-Allied army was over 15,000; of the Prussians 6700, of whom the greater portion belonged to Bülow's corps.[1]

No battle they ever gained added more to the glory of the French soldiery than their defeat at Waterloo. For nearly nine hours with unflinching valour they delivered attack after attack, until nearly half of their strength lay dead or dying; beaten but not disgraced, their courage still forms a bright example to their descendants.

---

[1] These losses have been taken, with regard to the French, from Martinien's 'Tableau par corps des Officiers tués et blessés pendant les guerres de l'Empire, 1805-1815,' and from Couderc de St Chamant's 'Dernières armées de Napoléon,' following in the main the calculations of Professor Oman as given in 'The English Historical Review,' October 1904. See also Houssaye, p. 453, footnote 4. The British casualties are taken from official returns, as also are those of the King's German Legion and other German auxiliaries. Those of the Prussians are to be found in Plotho, Appendix XIX., p. 97 *et seq.*

They were met by worthy foemen. For the English and their German fellow-subjects resisted without a thought of retreat the repeated assaults of their gallant foe, maintaining their ground throughout this terrible day. That they did so was largely due to the personal influence of the Great Duke, who "taught the furious battle where to rage," who was everywhere where he was wanted, encouraging, directing, and even leading up the troops himself when necessary.

The Prussian army gave the final blow which turned defeat into disaster. In this case also personal influence played an important part, for to Blucher himself was mainly due the success gained. Never was a more loyal and gallant ally than old Marshal "Vorwarts." Defeat never daunted him, and in Prussia's darkest days he had never despaired. For three years he had been the inspiring spirit of the army he commanded, an ideal leader for his country's national upheaval, which itself so largely contributed to the final overthrow of the Oppressor of Europe. The victory of Waterloo formed a fitting termination to a career of military capacity and dogged courage which never yielded to fear whatever the odds against it.

While the battle at Waterloo was proceeding, Grouchy's force continued to advance towards Wavre. As early as 10 A.M. Exelmans' scouts had reported Prussian troops in force on the heights beyond the Dyle. Not liking to cross the river with cavalry only, he sent back to inform Grouchy, holding in the meantime a line from La Plaquerie to Neuf Sart.

In the meantime Ledebur had remained at Mont

St Guibert without knowing that the French had pushed past him and threatened his retreat. But shortly after one he began to appreciate the situation in which he was placed, and fell back to the Huzelle wood and took up a position in its border to hold the approaches to the road to Wavre, which passes through it. About 2 P.M., when the brigades of Brause and Bose were still on the eastern side of the Dyle, Exelmans' cavalry, supported by Vandamme's corps, came into action against Ledebur's detachment, now strengthened by two battalions of Brause's brigade. The Prussians successfully resisted the French attack, and made good their retreat across the Dyle at Wavre. Leaving three battalions of infantry and a squadron of cavalry to hold Wavre, Theilmann took up a position to protect the passages over the Dyle from Wavre to Bierges.

For to the III. Corps had been intrusted the duty of covering the other three corps on their march to join the Anglo-Allies. Deceived by the slowness of the French advance, and the fact that the passages over the Dyle had not been occupied, and seeing, moreover, that the Prussian cavalry had a clear range of the ground between the forces as far as Maransart and almost up to the rear of the French,[1] Thielmann believed at first that only a weak force was before him. But when the French advanced in

[1] This boldness of the Prussian cavalry, and the inaction of the French, prevented that close connection between the Emperor and his lieutenant so essential to combined action, and, moreover, necessitated messengers passing by a wide *détour*, by Quatre Bras and Sombreffe, to keep up communication. Hence it was that Napoleon's messages took six and five hours to reach Grouchy.

GROUCHY CAPTURES WAVRE

strength he found himself compelled to give up all idea of marching on Waterloo, and disposed his available troops to dispute the bridges over the Dyle, having altogether about 14,000 men to resist Grouchy's 33,000. Thus attacked by superior forces, he had the greatest difficulty in holding the debouches over the river.

About 4 P.M. Grouchy received Napoleon's first communication sent off at 10 A.M., which enjoined him to push before him the corps at Wavre. This confirmed him in his view that his duty was to attack the force in front of him and not move directly to help the Emperor as his subordinates wished. At 6 P.M. Napoleon's despatch of one o'clock reached Grouchy ordering him to attack Bülow.[1] He therefore pressed the fight; and when he was informed by Vallin that the bridge at Limal was open, he sent across there the 12th and 13th Divisions of Gérard's corps, thus threatening Thielmann's right, while the suburb of Wavre on the eastern bank of the river was also captured. Darkness and the vigorous resistance of the Prussians prevented him making further progress that evening, and, not knowing the result of the battle fought at Waterloo, he determined to bivouac on the positions he had won from the Prussians during the day.

---

[1] Houssaye thinks this despatch arrived at 5 P.M., and gives his reasons on p. 465, footnote 2. It seems to me that if it had arrived at that hour the attack at Limal would have begun in sufficient time to have been more decisive; and, moreover, I doubt if it would have been possible for the messenger who bore it to cross, as Houssaye suggests, at Ottignies or Limalette, as the Prussian cavalry reached these points.

CHAPTER VIII.

COMMENTS ON THE BATTLE OF WATERLOO—GENERAL COMMENTS ON THE WAR UP TO THE 18th JUNE.

THE first point worthy of comment with regard to the battle is the delay in beginning it. Napoleon gave as his reason that he waited for the ground to harden to enable the artillery to move over it. This may have been the case, but the result was fatal to him, because it allowed the Prussians to come up in time to aid the Anglo-Allies and turn what otherwise might have been a drawn battle, or perhaps a defeat, into a crushing disaster.

The position held by Wellington was a suitable one for his forces. But the right being thrown forward was somewhat exposed when the troops were withdrawn from Braine-l'Alleud, and it seems curious that no effort was made by the concentration of the artillery on the left of Reille's corps to bring a fire to bear on this portion of the Anglo-Allied line.[1] Considering

---

[1] This was partially done (see *ante*, p. 244), but not to any great extent. With the superiority in guns which Napoleon possessed he could have used thirty or forty for this purpose. In this case Wellington must have attacked them or have thrown back his right wing. The latter alternative would not have suited his plan of battle, as it would have offered a salient to the French attack from Napoleon's centre. Had he diverted

the large number of guns Napoleon had present at the battle, he might easily have done this without diminishing the artillery strength too much on other portions of the field, and this manœuvre would have rendered it difficult to support Hougomont. Such a movement might well have been supported by a part of his numerous cavalry.

Hougomont was, in 1815 (Sketch No. I.), a very strong position indeed, the buildings and garden wall were substantially built, and the latter was quite safe from the artillery fire. It was the garden wall with the hedge in front of it, and hedge which formed the northern boundary, to which the strength of this position was due. The Guards inside the garden suffered but little from the French attacks. The moment the latter got past the south garden wall and passed up by the east wall, a cross fire thence, and from the northern hedge, met them, and they never penetrated farther. Covered by artillery fire, Reille was enabled to push his troops more home on the western side of the chateau. But the attack does not seem to have been carried out vigorously in this direction. It is possible that this was due to 'the troops getting engaged against the southern wall, and also to the strength of the English position on the plateau behind. The waste of life in the French frequent attacks on Hougomont—a waste quite incommensurate with the results obtained—shows very faulty leading on the part of the officers at this portion

troops to attack them he would have disturbed the general idea of his battle, which was to act defensively till the flank attack of the Prussians developed.

of the field. Two-thirds of Reille's corps was absorbed in them, and it was of little or no assistance to Napoleon in the general object of the battle.

La Haye Sainte should, in the manner it was attacked, never have fallen into the hands of the enemy; that it did do so was owing to the neglect to properly prepare it for defence and to send supplies of ammunition when called for by Baring. Wellington later in life said this was owing to there being no communication with the rear of the farm. Shaw Kennedy points out most distinctly this was not the case, and it appears Baring sent several times for ammunition, but owing to some misunderstanding none was sent him. La Haye Sainte might have been overwhelmed by shell fire, but it was not, and it is inexplicable that little or no artillery was ever brought to bear on it. The history of its defence shows that, attacked as it was by infantry only, the Frenchmen would not have captured it had not the brave defenders been at last shot down without the possibility of returning their enemies' fire.

Napoleon's plan to feint on the right and attack the left centre was judicious. By seizing the Brussels *chaussée* he would cut off Wellington from the Prussians, and thus the object of keeping the Allies separate would have been gained. Moreover, penetration of the centre of the Anglo-Allied army would have been disastrous to it. Its execution in detail, however, leaves a great deal to desire. For Reille, instead of a holding fight, used two-thirds of his corps against Hougomont without obtaining any success; while the formation of d'Erlon's corps was very

THE CAVALRY CHARGES 279

bad and clumsy, and to this was largely due the defeat it suffered. D'Erlon's defeat and that of the Imperial Guard form a triumphant justification of the line against the column. The general conduct of the battle shows plainly that Napoleon on this day was not tactically at his best, although he personally directed many of the movements.[1] All day long he acted as a rash gambler rather than as a great general.

After the attack on the Anglo-Allies left came the cavalry charges. The net result of the expenditure of the magnificent cavalry which he had on the field was nothing. No square was broken, and the only instances in which the French cavalry gained any success were when the German battalions were

[1] Borodino is, however, a similar instance, where illness in all probability obscured the clear judgment and rapid decision which he usually displayed. Houssaye points out that: At eleven o'clock the Emperor dictated his dispositions for the attack. At 11.15 he ordered the demonstration against Hougomont. At one o'clock he wrote to Grouchy. At 1.30 he ordered Lobau to take up a position to stop the Prussians, and ordered Ney to commence the attack on Mont St Jean. In the interval he ordered the bombardment of Hougomont by a battery of howitzers. At three o'clock he sent a brigade of cuirassiers against Ponsonby's cavalry, after they had defeated d'Erlon's men. At 3.30 he ordered Ney to carry La Haye Sainte. At 4.30 he ordered up the Guard close to La Belle Alliance. At five o'clock he ordered the Young Guard to help Lobau. At 5.30 he ordered Kellerman to support the charges of Milhaud. At six o'clock he renewed the order to attack La Haye Sainte. Shortly afterwards he detached two battalions of the Old Guard to drive the Prussians from Plancenoit. At seven o'clock he led his Guards to the hill below La Haye Sainte for the final assault, and on the right harangued the soldiers of Durutte who were falling back and sent them forward again. He then ordered officers to go along the line of battle and announce the approach of Grouchy. At dusk he formed the Reserve of the Guard into squares, and disputed the advancing English. See Houssaye, pp. 519, 520. I do not think Lobau took post on the French right flank till 3.30 or four. He would before that hour have been mixed up with the retreating troops of d'Erlon and the cavalry *mêlée*.

foolishly opposed to their onslaught in a formation which invited disaster.[1] The Allied infantry no doubt suffered, but they suffered from the artillery fire and not from the charges of the French horsemen. Indeed there is no point more certain about the battle than that our foot soldiers looked upon the cavalry charges as periods of relief from the cruel artillery fire to which they were exposed.

Once Napoleon had gained possession of La Haye Sainte he should have pushed on his remaining infantry against the Anglo-Allied centre from the point of vantage he had thus obtained. But he did not do so, and his final efforts were made against that portion of the line which, although it had suffered severely, was in capital condition of *moral*, and perfectly prepared to meet any French infantry sent against it.

The final cause of the French disaster was the defeat

---

[1] Houssaye states (p. 383) that many of the squares were disordered, partially broken, if not crushed in and dispersed. This is quite at variance with fact. No English square was broken; one or two of Kielmansegge's were severely handled by artillery and infantry fire, but were not forced by cavalry. No English colour was captured, and probably not more than one Hanoverian, viz., the King's colour of the 8th King's German Legion (see Cotton's 'Voice from Waterloo,' 6th edition, p. 90). Houssaye's argument on this head is peculiar. He says (p. 383), (1) that the squares must have been broken or the colour taken by the 9th Cuirassiers could not have been captured; (2) that the colour must have been English, because Delort gave a receipt for one. Now, as the King's German Legion colours were like the English, Delort's statement is valueless, and therefore the deduction from it that squares were broken, "des carrés . . . été au moins entamés," is equally without value. Delort, according to Houssaye, "dit expressement que plusieurs carrés furent entamés." Against this we have the English statement that none were injured. He adds that Jomini acknowledges that "trois carrés furent rompus." As Jomini was not at Waterloo and gives no authorities, his evidence is mere hearsay, and therefore worthless.

NAPOLEON'S CHANCES OF SUCCESS

of the Imperial Guard, followed immediately by the British advance, while a little later the Prussians were successful against the French right. Thus on both wings the French were thrust back, and a general retreat ensued. It is by no means certain that even if the French Guard had succeeded in penetrating the British centre a like result would not have been attained, because there is no reason to believe that the troops who fought so bravely during the battle would have fled without one more effort; and it must be remembered that part of Lambert's and Pack's brigades was here and ready to attack them in flank, while they would also have suffered from the intact cavalry force under Vivian and Vandeleur.[1]

The fact of the matter is that the Emperor never had much of a chance of winning the battle. By his own misdirection of Grouchy and the delay in beginning the fight, he had allowed the Prussians to help their allies. The whole plan of the campaign was based on the mutual co-operation of the two armies, whose forces were double the strength of the Emperor's, and the natural result was seen in the terrible defeat inflicted upon the French. No doubt had the Prussians not come up the troops used to defend the French right would have been used against the Anglo-Allies; but it must always be a matter of mere academical interest to discuss what might have

---

[1] The 4th British, the 3rd and 5th Hanoverian infantry brigades, with Vivian's and Vandeleur's cavalry, were practically uninjured; the 3rd British infantry brigade was also perfectly capable of strenuous fighting, while three battalions of the 10th and three of the 9th Brigade were also available.

happened had Wellington and Blucher acted independently instead of in co-operation. The object of the campaign was to destroy Napoleon's army; that destruction could only be attained by the Allies acting as they did. The Emperor's knowledge of war was too great for him not to have recognised this, and he ought to have made his arrangements accordingly. He did not do so, and he very properly suffered for his want of foresight.

It is of no more value to discuss what might have happened had the Allies not carried out their plan than it is to discuss what the result would have been had Napoleon commanded the Anglo-Allies and Wellington the French. One thing is certain, the French were defeated, and that defeat was due in the first instance to the British and German bravery, which bore without flinching the ardent attacks of the French, and to the German determination and courage, as shown by the exertions of the Prussians in their march to the field, and by their gallant attack when they reached it.

The Prussian part in the battle was an important one. They held at least 16,000 men firmly fixed, and to the direction of their attack was absolutely due the complete annihilation of the Emperor's forces as an organised army. It is impossible to say whether the English would have defeated Napoleon without the aid of the Prussians; they might or they might not, but the problem, though often discussed, is absolutely insoluble. The English and Germans of Wellington's army fought as well as any troops could fight, and it is perfectly impossible to predict whether

LATE ARRIVAL OF THE PRUSSIANS 283

they would have even been defeated by the additional French force which would have been available had not the Prussians attacked Napoleon.

The late arrival of the Prussians was entirely due to Gneisenau. Yet it was not without advantage, for when the French had been beaten off by Wellington the Prussian success turned defeat into disaster. An earlier success might have led to Napoleon's retreat when he still had the Guard intact. It would, however, have been better for Blucher to have directed his movement against Lobau's left, thus keeping the Prussian flank attack more in connection with the Anglo-Allied front. If this had been done Napoleon would have been defeated earlier and with less risk.[1]

A point on which no satisfactory explanation has ever been given by Wellington is the maintenance of 18,000 men at Hal and Tubize, some eleven and eight miles from the field, when he had an officer with him who belonged to these troops, and whom he might have sent at any moment of the battle to hurry them up. The action of even Colville's division on the French left would probably have been decisive at any moment of the fight; and it is as extraordinary a thing that Wellington should have allowed the forces to remain inactive where they were, as that they should have heard no sound of the battle. There is only one possible reason his doing so: he fought the battle entirely himself. Every point of the line had to be watched with more than usual vigilance, because of the large proportion of unreliable troops in his army. In the constant tension of his mind he probably forgot for a time the

[1] See Hofmann, pp. 117, 118.

existence of this body, until it was too late for them to reach the battlefield.[1]

Wellington has been censured for fighting in front of the Forest of Soignes. The unfavourable criticism has no sound foundation. The wood was easily traversable by troops of all arms, and its border would have made a good defensive position for a rear-guard. Wellington himself has stated that he did not mean to retreat in this direction, but that he had stationed the troops at Hal and Tubize as he intended to fall back in that direction. It is difficult to understand how he could have taken off the whole Anglo-Allied army in case of defeat right away to his right flank. Possibly he meant that he would have withdrawn the right towards Hal while the left might have fallen back towards the Prussians. The contemporary evidence seems to show that the line of retreat was back on Antwerp, which was a fortress and a port in communication with England, as all the baggage and trains were sent in that direction.

Napoleon as usual made free use of his artillery, and the great battery which he formed opposite the centre and left is a good instance of the employment of this arm in the attack. But no proper artillery fire was ever directed against La Haye Sainte, and the howitzer fire against Hougomont seems to have been of brief duration. Wellington's dispositions of his guns serves as an excellent example of their proper use on the defensive. Part placed so as to defend the approaches to the position and the re-

---

[1] He said to de Constant Rebecque when returning after the battle, "By God! I saved the battle four times myself." See de Bas, p. 758.

mainder kept back to be brought up, as it was here to the Anglo-Allied centre and right, the moment the enemy's object became evident.

Both the French and Prussian artilleries contained 12-pounder guns; the English had nothing heavier than 9-pounders, the three batteries of 18-pounders not having been brought into the field. Had these guns been on the height behind La Haye Sainte they would have been of the greatest service.

The English cavalry again displayed their strong and weak points. Their strong, in the way in which they defeated without difficulty the infantry and cavalry opposed to them. Their weak, in the too prolonged advance in disordered array which led to the enormous losses of the Union Brigade.

The pursuit was, as we have seen, taken up by the Prussian cavalry. It practically ceased at Genappe, because the small force of cavalry which rode on beyond could not have had a very serious effect on the flying French. But Waterloo will always be quoted as a case of successful pursuit, although it seems rather to be a case, as at Jena and Auerstadt in 1806, of an army which has resisted for long an overwhelming force losing suddenly all courage and flying from the field.

It is remarkable that Napoleon had taken no precautions for a possible retreat. Had Genappe been protected and Girard ordered up there to hold the village, it is possible that the army might have been rallied on the other side of the Dyle. It would, however, have been better for the Emperor to have retreated by the Binche road, when he became aware of the Prussian advance. He had ordered bridge-heads to be thrown up at Thuin and Abbaye d'Aulne, thus showing he had some idea of retiring in that direction; to retreat through the narrow defile of Genappe, in the face of a pursuing enemy, especially when no steps had been taken to occupy and defend it, was to court disaster. But, like a desperate gambler, he risked everything on the issue of the fight, and when that went against him all further hope of resistance seems to have died out. Thus he lost for the second and last time the Imperial throne to which the French army had called him.

From what has been said, it will be seen that the result of the battle was the total rout of the French army. Of the 125,000 men with which Napoleon crossed the frontier, not more than 50,000 were with the colours when the remains of the Army of the North were got together again under Soult and Grouchy. But it would be a mistake to think that the downfall of Napoleon was due simply to the result of the battle. From the moment the campaign began the chances in the Emperor's favour were few, and it was only possible for him to succeed by acting with the greatest skill and energy. These qualities he failed to display, though his general idea was sound and soldierly. The situation demanded rapid and concentrated employment of his force on interior lines against his separated opponents. When, on the night of the 15th, a large portion of his force were still on the right bank of the Sambre, the possibility of success was greatly diminished. That his army had not crossed the river was entirely his own fault. To begin

NAPOLEON'S MISTAKES 287

with, the late arrival of the 4th Corps and the 14th cavalry division at Philippeville delayed its progress on the opening day of the campaign. The mistake of directing it on Charleroi, where one narrow bridge only was available, was, it is true, by an afterthought which directed it to Chatelet, somewhat obviated. But, speaking broadly, it is perfectly evident that the number of passages over the Sambre used by the French army was insufficient to ensure a rapid passage over the river. Had the 3rd Corps been sent to Marchiennes and followed by part of the reserve cavalry, while the 1st and 2nd Corps crossed somewhat higher up the river, or if the 3rd Corps had been sent with the 4th to Chatelet, more rapid progress would have been made. The delay in Vandamme's march was, of course, entirely due to bad staff arrangements. The slowness of the concentration for dealing the first blow, which the Emperor had determined to give against the Prussians, took off a considerable percentage of the chances in the Emperor's favour.

They were again still further diminished by his delay in beginning the battle of Ligny. Had it been begun at ten instead of two o'clock, Blucher's army would most certainly have been defeated. A little more energy on the part of Ney would have ensured the defeat of Perponcher's Division. The wanderings of d'Erlon were largely the Emperor's own fault. He totally misjudged the strategical situation in thinking that neither Wellington nor Blucher could bring any considerable force against him, while he vacillated all through the day as to the task that should be imposed on Ney. Believing that the latter was likely to meet with but very little opposition, he ordered him to get into position for an advance to Brussels; then he was to manœuvre to help Napoleon, quite regardless as to what Wellington might be doing to stop him; finally, whether by his own, and by his aide-de-camp's mistake, d'Erlon was so directed that he was of no use either to Ney or to himself. On the night of the 16th, therefore, Napoleon's chances of success were again lessened. On the 17th, by his own fault, they vanished almost entirely.

Instead of keeping touch with the Prussians, which he could easily have done with his numerous cavalry, he allowed them to disappear altogether from his ken. They *ought* to retire on their communications, or what the Emperor thought were their communications, although, as a practical fact, they were not, therefore they *must* be going in that direction. Grouchy's task was therefore a simple one—to act as a screen to prevent their return whilst Napoleon chastised the bold Englishman. Even yet victory was within his grasp, but he failed to seize it, for it would have been quite possible on the 17th to have defeated Wellington severely. He failed, however, to send instructions to Ney early in the morning to move against the Duke, nor did he take any steps whatever to do so himself till the afternoon. As has been said (p. 30), the Emperor's plan was a good one, but it was badly carried out, and this must be the verdict of every impartial critic.

When the Prussians retreated on Wavre, although

COURSES OPEN TO NAPOLEON

it was possible to join Wellington, as they did the next day, by a cross-country march, still for the 17th Napoleon was free from all chance of interruption from them, and could therefore have used his whole force, or nearly so, against the Anglo-Allies; but had he followed the Prussians with the bulk of his forces he must have left Ney to occupy Wellington and prevent his attacking the rear of the French. Ney, with d'Erlon's corps, had altogether about 37,000 men on the morning of the 17th at Quatre Bras, Wellington had 45,000, and during the day would have had his whole army there, so that he must inevitably have defeated the French force. Having done this, he would have marched after Napoleon, who would then have had, with an army of 63,000 men, to fight at least 90,000 Prussians in front with the Anglo-Allied army of 70,000[1] close to his rear. Even if the Emperor had again defeated the Prussians, it is improbable, considering the disparity in numbers, that the defeat would have been a bad one, and he would then have had to deal with Wellington. Can it be doubted, after deducting the losses the French would necessarily have sustained in their fight with the Prussians, that the Anglo-Allied force would have defeated them? Then, with their line of communications cut, and placed between

---

[1] Original strength 93,000
    Deduct losses at Quatre Bras 4,000
    Ditto in supposed fight with Ney on 17th . 5,000
    Force pursuing Ney and guarding communications 14,000
        Total deductions . . . . ——— 23,000
        93,000 less 23,000, equal . . 70,000

two hostile forces, the drama of Waterloo would have been played at Wavre, and with a like result —annihilation for the French.

But supposing Napoleon, after Ligny, had sent the cavalry force he afterwards detached with Grouchy immediately in pursuit of the Prussians, to ascertain their line of retreat, and had supported this force with Lobau's corps, which had not been engaged, he would then have learnt that Blucher was retiring on Wavre, and must at once have known his object was to unite as soon as possible with Wellington. Now even before he knew the direction of the Prussian retreat, the fact that they were retreating must have shown him that for that day at least he was safe from attack from them, and he should at once have turned his attention to the Anglo-Allies. Wellington was at Quatre Bras, with a defile in rear of him and a very difficult country on his left. On his right there were no roads, except very circuitous ones, by which to retire on Brussels. Ney had, we have seen, 37,000 men, and he might have attacked soon after daybreak, for d'Erlon's corps, though it had marched fourteen miles the day before, had done no fighting. This force would have kept Wellington's troops, or at least the greater part of them, fast at Quatre Bras, and in the meantime Napoleon might have marched perpendicularly on their flank by a broad paved road. From Ligny to Quatre Bras is but seven miles, and by six or seven A.M. the Emperor might have had such a force on the field as would have crushed the Anglo-Allies had they remained to fight, or have caused them enormous loss in the retreat through the difficult ground behind them.

Assuming the latter supposition to be true, Wellington would have retreated on Waterloo, Napoleon would have followed him, having in the meantime learnt the line of the Prussian retreat. A reference to any large scale map of the country between Wavre and Waterloo (such as that published by the Belgian Government on a scale of $\frac{1}{20000}$) will show that the ground between Wavre and Waterloo is very difficult. In 1815 the roads were few, and the Prussians in advancing were obliged to cross the Lasne at Genval, St Lambert, Lasne, or, lower down, by Maransart. They chose the three former passages as leading more directly on their object. But the roads were so bad (the country is in parts marshy) that their advance was much retarded, and there is little doubt that a comparatively small force could have stopped the crossing of the Lasne, or at any rate have hindered the Prussians making any rapid progress towards Waterloo. Such a force would have held the ground between Lasne and Ohain. Wellington could not have detached any troops against it, as he would have been fully occupied with the main body of the French army, and it would have compelled the Prussians to deploy to attack it before advancing to aid their allies, and thus have considerably delayed them.[1]

---

[1] Napoleon in his 'Mémoires,' vol. v. p. 154, states that he sent on the 17th at 10 P.M. an order to Grouchy, whom he supposed to be at Wavre (Gourgaud says, 'La Campagne de 1815,' p. 69, "with the Prussian army in front of him"), to despatch 7000 men and 16 guns before daybreak to St Lambert to join the right of the French army, and that as soon as he was sure Blucher had evacuated Wavre he was to march with

Now the whole of Bülow's corps did not reach St Lambert till 3 P.M.[1] It would then have had to cross the Lasne and force its way up the steep slopes beyond, in the face of a strong opposition. It could look for no aid for two or three hours, and it is therefore pretty certain that it could not have proceeded onwards in the teeth of 20,000 men holding the position we have indicated. Had Bülow's force been checked, Wellington would have received no help till 7 P.M., when Zieten arrived.

But is it not more probable, had this General when advancing through Genval found his colleague engaged in a hot contest on his left, that he would have turned off to help him rather than have marched on to Waterloo, thus exposing his flank to the enemy at Lasne? Judging from Blucher's order to him

---

the majority of his troops to support the detachment he had sent to St Lambert. At 11 P.M. a despatch from Grouchy sent at 5 P.M. was received (see *op. cit.*, p. 155), and then Napoleon at 4 A.M. sent a duplicate of the 10 P.M. order. Gourgaud makes a similar statement, pp. 69, 70, but there is not the slightest evidence to believe either. The best proof of it not having been done is Napoleon's letter to Grouchy of 10 A.M. on the 18th (see *ante*, p. 195), which says nothing about it. Possibly the Emperor writing at St Helena, and recognising the value of holding St Lambert, as events subsequently showed, thought he might as well claim the credit of ordering it, while the non-performance of his instructions would be another point for blame against the man he chose to make the scapegoat of his own errors. Soult (see Houssaye, p. 278, footnote) suggested to the Emperor, in the evening of the 17th, the desirability of recalling part of Grouchy's force; but nothing was done because Napoleon assumed the Prussians had been so thoroughly defeated at Ligny that they would not be ready to fight again. This, as we have seen, was in spite of Milhaud's information as to a Prussian force retiring on Wavre and of the intelligence his brother had brought him that the Prussians had gone to Wavre with the intention of joining the English. See *ante*, p. 194.

[1] The first part arrived by noon, but the 14th Brigade only at 3 P.M.

SUGGESTED FRENCH ACTION 293

when he did arrive on the field of Waterloo, the latter would have ordered him to do so. Admitting this, it would have been eight o'clock at the earliest before Bülow and Zieten, having driven in the detached French force, could have arrived on the field of Waterloo, by which time the battle would have been decided.

It is then necessary to ascertain whether, following out the line of argument now adduced, Napoleon could have detached such a force, and with what numbers the Battle of Waterloo would then have been fought.

On the morning of the 17th—

Napoleon had . . .	66,000 men [1]
Wellington had . . .	45,000 [2]
Ney had	37,000 [2]

It may be assumed that the events of the day would have gone somewhat as follows:—

Early in the morning Ney would have attacked Wellington vigorously at all points, manœuvring so as to gain the Nivelles road on his (Ney's) left, and considering the composition of the Anglo-Allied force it cannot be held to have been much superior in fighting power, though slightly so in numbers, to the two French corps opposed to it. Ney then would have held Wellington fast at Quatre Bras. In the meanwhile Napoleon would have put his army in motion at daybreak, and by 6 A.M. he might have had at least 20,000 acting on Wellington's flank. This would have compelled the latter to re-

[1] Including Lobau.   [2] Deducting losses up to date.

treat, and a retreat through the narrow defile of Genappe could only have succeeded after great loss and the probable total demoralisation of the Dutch-Belgians. Wellington could not have carried off any large proportion to his left through the difficult country found there, more especially in the face of a hostile force such as Napoleon would have sent after him. On his right there were no good roads available, except the one to his flank on Nivelles.[1]

While this action was going on Napoleon would have learnt the direction of the Prussian retreat, and would necessarily have divined their object.[2] Lobau's corps would then have been ordered to cross the Dyle at Mousty and to march towards Napoleon. Taking into consideration the nature of the roads, it would not have advanced farther than Lasne from Mont St Guibert, and may be assumed to have reached the former place in the course of the morning of the 18th or evening of 17th.

The situation, then, on the night of the 17th would have been thus: Wellington at Waterloo with a loss of 10,000 men, reducing his force to 60,000; Napoleon at Waterloo with 77,000 men, deducting losses on the 17th, estimated at 5000, and allowing for 8000 men sent to the support of Lobau. This force would have been diverted from the Waterloo-

---

[1] He *might* possibly have retired on Nivelles to avoid the Genappe defile, though this movement to a flank in face of the enemy would have been very dangerous, would have kept him away from the Prussians, and have uncovered Brussels.

[2] See *ante*, p. 290, for proposed action of Lobau's corps.

Genappe road about Glabais, and would have reached Lasne that night, though late.[1]

On the 18th, then, Wellington would have had 60,000 men to fight the battle against Napoleon with 77,000. A strong corps of 20,000 men would have opposed the advance of the Prussians, having previously destroyed the bridges over Lasne. The banks of this river are marshy, and pontoon bridges could only have been made with difficulty, and, even if made, would have delayed the Prussians in their advance, and soon after crossing they would have had to force their way against a well-posted enemy.[2] Is it too much to assume, then, that Wellington would have had to fight alone? His force diminished by 10,000, Napoleon's increased by the same amount, what would have been the result of the battle?

It is assumed in this argument that Wellington still maintained his detachments at Hal and Tubize, because there is no reason in what we have said why the motives which caused him to do so should not still have had the same effect. That his doing so was a mistake—at any rate after the morning of the 18th—is generally admitted, and is only to be excused on the want of information brought in by his cavalry, for which this force is much to blame. It is rendered more curious by the fact that General Colville sent in an officer to Wellington for instructions (Lieutenant-Colonel Woodford), who remained with the Duke on the field of battle by his express

---

[1] Glabais to Lasne, four miles; Ligny to Glabais, ten miles.

[2] As a practical fact the Prussians were deficient in bridge equipment, which defect would still further have hampered them.

orders, and did not rejoin the 4th Division till the next day. It is stated that these troops heard nothing of the fight, although they were at Tubize and Hal—only eight and eleven miles off respectively.

We have seen (*ante*, p. 198) that Grouchy could not have saved Napoleon by marching off to his assistance at twelve o'clock on the 18th July, but it is impossible to absolve him from all blame for not having moved towards the Emperor earlier in the day. He had information which showed him that in all probability the Prussians were going to help Wellington, at any rate with part forces. Would it not have been better for him therefore to have left a retaining force to hold Blucher and have moved by the shorter or interior line with the remainder to Napoleon's aid early on the morning of the 18th? There is this to be said for him, that his instructions implied he was to hang on to the skirts of the retreating Prussians, but a general in his position must act to some extent independently. He had cavalry enough to keep up touch with Napoleon, and even if the Prussians had defeated the retaining force, it was far more desirable to run this risk by helping Napoleon to crush Wellington. Both Napoleon and Grouchy must be censured for not using their cavalry strength to keep in touch with one another. Had this been done each would have known what the situation was with the other.

Grouchy's failure was undoubtedly an error, and it can only be said he was not a man equal to the situation, although his subsequent conduct in handling his troops during the retreat shows that he was not without a certain amount of military capacity.

One point that has never been cleared up is, why Napoleon made so little use of his cavalry. He had over 22,000, all good and efficient men. To oppose him Wellington had only about 11,000 on whom he could rely, and the Prussians about 13,000, but these were very largely untrained troops. Yet with all this superiority Napoleon's cavalry did nothing. A cavalry raid against the advanced troops of Wellington in the direction of Binche, carried out by three or four thousand men, would have beaten back the Dutch-Belgian cavalry and have put Wellington into doubt as to whether the attack was not intended to be against him rather than against the Prussians. A similar force pushed between Wellington and Blucher on the 16th could have been used with effect against either army, and would have prevented all communication between the two Allied Commanders. The handling of the French cavalry was very different to what it was in 1805 or 1806; and even in 1814 when his horsemen were no longer the highly-trained men of former years, he obtained greater results from them. In 1815 he was unable to employ them as he had done in previous wars, because he kept them behind the army, committing the fault of the Prussians and the Austrians in 1866. This was his own fault, and was the result of selecting too few places of crossing over the Sambre.

It will be observed that Wellington's outposts on the frontier, where they were not in the hands of the Dutch-Belgians, were entrusted to the King's German Legion. This was in accordance with Wellington's practice in the Peninsula, because he found that the English King's German subjects did this duty so much better than the

British. The reason of this is not far to seek. The German cavalry officers were better trained and taught. It would be a mistake to look upon a British army of a hundred years ago as absolutely uneducated. On the contrary, there was in those days a considerable English military literature, not one of a mere text-book character, but solid works, worthy of study by all soldiers, but among them few, very few, dealt in any way with the question of cavalry. The teaching of Frederick the Great still influenced the German military world. In France, good light cavalry leaders had shown what the proper employment of cavalry with an army was and had written about it, but such men were not to be found in the British army.

The four-deep formation of the infantry at Waterloo during the latter portion of the battle is by some thought to have been an innovation introduced by Wellington. This is not the case. It was an ordinary drill manœuvre, and had been constantly used in Spain.[1]

This may be an appropriate place to deal with the question of staff duties. It is not too severe a criticism to say that they were not particularly good in either French, Prussian, or Anglo-Allied armies. Napoleon had allowed Gérard to start a day too late from Metz, hence he was behindhand in the strategical concentration. The Emperor suffered from the fact that Soult was not practised in the business of his post; he failed to send duplicate messages, hence Vandamme's late-

---

[1] See 'Mémoires du General Marbot,' vol. ii. p. 484—"English infantry doubling their files in an instant, formed four deep to receive a charge, and *never* have our squadrons been able to surprise them in two ranks, a disposition which they quickly assume as soon as it is necessary to fire."

ness in starting on the 15th. Ney was given no staff when he received the command of the left wing, and he had to improvise it as best he could. The wanderings of d'Erlon were largely due to the fact that the instructions to Ney were not definite. It is a queerly conducted staff in which the commanding general has to write to one of his subordinates that his personal staff officers will take the messages better than those of the Chief-of-the-Staff himself! Again, on the 17th Soult did not know whether he had written to Ney or not to tell him the situation! Ney may be possibly excused for not reporting frequently during the 16th to Napoleon, as he had no proper staff to do his work, but there is certainly no excuse for the Emperor's not letting the commander of the left wing know what the right wing was doing. Contrast this with Wellington and Blucher, who kept in touch with one another during the whole day.

In the Prussian army Bülow's non-arrival at Ligny was due to bad staff arrangements. The orders for the advance to Waterloo form even a worse example of want of knowledge of how military business should be carried on. The muddle made about Bülow, Gneisenau appears to have kept to himself, because, had he told Blucher what he had done, the latter would not have expected the IV. Corps to arrive in time for the battle; while, had Blucher known what the first instructions sent to Bülow were, he certainly would have sent him additional and more definite orders. The result of this want of care was the loss of the battle of Ligny. It is a high price to have paid for misplaced courtesy, nor is the excuse that it was inexpedient to wake the old Marshal worthy of consideration for a moment, and he emphatically would have been the first man to repudiate it.

In the case of the staff duties of the Anglo-Allied forces it is difficult to speak with great precision, because the memoranda issued by the Duke are not the elaborate orders issued to the troops, the originals of which were lost with Sir W. De Lancey's baggage.

But the so-called "disposition" is proof positive that some of the members of the Duke's staff were either lacking in military knowledge, or else very careless in carrying out their duties. Wellington's opinion of them has already been quoted.

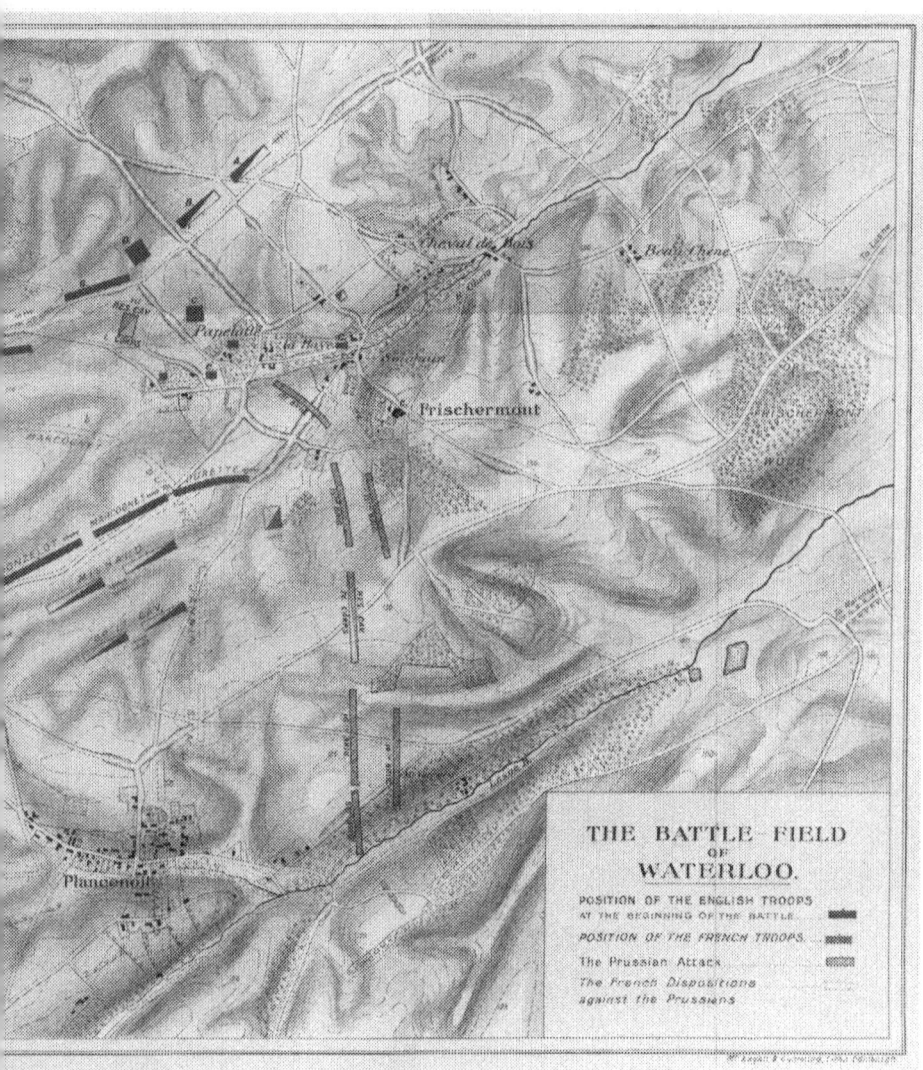

CHAPTER IX.

GROUCHY'S ADVANCE TO WAVRE — GROUCHY'S RETREAT FROM WAVRE TO NAMUR — THE INVASION OF FRANCE — THE CAPTURE OF PARIS AND END OF THE WAR.

AFTER the battle the position of the troops was briefly as follows:—

Wellington's troops bivouacked in the field, part holding the positions of the French in the morning. The French, under Napoleon, were fleeing in disorder to the frontier, and Grouchy's force was about Wavre. Of the Prussians, the IV. Corps and the 5th Brigade halted at Genappe. The Prussian cavalry and the two infantry regiments which had followed the retreating French ceased the pursuit after Frasnes. The I. Corps bivouacked at La Maison du Roi. The III. Corps was about Wavre, except the 9th Brigade which passed the night at Ohain.

Blucher had not forgotten the French force before Wavre, and issued orders for the 6th, 7th, and 8th Brigades of the II. Corps to march during the night across the Dyle and act against Grouchy with Thielmann, whom he was to inform of the Allies' victory. The three brigades started at midnight, passed the river at Bousval, and reached Mellery at 11 A.M. on the 19th, where they halted for the day.

19th June.—On the morning after Waterloo, both Grouchy and Thielmann were ignorant of the result of the battle fought so few miles away from them, and each prepared to renew the struggle of the previous day. Thielmann commenced at dawn to attack the French, but was beaten back by Grouchy, who had moved his troops across the Dyle during the night, and now drove his opponents steadily before him until he captured Wavre. The Prussians continued their retreat on the Louvain road to Rhode St Agathe, where they halted. During the fight each side learned the result of the previous day's battle, Thielmann at 8 A.M., Grouchy about 10.30, when he was preparing to press back the Prussians along the Brussels road. Grouchy at once determined to retreat on Namur, which had been abandoned by the Prussians when they advanced. He was already in a very dangerous position, for Pirch with his three brigades was now at Mellery. Leaving Vandamme at Wavre to cover the retreat, he sent on Exelmans with his cavalry to seize Namur, while he followed with the rest of the troops. He reached the neighbourhood of Sombreffe that evening; Exelmans took possession of Namur, and Vandamme arrived at Tembloux about midnight; the rear-guard, consisting of the 4th Cavalry Division and Teste's infantry, taking up positions at Gembloux.

Of the main body of the Prussians the I. Corps marched to Charleroi; the IV. to Fontaine L'Evêque;

the 5th Brigade to Anderlues. The Anglo-Allied advanced to Nivelles.

20th June.—The French continued their retreat on Namur about 7 A.M., and Grouchy was overtaken near the town by the advance-guard of Pirch, which had left Mellery early in the morning. Thielmann, also joining the pursuit, pushed on his cavalry, which came upon Vandamme after passing through Gembloux, where the bulk of the III. Corps rested. The Prussians were unable to make any serious attack, and the French reached Namur with but little loss. Pirch now directed an assault on the town, which was repulsed by Teste's division, left behind as a rear-guard, and Grouchy was enabled to withdraw his whole force by the left bank of the Meuse to Dinant, and thence to Philippeville, which he reached unmolested on the 21st. The II. Corps remained at Namur, the III. at Tembloux and Gembloux.

The I. Corps advanced to Beaumont, the IV. to Colleret, and the 5th Brigade to Maubeuge. The Anglo-Allied army marched to Binche and Mons. The remains of the Grand Army were continuing their disordered retreat, in which was included Girard's division left behind at Ligny, towards Laon, Philippeville, and Avesnes.

21st June.—Wellington's army reached Valenciennes-Bavay. Blucher with the I. and IV. Corps was near Avesnes; the II. Corps at Thuin, while the 5th Brigade blockaded Maubeuge; the III. Corps moved to Charleroi. Avesnes was captured by the I. Corps, and used as a depôt and hospital.

22nd June.—Wellington advanced to Le Cateau, having masked Valenciennes and Quesnoy by detachments. The I. and IV. Prussian Corps marched to Etrœung-Fesmy, the III. to Beaumont, and the II. was detached from the army to operate against the northern fortresses. Soult arrived at Laon and began concentrating the remains of the Waterloo army there. Grouchy was at Rocroi and Mezières on the 23rd, and received urgent messages from Paris to unite all the troops he could to oppose the invaders.

23rd June.—This was a day of rest for the Allies; the III. Prussian Corps only marched to Avesnes to be nearer the I. and IV., with which it was intended to advance on Paris. A British force was also detached to take Cambray, which fell on the 24th.

Blucher and Wellington met and arranged their plan of operations. This was to press forward on Paris after leaving detachments to mask or besiege the different fortresses. Hearing that the enemy was concentrating on Laon-Soissons, it was arranged to advance on Paris by the right bank of the Oise, which was to be crossed at Compiègne and lower down, thus turning the French flank. To deceive the enemy the Prussian cavalry was to be used to demonstrate towards the position they then held. The three Prussian corps, with the Anglo-Allied force, amounted altogether to about 120,000 men.

24th June.—The advance was again begun. The Prussians marched in two columns, the left formed by the I. and III., the right by the IV. Corps. The I. Corps was directed on Guise; the III. Corps by Nouvion on Compiègne; the IV. Corps by St Quentin on Pont St Maxence. The bulk of the Anglo-Allied forces was on this date about Le Cateau, except the reserve, which was at Englefontaine. Wellington's delay was caused by his waiting for his bridge-train to come up. Grouchy reached Réthel, Soult Soissons.

25th June.—The Anglo-Allied force, now fully concentrated, held the line Serain - Prémont. The Prussian I. Corps reached Cérisy, the III. Origny and its neighbourhood, the IV. Essigny. Grouchy, hearing Soult had gone to Soissons, sent Vandamme with the 3rd and 4th Corps to Reims, and with the rest moved to Soissons.

26th June.—Continuing the movement, the I. Corps reached Chauny, one brigade pushing on to Compiègne to stop Grouchy, who had now taken command from Soult. It arrived half an hour before the French reached the town. The III. Corps marched to Guiscard; the IV. to Ressons, whence Bülow sent out reconnoitring parties down the Oise as far as Creil. Wellington's troops were between Péronne and Vermand, having captured the former place by assault.[1]

27th June.—Grouchy, who had now taken over command of Soult's troops, fearing for his left, now ordered d'Erlon and Kellermann with the remains of their corps to Compiègne. They reached this place early on the 27th, only to find it occupied by the Prussians. After a brief engagement, seeing the

---

[1] He had ordered a brigade of Dutch-Belgians to start at daybreak to aid the Guards. They only commenced their march at 9 P.M. — *i.e.*, after Péronne had been captured! See 'Wellington Despatches,' vol. xii. p. 514.

large force opposed to them, the French retired towards Senlis, where they would be in a position to check the Prussians crossing the river; but finding this point also held by the enemy, they drew off to Mont L'Evêque, where they halted. This day the Prussians captured the passages over the Oise, and Grouchy, finding himself in danger of being cut off from Paris, ordered Vandamme to retire by La Ferté Milon on Paris, while he himself led the rest of the army by Villers Cotteret, his intention being to gain Dammartin.

The Prussians this night were placed as follows: The III. Corps at Compiègne; the I. Corps had its main body at Gillcourt, with the 2nd Brigade and the Reserve cavalry towards Villers Cotteret; the IV. Corps at St Maxence, with a brigade at Senlis. Wellington's army was about the line Roye-Ham.

28th June.—The Prussians advanced the next day, but Pirch II. was driven back by Grouchy's troops, who then continued their retreat. The Prussians acting perpendicularly to the line the latter went by, drove them repeatedly from it, and compelled them to make considerable *détours*, but eventually the greater part of the French army was assembled about Gonesse, whence it moved into the lines north of Paris the next day. Vandamme, who joined in the evening of the 29th, was ordered to the south of Paris. The Prussians reached the following points: The I. Corps, Nanteuil; the III., Crépy; the IV., Marly-la-Ville; the Anglo-Allied on the line Crèvecœur-Ressons.

29th June.—The I. Prussian Corps moved on to

Blancménil; the III. to Dammartin; the IV. to Le
Bourget; Wellington advanced to Clermont-St Martin
Longeau-St Maxence. The French remained about
Paris.

The Allies were now before the French capital,
and the war approached its close. Within the city
the uncertainty of the situation was the cause of
considerable alarm, but Napoleon, who had abdicated
on the 23rd, had no following of importance left,
at any rate among the civil population, and the
chances of resistance were therefore small. Moreover, Fouché, as head of the Provisional Government,
with Davoust as war minister, was in a position to
prevent the army taking any very serious steps to
upset the consummation he was working for—the
return of the Bourbons.

But the troops in Paris were still capable of
checking the invaders' advance. For the lines
thrown up to the north of Paris, on the heights
from Montmartre to Belleville, could not be forced
without loss, as a reconnaissance in force against
Aubervilliers showed Blucher on the night of the
29th. It was therefore determined by the Allied
commanders to transfer the Prussians to the south
of the town, which was unfortified.

In the meantime attempts had been made at
negotiation, but Wellington refused to treat while
Napoleon remained in Paris. Persuaded by his
personal adherents, and fearing capture, he left on
the 29th, and commenced that journey which ended
only at St Helena.

30th June.—The Prussian I. and III. Corps marched

to the neighbourhood of St Germain. The IV. Corps remained in front of Le Bourget to rivet the French attention.

The Anglo-Allied 1st Corps occupied the road Senlis-la Chapelle; the 2nd Corps Chantilly. The cavalry pushed on to Verlau, and the Reserve advanced to Fleurines.

1st July.—The Prussian I. Corps crossed the river and halted about Carrières; the III. Corps marched to Rocquancourt; the IV. set out for St Germain.

The 1st and 2nd Corps of Wellington's army closed up to the positions previously held by the Prussians on the north of Paris, the Reserve being in their rear to support them.

The 3rd and 4th French Corps and the Imperial Guard were sent to the south of Paris to hold the ground against the Prussians, and on this day Sohr's brigade of cavalry marching towards Versailles was cut to pieces by Exelmans' cavalry.

2nd July.—The Anglo-Allied army remained in the same positions, in front of the northern fortification of Paris by St Denis, and bridged the Seine. The Prussians continued their march round the south of Paris and reached a line from Clamart to Rocquancourt. The French attacked the Prussians but were driven back.

3rd July.—A council of war was now held in Paris, and it was resolved that further resistance was useless; negotiations were therefore entered into with the Allies, who agreed to suspend hostilities on Paris being surrendered and the French army marched beyond the Loire.

To enter into the details of the peace which restored the Bourbons to the throne and thrust back France within her pre-revolutionary limits, is beyond the scope of this work; and in conclusion, therefore, it is only necessary to say a few words of comment on the operations since the 18th June, on which date the issue of the war was practically determined.

It seems curious that both Grouchy and Thielmann knew nothing of the result of the Battle of Waterloo. Pirch I. was instructed to tell his brother corps-commander, but did not do so till the next day. It must be admitted that the movements of the II. Corps were lacking in judgment. Not only should Pirch at once have sent to tell Thielmann, but he should also have concerted with him his movements for the next day (the 19th) against Grouchy. He did not do so, but let the French pass by him without in the least attempting to hinder them, nor was it till the 20th that he made any effort to follow them up. Had he pushed on from Mellery, where he arrived at 11 A.M., to Gembloux, only six miles off, he would have stood between Grouchy and Namur. But his force, three brigades only, was much smaller than Grouchy's, and as he had failed to concert measures with Thielmann, and his troops were tired, he was perhaps wiser to avoid so bold a step. Yet certainly he might have annoyed the French flank. After Grouchy had passed through Namur there was no object in following him. The right course for the Allies was to advance at once on Paris, and they did so.

The reason for the comparative slowness of Wellington's advance compared with Blucher's is not evident.[1] Had the Napoleon of 1814 commanded the army at Soissons on the 26th, he might once more have delivered against the extended and unsupported Prussians the lightning-like strokes which then paralysed his enemies, though success, as in the former campaign, could only have retarded, not averted, the final disaster. It was a mistake for the French not to have destroyed the bridges over the Oise (Compiègne, St Maxence, Creil, &c.), and, lastly, they might have attacked with advantage the Prussians while executing their flank march round from the north to the south of Paris.

Grouchy undoubtedly deserves considerable credit for the retreat under circumstances difficult at first, though afterwards easy.

Further criticism is unnecessary; the operations in France after Waterloo are of no real interest; once that great fight had been gained and Napoleon driven headlong from the field, the days of the Empire were numbered. The subsequent movements were but the dying convulsions of the body which had received its death-blow on the battlefield of Flanders.

[1] Müffling, p. 251, says that Wellington told him this was due to the necessity of attending to the comfort of the men. It is far more probable that the want of discipline in the Dutch-Belgian force was the real reason. But the Duke was always desirous of saving the feelings of the Netherlands King and Princes, and, unless compelled to do so, as in his general order of the 27th June, did his best to conceal their shortcomings.

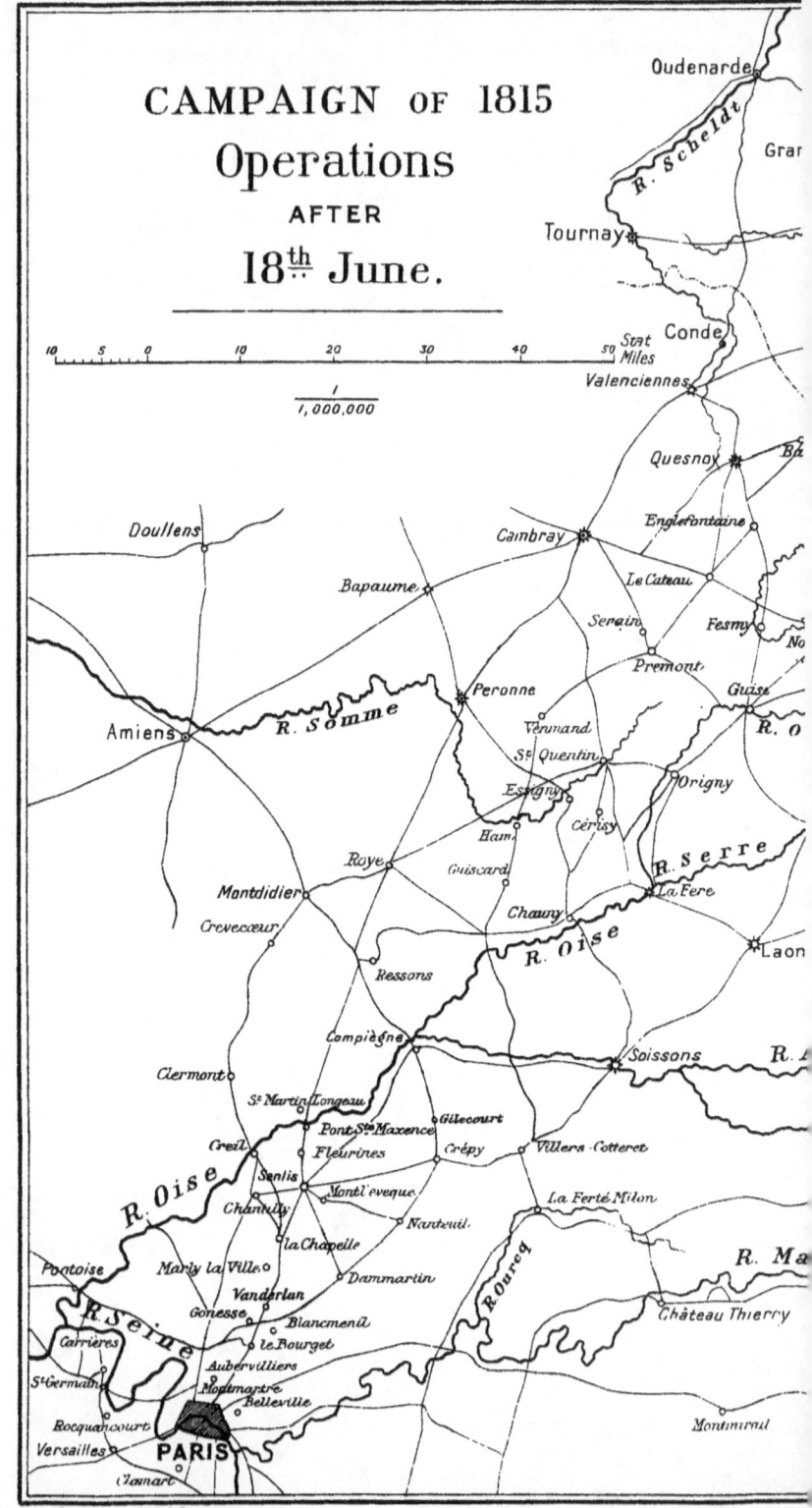

Lieut. Col. W.H. James, 1815 Campaign.

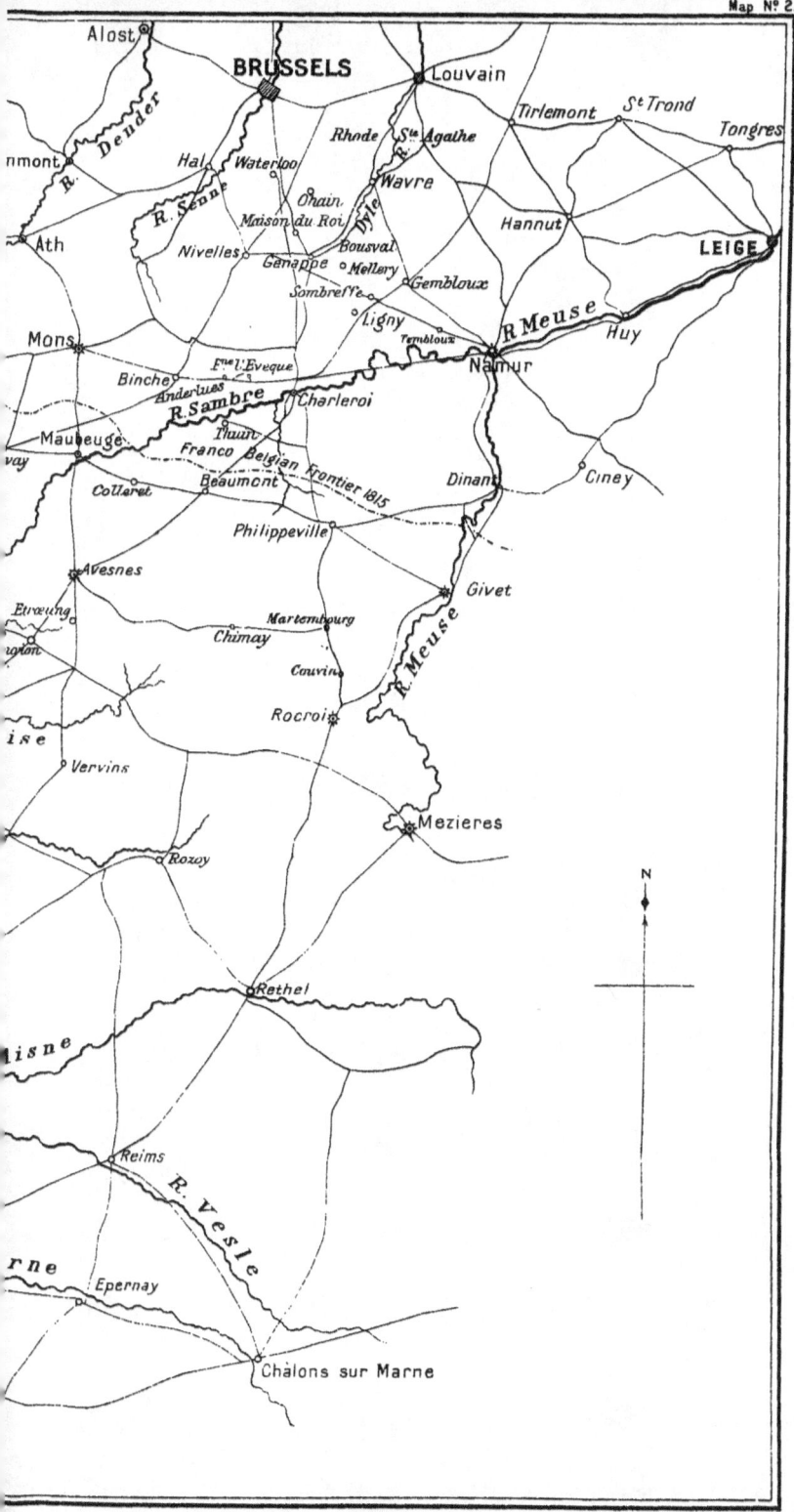

Map No 2.

APPENDIX.

WELLINGTON DESPATCH TO THE EARL BATHURST.

WATERLOO, 19*th June* 1815.

MY LORD,—Bonaparte, having collected the 1st, 2nd, 3rd, 4th, and 6th corps of the French army, and the Imperial Guards, and nearly all the cavalry, on the Sambre, and between that river and the Meuse, between the 10th and 14th of the month, advanced on the 15th and attacked the Prussian posts at Thuin and Lobbes, on the Sambre, at daylight in the morning.

I did not hear of these events till in the evening of the 15th; and I immediately ordered the troops to prepare to march, and afterwards to march to their left, as soon as I had intelligence from other quarters to prove that the enemy's movements upon Charleroi was the real attack.

The enemy drove the Prussian posts from the Sambre on that day; and General Zieten, who commanded the corps which had been at Charleroi, retired upon Fleurus; and Marshal Prince Blücher concentrated the Prussian army upon Sombref, holding the villages in front of his position of St Amand and Ligny.

The enemy continued his march along the road from Charleroi towards Bruxelles; and, on the same evening, the 15th attacked a brigade of the army of the Netherlands, under the Prince de Weimar, posted at Frasne, and forced it back to the farmhouse, on the same road, called Les Quatre Bras.

The Prince of Orange immediately reinforced this brigade with another of the same division, under General Perponcher, and, in the morning early, regained part of the ground which had been lost, so as to have command of the communication leading from Nivelles and Bruxelles with Marshal Blücher's position.

In the meantime, I had directed the whole army to march upon Les Quatre Bras; and the 5th division, under Lieut.-General Sir Thomas Picton, arrived at about half-past two in the day, followed by the corps of troops under the Duke of Brunswick, and afterwards by the contingent of Nassau.

At this time the enemy commenced an attack upon Prince Blücher with his whole force, excepting the 1st and 2nd corps and a corps of cavalry under General Kellermann, with which he attacked our post at Les Quatre Bras.

The Prussian army maintained their position with their usual gallantry and perseverance against a great disparity of numbers, as the 4th corps of their army, under General Bülow, had not joined; and I was not able to assist them as I wished, as I was attacked myself, and the troops, the cavalry in particular, which had a long distance to march, had not arrived.

We maintained our position also, and completely defeated and repulsed all the enemy's attempts to get possession of it. The enemy repeatedly attacked us with a large body of infantry and cavalry, supported by a numerous and powerful artillery. He made several charges with the cavalry upon our infantry, but all were repulsed in the steadiest manner.

In this affair, his Royal Highness the Prince of Orange, the Duke of Brunswick, and Lieut.-General Sir Thomas Picton, and Major-General Sir James Kempt, and Sir Dennis Pack, who were engaged from the commencement of the enemy's attack, highly distinguished themselves, as well as Lieut.-General Charles Baron Alten, Major-General Sir C. Halkett, Lieut.-General Cooke, and Major-Generals Maitland and Byng, as they successively arrived. The troops of the 5th division and those of the Brunswick corps were long and severely engaged, and conducted themselves with the utmost gallantry. I must particularly mention the 28th, 42nd, 79th, and 92nd regiments, and the battalion of Hanoverians.

Our loss was great, as your lordship will perceive by the enclosed return; and I have particularly to regret His Serene Highness the Duke of Brunswick, who fell fighting gallantly at the head of his troops.

Although Marshal Blücher had maintained his position at Sombref, he still found himself much weakened by the severity of the contest in which he had been engaged, and, as the 4th corps had not arrived, he determined to fall back and to concentrate his army upon Wavre; and he marched in the night, after the action was over.

This movement of the Marshal rendered necessary a corresponding one upon my part; and I retired from the farm of Quatre Bras upon Genappe and thence upon Waterloo, the next morning, the 17th, at ten o'clock.

The enemy made no effort to pursue Marshal Blücher. On the contrary, a patrole which I sent to Sombref in the morning found all quiet; and the enemy's vedettes fell back as the patrole advanced. Neither did he attempt to molest our march to the rear, although made in the middle of the day, excepting by following, with a large body of cavalry brought from his right, the cavalry under the Earl of Uxbridge.

This gave Lord Uxbridge an opportunity of charging them with the 1st Life Guards, upon their *débouché* from the village of Genappe, upon which occasion his Lordship has declared himself to be well satisfied with that regiment.

The position which I took up in front of Waterloo crossed the high roads from Charleroi and Nivelles, and had its right thrown back to a ravine near Merke Braine, which was occupied, and its left extended to a height above the hamlet Ter la Haye, which was likewise occupied. In front of the right centre, and near the Nivelles road, we occupied the house and gardens of Hougoumont, which covered the return of that flank; and in front of the left centre we occupied the farm of La Haye Sainte. By our left we communicated with Marshal Prince Blücher at Wavre, through Ohain; and the Marshal had promised me that, in case we should be attacked, he would support me with one or more corps as might be necessary.

The enemy collected his army, with the exception of the 3rd corps, which had been sent to observe Marshal Blücher, on a range of heights in our front, in the course of the night of the 17th and yesterday morning, and at about ten o'clock he commenced a furious attack upon our post at Hougoumont. I had occupied that post with a detachment from General Byng's brigade of Guards, which was in position in its rear; and it was for some time under the command of Lieut.-Colonel Macdonnell, and afterwards of Colonel Home; and I am happy to add that it was maintained throughout the day with the utmost gallantry by these brave troops, notwithstanding the repeated efforts of large bodies of the enemy to obtain possession of it.

This attack upon the right of our centre was accompanied by a very heavy cannonade upon our whole line, which was destined to support the repeated attacks of cavalry and infantry, occasionally mixed, but sometimes separate, which were made upon it. In one of these the enemy carried the farmhouse of La Haye Sainte, as the detachment of the light battalion of the German Legion, which occupied it, had expended all its ammunition; and the enemy occupied the only communication there was with them.

The enemy repeatedly charged our infantry with his cavalry, but these attacks were uniformly unsuccessful; and they afforded opportunities to our cavalry to charge, in one of

APPENDIX 315

which Lord E. Somerset's brigade, consisting of the Life Guards, the Royal Horse Guards, and 1st Dragoon Guards, highly distinguished themselves, as did that of Major-General Sir William Ponsonby, having taken many prisoners and an eagle.

These attacks were repeated till about seven in the evening, when the enemy made a desperate effort with cavalry and infantry, supported by the fire of artillery, to force our left centre, near the farm of La Haye Sainte, which, after a severe contest, was defeated; and having observed that the troops retired from this attack in great confusion, and that the march of General Bülow's corps by Frischermont, upon Planchenois and La Belle Alliance, had begun to take effect, and as I could perceive the fire of his cannon, and as Marshal Prince Blücher had joined in person with a corps of his army to the left of our line by Ohain, I determined to attack the enemy, and immediately advanced the whole line of infantry, supported by the cavalry and artillery. The attack succeeded in every point; the enemy was forced from his positions on the heights and fled in the utmost confusion, leaving behind him, as far as I could judge, 150 pieces of cannon, with their ammunition, which fell into our hands.

I continued the pursuit till long after dark, and then discontinued it only on account of the fatigue of our troops, who had been engaged during twelve hours, and because I found myself on the same road with Marshal Blücher, who assured me of his intention to follow the enemy throughout the night. He has sent me word this morning that he has taken 60 pieces of cannon belonging to the Imperial Guard, and several carriages, baggages, &c., belonging to Bonaparte, in Genappe.

I propose to move this morning upon Nivelles and not to discontinue my operations.

Your lordship will observe that such a desperate action could not be fought and such advantages could not be gained without great loss; and I am sorry to add that ours had been immense. In Lieut.-General Sir Thomas Picton his Majesty has sustained the loss of an officer who has frequently distinguished himself in his service, and he fell gloriously leading his division to a charge with bayonets, by which one of the most serious attacks made by the enemy on our position was repulsed. The Earl of Uxbridge, after having successfully got through this arduous day, received a wound by almost the last shot fired, which will, I am afraid, deprive his Majesty for some time of his services.

His Royal Highness the Prince of Orange distinguished himself by his gallantry and conduct till he received a wound from a musket ball through his shoulder, which obliged him to quit the field.

It gives me the greatest satisfaction to assure your lordship that the army never, upon any occasion, conducted itself better. The division of Guards, under Lieut.-General Cooke, who is severely wounded, Major-General Maitland, and Major-General Byng, set an example which was followed by all, and there is no officer nor description of troops that did not behave well.

I must, however, particularly mention, for his Royal Highness's approbation, Lieut.-General Sir H. Clinton, Major-General Adam, Lieut.-General Charles Baron Alten (severely wounded), Major-General Sir Colin Halkett (severely wounded), Colonel Ompteda, Colonel Mitchell (commanding a brigade of the 4th Division), Majors-General Sir James Kempt and Sir D. Pack, Major-General Lambert, Major-General Lord E. Somerset, Major-General Sir W. Ponsonby, Major-General Sir C. Grant and Major-General Sir H. Vivian, Major-General Sir O. Vandeleur and Major-General Count Dornberg.

I am also particularly indebted to General Lord Hill for his assistance and conduct upon this as upon all former occasions.

The artillery and engineer departments were conducted much to my satisfaction by Colonel Sir George Wood and

APPENDIX

Colonel Smyth, and I had every reason to be satisfied with the conduct of the Adjutant-General, Major-General Barnes, who was wounded, and of the Quartermaster-General, Colonel De Lancey, who was killed by a cannon shot in the middle of the action. This officer is a serious loss to his Majesty's service and to me at this moment.

I was likewise much indebted to the assistance of Lieut.-Colonel Lord FitzRoy Somerset, who was severely wounded, and of the officers composing my person staff, who have suffered severely in this action. Lieut.-Colonel the Hon. Sir Alexander Gordon, who has died of his wounds, was a most promising officer, and is a serious loss to his Majesty's service.

General Kruse, of the Nassau service, likewise conducted himself much to my satisfaction, as did General Tripp, commanding the heavy brigade of cavalry, and General Vanhope, commanding a brigade of infantry in the service of the King of the Netherlands.

General Pozzo di Borgo, General Baron Vincent, General Müffling, and General Alava were in the field during the action, and rendered me every assistance in their power. Baron Vincent is wounded, but I hope not severely, and General Pozzo de Borgo received a contusion.

I should not do justice to my own feelings, or to Marshal Blücher and the Prussian army, if I did not attribute the successful result of this arduous day to the cordial and timely assistance I received from them. The operation of General Bülow upon the enemy's flank was a most decisive one; and even if I had not found myself in a situation to make the attack which produced the final result, it would have forced the enemy to retire if his attacks should have failed, and would have prevented him from taking advantage of them if they should unfortunately have succeeded.

Since writing the above I have received a report that Major-General Sir William Ponsonby is killed, and in announcing this intelligence to your lordship, I have to add the expression of my grief for the fate of an officer who had already rendered very brilliant and important services, and was an ornament to his profession.

I send with this despatch two eagles,[1] taken by the troops in this action, which Major Percy will have the honour of laying at the feet of his Royal Highness. I beg leave to recommend him to your lordship's protection.

I have the honour to be, &c.,

WELLINGTON.

Earl BATHURST.

---

[1] In both editions of the 'Despatches' the number of eagles is given as three. In the original despatch it is two, and this is the number given in the newspapers of the period.

APPENDIX

STRENGTH OF ANGLO-ALLIED, PRUSSIAN, AND FRENCH FORCES.

Composition of the Anglo-Allied Army under the Command of Field-Marshal the Duke of Wellington.

1ST CORPS—H.R.H. THE PRINCE OF ORANGE.[1]

1st Division, Major-Gen. Cook
- 1st British Brigade, Major-General Maitland
  - 2nd Batt., 1st Guards.
  - 3rd ,, ,,
- 2nd British Brigade, Major-Gen. Sir John Byng
  - 2nd Batt., Coldstream Guards.
  - 2nd ,, 3rd Guards.
- Artillery, Lieut.-Colonel Adye
  - Sandham's British Field Battery.
  - Kuhlmann's K.G. Legion Field Battery.

Total, 4061 infantry, 12 guns.

3rd Division, Lieut.-Gen. Sir Charles Alten
- 5th British Brigade, Major-General Sir Colin Halkett
  - 2nd Batt., 30th Regt.
  - 33rd Regt.
  - 2nd Batt., 69th Regt.
  - 2nd ,, 73rd ,,
- 2nd Brigade K.G. Legion, Colonel von Ompteda
  - 1st Light Batt.
  - 2nd ,, ,,
  - 5th Line ,,
  - 8th ,, ,,
- 1st Hanoverian Brigade, Major-General Count Kielmansegge
  - Field Batt., Bremen.
  - ,, ,, Verden.
  - ,, ,, York.
  - ,, ,, Lüneberg.
  - ,, ,, Grubenhagen.
  - ,, Jäger Corps.
- Artillery, Lieut.-Col. Williamson
  - Lloyd's British Field Battery.
  - Cleeve's K.G. Legion Field Battery.

Total, 6970 infantry, 12 guns.

2nd Dutch-Belgian Division, Lieut.-Gen. Baron de Perponcher-Sedlnitzky.
- 1st Brigade, Major-General Count de Bijlandt
  - 7th Line Batt.[2]
  - 27th Chasseur Batt.
  - 5th Militia Batt.
  - 7th ,, ,,
  - 8th ,, ,,
- 2nd Brigade, H.R.H. The Prince Bernhard of Saxe-Weimar
  - 2nd Regt. of Nassau, 3 Batts.
  - Regt. of Orange-Nassau, 2 ,,
  - 1 Co. Jägers.
- Artillery, Major von Opstall
  - Stievenart's Belgian Field Battery.[3]
  - Bijleveld's Dutch Horse Battery.[3]

Total, 7700 infantry, 16 guns.

[1] The Prince of Orange had a staff of his own. Major-General Baron de Constant Rebecque was Quartermaster-General, *i.e.* Chief of the Staff; Major-General Jonkheer van der Wijck, Adjutant-General.

[2] Belgian. [3] Six guns, two howitzers.

APPENDIX

3rd Dutch-Belgian Division, Lieut.-Gen. Baron Chassé
- 1st Brigade, Major-General Detmers
  - 2nd Line Batt.
  - 35th Chasseur Batt.
  - 4th Militia Batt.
  - 6th ,, ,,
  - 17th ,, ,,
  - 19th ,, ,,
- 2nd Brigade, Major-General d'Aubremé
  - 3rd Line Batt.[1]
  - 12th ,, ,,
  - 13th ,, ,,
  - 36th Chasseur Batt.[1]
  - 3rd Militia Batt.
  - 10th ,, ,,
- Artillery, Major van der Smissen
  - Krahmer de Bichin's Belgian Horse Battery.[2]
  - Lux's Belgian Field Battery.[2]

Total, 6669 infantry, 16 guns.
Total 1st Corps, 25,400 infantry and 56 guns.

2ND CORPS—LIEUT.-GENERAL LORD HILL.

2nd Division, Lieut.-Gen. Sir H. Clinton
- 3rd British Brigade, Major-General Adam
  - 1st Batt., 52nd Regt.
  - 1st ,, 71st ,,
  - 2nd ,, 95th ,,
  - 3rd ,, 95th ,,
- 1st Brigade K.G. Legion, Colonel Du Plat
  - 1st Line Batt.
  - 2nd ,, ,,
  - 3rd ,, ,,
  - 4th ,, ,,
- 3rd Hanoverian Brigade, Colonel Hew Halkett
  - Landwehr Batt., Bremervörde.
  - ,, ,, Osnabrück.
  - ,, ,, Quackenbrück.
  - ,, ,, Salzgitter.
- Artillery, Lieut.-Colonel Gold
  - Bolton's British Field Battery.
  - Sympher's K.G. Legion Field Battery.

Total, 6833 infantry, 12 guns.

4th Division, Lieut.-Gen. Sir C. Colville
- 4th British Brigade, Colonel Mitchell
  - 3rd Batt., 14th Regt.
  - 1st ,, 23rd ,,
  - 51st Regt.
- 6th British Brigade, Major-General Johnstone
  - 2nd Batt., 35th Regt.
  - 1st ,, 54th ,,
  - 2nd ,, 59th ,,
  - 1st ,, 91st ,,
- 6th Hanoverian, Major-Gen. Sir James Lyon
  - Field Batt. Lauenburg.
  - ,, ,, Calenberg.
  - Landwehr Batt., Nienburg.
  - ,, ,, Hoya.
  - ,, ,, Bentheim.
- Artillery, Lieut.-Colonel Hawker
  - Brome's British Field Battery.
  - Rettberg's Hanoverian Field Battery.

Total, 7217 infantry, 12 guns.

[1] Belgian   [2] Six guns, two howitzers.

APPENDIX

CORPS OF PRINCE FREDERICK OF THE NETHERLANDS.

1st Dutch-Belgian Division, Lieut.-Gen. Stedman
- 1st Brigade, Major-General d'Hauw
  - 4th Line Batt.[1]
  - 6th ,,   ,,
  - 16th Chasseur Batt.
  - 9th Militia ,,
  - 14th ,,   ,,
  - 15th ,,   ,,
- 2nd Brigade, Major-General de Eerens
  - 1st Line Batt.[1]
  - 18th Chasseur Batt.
  - 1st Militia ,,
  - 2nd ,,   ,,
  - 18th ,,   ,,
- Artillery, ... Wijnand's Dutch Field Battery.[2]

Total, 6437 infantry, 8 guns.

Dutch-Belgian Indian Brig., Lieut.-General Anthing
- 5th East Ind. Regt., 2 Batts.
- Flankers.[1]
- 10th West Ind. Chasseur, 1 Batt.
- 11th ,,   ,,   ,,

Artillery, ... Riesz's Dutch Field Battery.[2]

Total, 3499 infantry, 8 guns.
Total 2nd Corps, 23,986 infantry, and 40 guns.

RESERVE.

5th Division, Lieut.-Gen. Sir Thomas Picton
- 8th British Brigade, Major-General Sir James Kempt
  - 1st Batt., 28th Regt.
  - 1st ,, 32nd ,,
  - 1st ,, 79th ,,
  - 1st ,, 95th ,,
- 9th British Brigade, Major-Gen. Sir Denis Pack
  - 3rd Batt., 1st Regt.
  - 1st ,, 42nd ,,
  - 2nd ,, 44th ,,
  - 1st ,, 92nd ,,
- 5th Hanoverian Brigade, Colonel von Vincke
  - Landwehr Batt., Hameln.
  - ,,   ,,   Gifhorn.
  - ,,   ,,   Hildesheim.
  - ,,   ,,   Peine.
- Artillery, Major Heisse
  - Roger's British Field Battery.
  - Braun's Hanoverian Field Battery.

Total, 7158 infantry, 12 guns.

6th Division, Lieut.-Gen. Hon. Sir L. Cole
- 10th British Brigade, Major-General Sir John Lambert
  - 1st Batt., 4th Regt.
  - 1st ,, 27th ,,
  - 1st ,, 40th ,,
  - 2nd ,, 81st ,,
- 4th Hanoverian Brigade, Colonel Best
  - Landwehr Batt., Verden.
  - ,,   ,,   Lüneburg.
  - ,,   ,,   Osterode.
  - ,,   ,,   Münden.
- Artillery, Lieut.-Colonel Brückmann
  - Unett's British Field Battery.
  - Sinclair's ,,   ,,

Total, 5149 infantry, 12 guns.

British Reserve Artillery, Major Drummond
- Five Batteries—viz., Ross's and Beane's Horse, Morisson's,[3] Hutchesson's,[3] and Ilbert's[3] Field, Batteries.

Total, 24 guns.

[1] Belgian.   [2] Six guns, two howitzers.   [3] Heavy batteries.

APPENDIX

Brunswick Corps, H.R.H. The Duke of Brunswick	Advanced Guard, Major von Rauschenplatt	Two companies Jägers, two companies Light Infantry, and Cavalry Detachment.
	Light Brigade, Lieut.-Colonel von Buttlar	Guard Batt. 1st Light Batt. 2nd ,, ,, 3rd ,, ,,
	Line Brigade, Lieut.-Colonel von Specht	1st Line Batt. 2nd ,, ,, 3rd ,, ,,
	Artillery, Major Mahn	Horse Battery, von Heinemann.[1] Field ,, Moll.[1]

Total, 5376 infantry, 16 guns.

Nassau Contingent, General von Kruse · · · 1st Regt., 3 Batts.

Total, 2841 infantry.
Total Reserve, 20,524 infantry, 64 guns.

CAVALRY.

British and King's German Legion	1st Brigade, Major-General Lord E. Somerset	1st Life Guards. 2nd ,, ,, Royal Horse Guards (Blue). 1st Dragoon Guards.
	2nd Brigade, Major-General Sir W. Ponsonby	1st (or Royal) Dragoons. 2nd Dragoons (Scots Greys). 6th (or Inniskilling) Dragoons.
	3rd Brigade, Major-General Sir W. Dörnberg	1st Light Dragoons, K.G. Legion. 2nd ,, ,, ,, ,, 23rd ,, ,,
	4th Brigade, Major-General Sir J. Vandeleur	11th Light Dragoons. 12th ,, ,, 16th ,, ,,
	5th Brigade, Major-General Sir Colq. Grant	2nd Hussars, K.G. Legion. 7th ,, 15th ,,
	6th Brigade, Major-General Sir H. Vivian	1st Hussars, K.G. Legion. 10th ,, 18th ,,
	7th Brigade, Col. Sir F. O. Arentsschildt	3rd Hussars, K.G. Legion. 13th Light Dragoons.

Total, 8471 men.

British Horse Batteries attached to the Cavalry — Six — viz., Bull's (howitzers) Webler-Smith's, Gardiner's Whinyates' (had also rockets), Mercer's, Ramsay's.

Hanoverian — 1st Brigade, Colonel von Estorff · Prince Regent's Hussars. Bremen and Verden Hussars. Cumberland Hussars.

Total, 1682 men.

Brunswick Cavalry · · · · Regiment of Hussars. Squadron of Uhlans.

Total, 922 men.

[1] Six guns, two howitzers.

APPENDIX 323

Dutch-Belgian
- 1st Brigade, Major-General Trip
  - 1st Dutch Carbineers.
  - 2nd Belgian ,,
  - 3rd Dutch ,,
- 2nd Brigade, Major-General de Ghigny
  - 4th Dutch Light Dragoons.
  - 8th Belgian Hussars.
- 3rd Brigade, Major-General van Merlen
  - 5th Belgian Light Dragoons.
  - 6th Dutch Hussars.
- Artillery . . . . Formed by half Gey van Pittius' Dutch Horse Battery, and half of Petter's do.[1]

Total, 3405 men, 8 guns.
Total Cavalry, 14,482 men, and 44 guns.

GARRISONS.

7th Division
- 7th British Brigade
  - 2nd Batt., 25th Regt.
  - 2nd ,, 37th ,,
  - 2nd ,, 78th ,,
- British Garrison Troops
  - 13th Veteran Batt.
  - 1st Foreign ,,
  - 2nd Garrison ,,

Total, 3233 men.

Hanoverian Reserve Corps, Lieut.-Gen. von der Decken
- 1st Brigade, Lieut.-Col. von Bennigsen
  - Field Batt., Hoya.
  - Landwehr Batt., Mölln.
  - ,, ,, Bremerlehe.
- 2nd Brigade, Lieut.-Col. von Beaulieu
  - Landwehr Batt., Nordheim.
  - ,, ,, Ahlefeldt.
  - ,, ,, Springe.
- 3rd Brigade, Lieut.-Colonel Bodecker
  - Landwehr Batt., Otterndorf.
  - ,, ,, Zelle.
  - ,, ,, Ratzeburg.
- 4th Brigade, Lieut.-Colonel Wissel
  - Landwehr Batt., Hannover.
  - ,, ,, Uelzen.
  - ,, ,, Neustadt.
  - ,, ,, Diepholz.

Total, 9000 men.
Total Garrisons, 12,233 men.

TOTAL STRENGTH.

Infantry	81,143
Cavalry	14,482
Artillery	8,969
Engineers, Waggon Trains, &c.	1,240
Grand Total	105,834 men and 204 guns.

The battalions of infantry and regiments of cavalry varied considerably in strength; some of the infantry being over 1000 men and some under 500. The proportion of artillery was small, and the arrangement of the corps, without cavalry, differed from the Prussian and French organisation. The actual strength with which Wellington took the field, exclusive of garrisons, and of

[1] Six guns, two howitzers.

three heavy batteries, each of four 18-pounders, left at Antwerp, was 68,910 infantry, 14,480 cavalry, and 192 guns, making a total of 83,392 men, excluding artillery, engineers, and train.

TOTAL STRENGTH BY NATIONALITIES.

	Infantry.	Cavalry.	Guns.
British	20,310	5,911	90
King's German Legion	3,285	2,560	18
Hanoverians	13,793	1,682	12
Brunswick	5,376	922	16
Nassau	7,308	...	...
Dutch-Belgians	18,838	3,405	56
	68,910	14,480	192

The numbers are chiefly taken from Siborne, van Löben-Sels, and de Bas. The actual numbers were slightly in excess of these, as officers are not counted except in the case of the Nassau and Dutch-Belgian troops.

Composition of the Prussian Army under the Command of Field-Marshal Prince Blucher von Wahlstadt; Chief of the Staff, Lieut.-General Graf von Gneisenau; Quartermaster-General, Maj.-Gen. von Grolmann.

I. ARMY CORPS—LIEUT.-GENERAL VON ZIETEN.

1st Brigade, Maj.-Gen. von Steinmetz .
{ 12th and 24th Line Regts.
1st Westphalian Landwehr Regt.
Two companies Silesian Sharpshooters.
4th Silesian Hussar Regt.
One Horse and one Field Battery.

Total, 9069 men, and 16 guns.

2nd Brigade, Maj.-Gen. von Pirch II. .
{ 6th and 28th Line Regts.
2nd Westphalian Landwehr Regt.
Westphalian Landwehr Cavalry Regt.
One Field Battery.

Total, 8018 men, and 8 guns.

3rd Brigade, Maj.-Gen. von Jagow .
{ 7th and 29th Line Regts.
3rd Westphalian Landwehr Regt.
Two companies Silesian Sharpshooters.
One Field Battery.

Total, 7146 men, and 8 guns.

4th Brigade, Maj.-Gen. Henckel von Donnersmarck
{ 19th Line Regt.
4th Westphalian Landwehr Regt.
One Field Battery.

Total, 4900 men, and 8 guns.

APPENDIX 325

Reserve Cavalry of the I. Corps—LIEUT.-GENERAL VON RÖDER.

Brigade of
Maj.-Gen. von Tresckow II.
{ Brandenburg Dragoons (No. 5).
1st West Prussian Dragoons (No. 2).
Brandenburg Uhlans.
One Horse Battery. }

Brigade of
Lieut.-Colonel von Lützow
{ 6th Uhlans.
1st and 2nd Kurmark Landwehr Regts.
1st Silesian Hussars. }

Total, 2175 men, and 8 guns.

Reserve Artillery of the I. Corps—MAJOR VON RENTZELL, six Batteries—viz., two 12-pdr., one 6-pdr., one 14-pdr. howitzer Field, and one Horse Battery. Engineers, one Field Company.

Total, 31,308 men, and 88 guns.

II. ARMY CORPS—GENERAL VON PIRCH I.

5th Brigade,
Maj.-Gen. von Tippelskirch
{ 2nd and 25th Line Regts.
5th Westphalian Landwehr Regt.
One Field Rifle Company.[1]
One Field Battery. }

Total, 7153 men, and 8 guns.

6th Brigade,
Maj.-Gen. von Krafft
{ 9th and 26th Line Regts.
1st Elbe Landwehr Regt.
One Field Battery. }

Total, 6762 men, and 8 guns.

7th Brigade,
Maj.-Gen. von Brause
{ 14th and 22nd Line Regts.
2nd Elbe Landwehr Regt.
One Field Battery. }

Total, 6503 men, and 8 guns.

8th Brigade,
Maj.-Gen. von Bose
{ 21st and 23rd Line Regts.
3rd Elbe Landwehr Regt.
One Field Battery. }

Total, 6584 men, and 8 guns.

Reserve Cavalry of the II. Corps—MAJOR-GENERAL VON WAHLEN-JÜRGASS.

1st Brigade,
Colonel von Thümen.
{ 1st Queen's Dragoons.
Silesian Uhlans.
6th Neumark Dragoons.
One Horse Battery. }

2nd Brigade,
Lieut.-Colonel von Sohr
{ 3rd Brandenburg Hussars.
5th Pomeranian   ,,
11th Hussars. }

3rd Brigade,
Col. Count v.d. Schulenburg
{ 4th and 5th Kurmark Landwehr Regts.
Elbe Landwehr Cavalry Regt. }

Total, 4471 men, and 8 guns.

Reserve Artillery of the II. Corps—MAJOR LEHMANN, five Batteries—viz., two 12-pdr., one 6-pdr. Field, and two Horse Batteries. Engineers, one Field Company.

Total, 31,473 men, and 72 guns.[2]

---

[1] Did not join till after the 18th June.   [2] Up to 18th June.

APPENDIX

III. ARMY CORPS—LIEUT.-GENERAL FREIHERR VON THIELMANN.

9th Brigade,
Major-General von Borcke
{ 8th and 30th Line Regts.
1st Kurmark Landwehr Regt.
Two Squadrons 3rd Kurmark Landwehr Cavalry.
One Field Battery. }

Total, 7262 men, and 8 guns.

10th Brigade,
Colonel von Kemphen
{ 27th Line Regt.
2nd Kurmark Landwehr Regt.
Two Squadrons 3rd Kurmark Landwehr Cavalry.
One Field Battery. }

Total, 4419 men, and 8 guns.

11th Brigade,
Colonel von Luck
{ 3rd and 4th Kurmark Landwehr Regt.
Two Squadrons 6th Kurmark Landwehr Cavalry.
One Field Battery.[1] }

Total, 3980 men, and 8 guns.

12th Brigade,
Colonel von Stülpnagel
{ 31st Line Regt.
5th and 6th Kurmark Landwehr Regts.
Two Squadrons 6th Kurmark Landwehr Cavalry.
One Field Battery.[1] }

Total, 6614 men, and 8 guns.

Reserve Cavalry of the III. Corps—MAJOR-GENERAL VON HOBE.

Brigade of
Colonel von der Marwitz
{ 7th Uhlans.
8th   ,,
12th Hussars.[1] }

Brigade of
Colonel Count von Lottum
{ 5th Uhlans.
7th Dragoons.
9th Hussars.
One Horse Battery. }

Total, 1981 men, and 8 guns.

Reserve Artillery of the III. Corps—MAJOR VON GREVENITZ, four Batteries—viz., two 12-pdr. Field, and two Horse Batteries. Engineers, one Field Company.

Total, 24,256 men, and 56 guns.[2]

V. ARMY CORPS—GENERAL COUNT BÜLOW VON DENNEWITZ.

13th Brigade,
Lieut.-General von Hake
{ 10th Line Regt.
2nd and 3rd Neumark Landwehr Regts.
Two Squadrons 2nd Silesian Landwehr Cavalry.
One Field Battery. }

Total, 6560 men.

---

[1] Did not join till after the 18th June.   [2] Up to 18th June.

APPENDIX 327

14th Brigade,
Major-Gen. von Ryssel I.
- 11th Line Regt.
- 1st and 2nd Pomeranian Landwehr Regts.
- Two Squadrons 2nd Silesian Landwehr Cavalry.
- One Field Battery.

Total, 7138 men.

15th Brigade,
Major-General von Losthin
- 18th Line Regt.
- 3rd and 4th Silesian Landwehr Regts.
- Two Squadrons 3rd Silesian Landwehr Cavalry.
- One Field Battery.

Total, 7143 men.

16th Brigade,
Colonel von Hiller
- 15th Line Regt.
- 1st and 2nd Silesian Landwehr Regts.
- Two Squadrons 3rd Silesian Landwehr Cavalry.
- One Field Battery.

Total, 6423 men.

Reserve Cavalry of the IV. Corps—GENERAL PRINCE WILLIAM OF PRUSSIA.

1st Brigade,
Col. Count von Schwerin
- 6th and 10th Hussars.
- 1st West Prussian Uhlans.
- 1st Silesian Landwehr Cavalry.

2nd Brigade,
Lieut.-Col. von Watzdorf
- 8th Dragoons.[1]
- 8th Hussars.
- One Horse Battery.

3rd Brigade,
Major-General von Sydow
- 1st and 2nd Neumark Landwehr Cavalry.
- 1st and 2nd Pomeranian ,, ,,
- One Horse Battery.

Total, 3321 men.

Reserve Artillery of the IV. Corps—LIEUT.-COLONEL VON BARDELEBEN, five Batteries—viz., three 12-pdr., one 15-pdr. howitzer,[1] and one 6-pdr. Field, with one Horse Battery. Engineers, one Field Company.

Total, 30,585 men, and 80 guns.

TOTAL STRENGTH.

	Infantry.	Cavalry.	Guns.
I. Army Corps	27,817	2,675	88
II. ,, ,,	25,836	4,471	72
III. ,, ,,	20,611	2,581	56
IV. ,, ,,	25,381	3,921	80
Total	99,645	13,648	296[2]

Total, 113,293 men, exclusive of gunners, engineers, and train, and 296 guns.[3]

These numbers have been taken from Lettow-Vorbeck, supplemented by reference to other Prussian authorities, chiefly von Ollech. It will be observed that the troops were organised in

---

[1] Did not join till after the 18th June.
[2] Up to the 18th June the usual statements include 8 which joined later.
[3] With train, &c., the Grand Total was about 124,000.

brigades, not in divisions, as in the modern Prussian army corps. Each corps was entitled to two engineer companies, but none of them had more than one when hostilities broke out.

Composition of the French Army under the Command of the Emperor Napoleon; Chief of the Staff, Marshal Soult, Duke of Dalmatia.

IMPERIAL GUARD—MARSHAL MORTIER, DUKE OF TREVISO.[1]

INFANTRY—

Lieut.-Gen. Count Friant . 1st,[2] 2nd,[2] 3rd,[3] and 4th[3] Grenadiers.
Total, 4140 men.

Lieut.-Gen. Count Morand . 1st,[2] 2nd,[2] 3rd,[3] and 4th[3] Chasseurs.
Total, 4603 men.

Lieut.-Gen. Count Duhesme[4] { 1st and 3rd Tirailleurs.
{ 1st and 3rd Voltigeurs.
Total, 4283 men.
Total, 13,026 men.

CAVALRY—

Lieut.-Gen. Lefebvre-Desnoëttes (Light Cavalry) } Lancers and Chasseurs à Cheval.

Lieut-Gen. Count Guyot (Heavy Cavalry) } Dragoons and Grenadiers à Cheval.

Colonel d'Autancourt (Heavy Cavalry) } Gendarmerie d'Elite.
Total, 4100 men.

ARTILLERY—

Lieut.-Gen. Desvaux de St Maurice } Thirteen Foot and three Horse Batteries.
Engineers and Sailors of the Guard.
Total, with train, 20,755 men, and 122 guns.

1ST CORPS D'ARMÉE—LIEUT.-GENERAL COUNT D'ERLON.

1st Division, Lieut.-General Allix[5] . { Brigades, Quiot and Bourgeois—54th, 55th; 28th and 105th of the Line.
Total, 4000 men.

2nd Division, Lieut.-Gen. Baron Donzelot { Brigades, Schmitz and Aulard—13th Light Infantry, 17th; 19th and 51st of the Line.
Total, 5132 men.

3rd Division, Lt.-Gen. Baron Marcognet { Brigades, Noguèz and Grenier—21st, 46th; 25th and 45th of the Line.
Total, 3900 men.

---

[1] He was not present during the campaign, and Druot, who was the commander of the artillery of the Guard, commanded the whole corps.
[2] Old Guard.   [3] Middle Guard.   [4] Young Guard.
[5] Allix did not join in time, and the division was therefore commanded by Quiot, who was the senior brigadier of this division.

APPENDIX

4th Division, Lieut.-Gen. Count Durutte { Brigades, Pégot and Brue—8th, 29th; 58th and 95th of the Line.
Total, 3853 men.

1st Cavalry Division, Lieut.-Gen. Baron Jacquinot { Brigade, Bruno—3rd Chasseurs, 7th Hussars. Brigade, Gobrecht—3rd and 4th Lancers.
Total, 1706 men.

Artillery . . . . { Five Foot and one Horse Batteries. One Foot Battery to each Division, the Horse Battery to the Cavalry, one Foot Battery Artillery Reserve.

Engineers . . . . Five companies.

Total, with train, 20,731 men, and 46 guns.

2ND CORPS D'ARMÉE—LIEUT.-GENERAL COUNT REILLE.

5th Division, Lieut.-Gen. Baron Bachelu { Brigades, Husson and Campy—2nd Light Infantry, 61st; 72nd and 108th of the Line.
Total, 4103 men.

6th Division, Prince Jerome Napoleon . { Brigades, Bauduin and Soye—1st and 3rd (Light); 1st and 2nd of the Line.
Total, 7819 men.

7th Division, Lieut.-Gen. Count Girard . { Brigade, Devilliers—11th (Light), and 82nd of the Line. Brigade, Piat—12th (Light), and 4th of the Line.
Total, 3925 men.

9th Division, Lieut.-General Count Foy . { Brigade, Gauthier—92nd and 93rd of the Line. Brigade, B. Jamin—4th (Light), and 100th of the Line.
Total, 4788 men.

2nd Cavalry Division, Lieut.-General Baron Piré . { Brigade, Hubert—1st and 6th Chasseurs. Brigade, Vathiez—5th and 6th Lancers.
Total, 2064 men.

Artillery . . . . { Five Foot and one Horse Batteries. One Foot Battery to each Division, Cavalry one Horse Battery, Reserve one Foot Battery.

Engineers . . . . Five companies.

Total, with train, 25,179 men, and 46 guns.

3RD CORPS D'ARMÉE—LIEUT.-GENERAL COUNT VANDAMME.

8th Division, Lieut.-General Baron Lefol { Brigades, Billard and Corsin—15th (Light), and 23rd; 37th and 64th of the Line.
Total, 4541 men.

10th Division, Lieut.-Gen. Baron Habert { Brigades, Gengoux and Dupeyroux — 34th, 88th; 22nd and 70th of the Line; 2nd Swiss Foreign Legion.
Total, 5024 men.

11th Division, Lieut.-General Berthezène . { Brigades, Dufour and Lagarde—12th, 56th; 33rd and 86th of the Line.
Total, 5565 men.

3rd Cavalry Division, { Brigade, Dommanget—4th and 9th Chasseurs.
Lieut.-Gen. Baron Domon { Brigade, Vinot—12th Chasseurs.
    Total, 1017 men.

Artillery . . . . { Four Foot and one Horse Batteries. One Foot Battery to each Division, one Horse Battery to the Cavalry, one Foot Battery Artillery Reserve.

Engineers . . . . Three companies.
    Total, with train, 18,105 men, and 46 guns.

4TH CORPS D'ARMÉE—LIEUT.-GENERAL COUNT GÉRARD.

12th Division, { Brigades, Romme and Schœffer — 30th, 96th;
Lieut.-Gen. Baron Pécheux { 63rd of the Line, and 6th Light Infantry.
    Total, 4719 men.

13th Division, { Brigades, Le Capitaine and Desprez—59th,
Lieut.-Gen. Baron Vichery { 76th; 48th and 60th of the Line.
    Total, 4145 men.

14th Division, { Brigades, Hulot and Toussaint—9th (Light)
Lieut.-Gen. de Bourmont[1] { and 111th; 44th and 50th of the Line.
    Total, 4237 men.

7th Cavalry Division, { Brigade, Vallin—6th Hussars, 8th Chasseurs.
Lieut.-General Maurin . { Brigade, Berruyer—6th and 16th Dragoons.
    Total, 1500 men.

Artillery . . . . { Five Foot Batteries. One to each Infantry Division, one Artillery Reserve, one Horse Battery with the Cavalry.

Engineers . . . . Three companies.
    Total, with train, 16,219 men, and 46 guns.

6TH CORPS D'ARMÉE—LIEUT.-GENERAL COUNT LOBAU.

19th Division, { Brigades, Bellair and M. Jamin—5th, 11th;
Lieut-Gen. Baron Simmer . { 27th and 84th of the Line.
    Total, 3953 men.

20th Division, { Brigades, Bony and Tromelin—5th (Light)
Lieut.-Gen. Baron Jannin . { and 10th; 47th and 107th of the Line.
    Total, 2202 men.

21st Division, { Brigades, Lafitte and Penne—8th (Light), and
Lieut.-Gen. Baron Teste . { 40th; 65th and 75th of the Line.
    Total, 2418 men.

Artillery . . . . { Four Foot Batteries. One to each Division, one Artillery Reserve.

Engineers . . . . Three companies.
    Total, with train, 10,821 men, and 32 guns.

RESERVE CAVALRY—MARSHAL GROUCHY.
1st Corps—LIEUT.-GENERAL COUNT PAJOL.

4th Cavalry Division, { Brigades, St Laurent and Ameil—1st; 4th and
Lieut.-Gen. Baron Soult . { 5th Hussars.

---

[1] When Bourmont deserted, Hulot took command.

APPENDIX

5th Cavalry Division, { Brigade, A. de Colbert—1st and 2nd Lancers.
Lieut.-Gen. Baron Subervie { Brigade, Merlin—11th Chasseurs.
Total, 2536 men.

Artillery . . . . Two Horse Batteries, one to each Brigade.

2nd Corps—LIEUT.-GENERAL COUNT EXELMANS.

9th Cavalry Division, { Brigades, Burthe and Vincent—5th, 13th ; 15th
Lieut.-General Strolz { and 20th Dragoons.
10th Cavalry Division, { Brigades, Bonnemains and Berton—4th, 12th ;
Lieut.-Gen. Baron Chastel { 14th and 17th Dragoons.
Total, 3116 men.

Artillery . . . . Two Horse Batteries, one to each Brigade.

3rd Corps—LIEUT.-GENERAL KELLERMANN (COUNT DE VALMY).

11th Cavalry Division,
Lieut.-Gen. Baron L'Heri-
tier
} Brigade, Piquet—2nd and 7th Dragoons.
Brigade, Guiton—8th and 11th Cuirassiers.

12th Cavalry Division,
Lieut.-Gen. Roussel d'Hur-
bal
} Brigade, Blancard—1st and 2nd Carabineers.
Brigade, Donop—2nd and 3rd Cuirassiers.

Total, 3400 men.

Artillery . . . . Two Horse Batteries, one to each Brigade.

4th Corps—LIEUT.-GENERAL COUNT MILHAUD.

13th Cavalry Division, { Brigades, Dubois and Travers—1st, 4th ; 7th
Lieut.-General Wathier { and 12th Cuirassiers.
14th Cavalry Division, { Brigades, Farine and Vial—5th, 10th ; 6th and
Lieut.-Gen. Baron Delort { 9th Cuirassiers.
Total, 2797 men.

Artillery . . . . Two Horse Batteries, one to each Brigade.
Total, without train, 11,849 men, and 48 guns.

TOTAL STRENGTH.

	Infantry.	Cavalry.	Artillery.	Engineers, &c.	Guns.
Imperial Guard	13,026	4,100	2,786	109	122
1st Corps d'Armée	16,885	1,706	1,096	330	46
2nd ,, ,,	20,635	2,064	1,700	409	46
3rd ,, ,,	15,130	1,017	1,084	146	38
4th ,, ,,	13,401	1,500	1,417	201	38
6th ,, ,,	8,573	...	765	189	32
Four corps of Reserve Cavalry	...	11,849	1,222	...	48
	87,650	22,236	10,070	1,384	370

Grand Total, including train not given above, 124,139 men, and 370 guns.

The above numbers are taken chiefly from Houssaye's 'Waterloo,' vol. ii., and 'L'Armée Française.' The figures in the latter work are said to be due to Colonel Perrier of the Depôt de la Guerre.

INDEX.

After-orders of 16th June, 162.
Allied army commanders prefer indirect defence to direct, 116.
   Allies, dispositions of, 46.
       " were they good, 46.
Allix, 81, 258.
Alten, C. von, 17.
   At Waterloo, 250, 252.
Anglo-Allied army—
   Composition of. *See* Appendix, 319.
   Distribution of, 27.
   Not really efficient fighting force, 15.
   Numbers of, 27.
   Position of, 17th June, 185.
      " 18th June, 209.
   Stations of, on 15th June, 55.
   Value of, at Waterloo, 216.
Arentsschildt, 17.
Armies, the three, organisations of, 38, 39. Also *see* Appendix.
Army, French, reduction of by Louis XVIII., 4.
Army of the Alps, 15.
Army of the North, situation in June, 14.
   Strength of, 13.

Bachelu, 70, 258.
   At Mellet, 81.
   At Waterloo, 235, 258.
Baltus, General, opinions on march to Waterloo, 198.
Barclay de Tolly, 40.
Bauduin, 146.
Belgium, invasion of, three different routes, 42.

Berkeley, letter to Lord FitzRoy Somerset, 86.
Bernhard, Prince, of Saxe-Weimar, 26, 73.
   Orders brigade to Quatre Bras, 101.
   Position at Quatre Bras, 15th June, 102.
   Position at Waterloo, 216, 217, 235 fn., 269.
Berthier, 14.
Berton, General, report of, June 17th, 175.
Blucher, 33, 34.
   Believed beat Napoleon alone, 15th June, 113.
   Determines to fight at Ligny, 103.
   Determines to assist Wellington, 199.
   Letter to Müffling, 9.30 A.M., 18th June, 202, 203.
   Letter to Wellington, 17th June, 200.
   Object of, to support Wellington, 44, 45.
   Orders for June 18th—
      I. Corps, 201.
      II. Corps, 201.
      III. Corps, 201.
      IV. Corps, 200.
   Reports to Wellington, 60-63.
   Reports to Wellington, 15th June, for II., III., IV. Corps to concentrate, 89.
Brunswick troops, composition of, 26.
Brussels, news from front, 15th June, sequence of, 90-92.

INDEX

Bülow, von, General, 18, 48.
   Instructions to Thielmann, June 17th, 177.
   Orders to, 14th June, 64, 65.
       „   18th June, 200.
   Reaches St Lambert, 254.
   Attacks Plancenoit, 257, 270.
Bussy, Mill of, 120.

Campaign, general comments on—
   Cavalry, French, little use of, 297.
   Faults of Emperor from beginning of campaign, 286-288.
Carmichael Smyth, 52.
Charleroi, 46, 53.
   Captured, 71.
   Firing heard at, by Steinmetz, 84.
Charleroi-Brussels highway, defence of, 50.
Chassé, 99.
   At Waterloo, 263 fn., 265-267.
Châtelet, Gérard's corps directed on, 70.
Clergy, the French, 3.
Colborne attacks Chasseur column, 264.
Communications, evil of exposed line of, 49.
   Alternative for Prussians, 45.
   English, 42, 43.
   Prussian, 43.
Condé, 52.
Constant de Rebecque, Baron, chief of the Dutch-Belgian Staff, 117.
   Orders to Perponcher, Chassé, and Collaert, 15th June, 84.
Corps I., Prussian—
   Attack on, 72.
   Distribution of, 69.
   Position of, at opening of campaign, 56.
   Position of, on June 15th, 82.
   Position of, on June 17th, 179.
Corps II., Prussian—
   Position of, at opening of campaign, 56, 57.
   Position of, on June 15th, 82.
   Position of, on June 17th, 179.
Corps III., Prussian—
   Position of, at opening of campaign, 57.
   Position of, on June 15th, 82.
   Position of, on June 17th, 179, 180.
Corps IV., Prussian—
   Position of, at opening of campaign, 57.
   Position of, on June 15th, 82.
   Position of, on June 17th, 179, 180.

De Behr, 99.
Debt left by Empire needed economy, 4.
D'Erlon, 54, 72, 81, 125, 168.
   Denied received orders to return Ligny, 157.
Delbrück, Professor, 163, 164.
Delort, 81.
De Salle, 157.
Despatch, Wellington's, after Waterloo, Appendix, 311-318.
Disposition of 16th June, Wellington's, 151.
Domon, 174.
Donzelot at Waterloo, 229, 231, 234, 236, 245, 258, 269.
   His skirmishers occupy Smohain and La Haye, 253.
Dörnberg, 56, 166.
   Colquhoun-Grant's letter to, 166.
   Ordered by Wellington to Waterloo, 100.
Durutte, 81, 125, 131.
   Fault of, at Ligny, 161.
   At Waterloo, 229, 234, 235, 240, 259.
Dutch-Belgians, 18.
   Army as it really was, 18.
   Attitude of troops, 20.
   Composition of, 18-21. Also *see* Appendix, 319-324.
   Desertions from, 21.
   Strength of, at Quatre Bras, 118.
   Waterloo, at, 216-221, 231, 232 and fn., 237, 247 and fn., 247-250, 263, 265 and fn., 265-267.
Dutch troops, composition of, 18, 21.

Ellesmere, Earl of, 16.
English infantry largely composed of 2nd battalions, 16.

INDEX 335

Eugen, Prince, 31.
Exelmans, 81, 175, 181, 182, 199.
   Reports on 17th June, 181.

Farine, 236.
Flahaut, Count, 107, 155, 171.
Fortifications of Belgium, 52.
Fortifications of French frontier, 52.
Foy, 81, 146.
   At Waterloo, 225 fn., 226, 258.
France, discontented at Bourbon rule, 3.
   Forces for invading, 40.
   Invasion of, postponed, 59.
French army assembled, 64.
   Army of the Rhine, 15.
   Composition of, 12. Also Appendix, 328-331.
   Concentration of, 53.
   Distrust of officers, 13.
   Enthusiasm of men, 13.
   Equipment insufficient, 13.
   Increase of, by Napoleon, 11.
   Position of, 14th June, at night, 54.
   Position of, 15th June, at night, 81.
   Position of, 17th June, at night, 190, 191.
   Strength in March, 11.
   Strength in June, 12.
   Strength in July, 12.
French Army Corps, composition of, 39.
French Guard, attack of, 259.
   Defeat of, 263-267.
   Formation of, 261, 262.
   Sketch illustrating attack, 260.

Gagern's, Captain Baron von, report, 99.
Gérard, 70, 81, 123, 124, 132, 182.
   Morning of 15th, 70.
Girard, 81, 112.
Gneisenau, 33.
   And Wellington, 203-205 fn.
   Fails Wellington, 15th June, 103.
   His capacity, 33.
   Orders assemblement of army, 64.
   Orders for Prussian march, 18th June, 206-208.
   Orders retreat on Tilly, June 17th, 176.

   Postscript to Blucher's letter, 203.
Gordon, Col. Sir Alexander, 185.
Gourgaud, report of, to Napoleon, 71.
Grant, 17.
Grant-Colquhoun, letter to Dörnberg, 166.
Groeben, Count von, 177.
   Report of, 7 A.M., 18th June, 202.
Grolmann, 33, 170.
   Gives orders for position of troops, June 17th, 176.
   Gives orders for advance on 18th June, 255, 256.
   Influences decision to retire on Wavre, 34.
Grouchy, 72, 107, 112, 172, 182.
   Captures Wavre, 301.
   Drives back Thielmann, 275.
   Hears sound of Waterloo guns, 198.
   Marches on Wavre, 273.
   Orders for 18th June, 193.
   Receives Napoleon's ten o'clock despatch, 18th June, 238, 275.
   Report of 6 A.M., 18th June, 194.
   Report of 11 A.M., 18th June, to Napoleon, 196.
   Retreats to Namur, 302, 303.
   6 P.M. receives Napoleon's one o'clock despatch, 275.
   10 P.M. report of, to Napoleon from Gembloux, 183.
Guard—
   Imperial, 11, 133, 222.
   Old, 11, 133.
      At Ligny, 133.
      At Waterloo, 259-267, 270.
   Young, 11.
      At Waterloo, 259, 270.
Guyot, 131.

Hanoverian troops, composition of, 25. Also Appendix, 319-324.
Haye-Sainte, La—
   Captured, 251, 252, 257.
   Description and plan of, 212, 213.
   Set on fire, 247.
Henckel, 128, 132.
Hill, Lord, 17.

INDEX

Hollert, notary of Sart-à-Walhain, 198.
Hougomont, 252.
    Attacks on, 224-227.
    Bombarded, 241.
    Sketch and description of, 211.

Imperial Guard, 11, 133.
    At Waterloo, 259-267.

Jacquinot, 81.
    At Waterloo, 236.
Jagow, 72, 132.
Jerome, 81.
    At Waterloo, 258.
Joseph, 30.
Jourdan, 30.
Jumet, 72, 81.
Junot, 30.
Jurgass, 127, 130.

Katzbach, battle of, 36.
Kellermann, 81, 112, 145, 154.
Kempt, 17.
    At Quatre Bras, 139, 140, 142.
    At Waterloo, 217, 233.
King's German Legion, 25.
Kleist, 40.
Krafft, 130, 132.
Krahmer, 263.
Kruse, 26.

Lamarque, 15.
Lancey, De, Col. Sir W., Quartermaster-General, 34.
Le Courbe's corps of observation, 15.
Lefebvre-Desnoëttes, 73.
    His report to Ney, 74, 75.
Lefol, 130.
Legion of Honour, 21.
Ligny, battle of, 16th June, 121-136.
    Comments on, 147-150.
    French losses at, 136.
    Napoleon's best plan, 147.
    Penetration of Prussian centre, 129.
    Position bad, 149.
    Prussians, strength of, 124.
    Prussian losses at, 136.
Lobau, 81.
    Reaches Fleurus, 125.
    At Waterloo, 240, 257, 270.
Lorière, Colonel, opinions on march to Waterloo, 198.

Louis XVIII., his opportunity, 2.
Lynedoch, Lord, 45, 59.

Maison du Roi, 5.
Marengo, anniversary of, and Friedland, 54.
Marcognet, 81, 234, 258.
    At Waterloo, 234, 236, 259.
Marlborough, 31.
Marmont, 8 fn., 30.
Marwitz, opinion on Prussian army, 131.
Massena, 30.
Merlen, van, 82, 84, 86, 99.
    At Quatre Bras, 139, 140.
    At Waterloo, 248 fn., 250 fn.
Milhaud, 131, 132, 237, 241.
Müffling, 88, 94, 113, 184, 186 fn.
    Reports to Blucher, Wellington in position at Waterloo, 200.

Namur-Liége road, Prussian communications, evil of, 49.
Napoleon—
    Allies contingents against, 10.
    Allies proclamation against, March 13th, 10.
    Army, strength of, 124.
    Attack against his communications, advantages of, 115.
    Chooses best line of attack, 45.
    Determines to attack Allies, selects Belgium, 42.
    Escapes from Elba, 1.
    Faults of advance arrangements, 69.
    General idea for 15th and 16th, 79.
    Gives instructions to Ney, 107-109.
    Good points of advance arrangements, 68.
    Grouchy, first letter to, 18th June, 194; second letter, 238.
    Health of, 35, 279 and fn.
    His plan of campaign, 50.
    Letter to Davout, 14th June, 78.
    Letter to Grouchy, 17th June, 174.
    Not to be trusted, 9.
    One o'clock despatch to Grouchy, 18th June, 238.

INDEX 337

Orders for advance, 15th June, 66-68.
Orders for defence of Paris, 41.
Orders Grouchy to pursue Prussians, 174.
Orders of, to Grouchy, 16th June, 109-111.
Plan of operation, June 17th, 169, 170.
Plans for invading Belgium, 42.
Position of troops at commencement of battle of Ligny, 126-128.
Progress to Paris, 10.
Reasons for his return to France, 2, 8.
Receives letter from Grouchy, written ten o'clock, 17th June, 183.
Situation, 15th June, night, favourable, 104.
Ten o'clock despatch to Grouchy, 18th June, 194.
The weak points in plan of campaign, 50, 51.
Thinks Prussians cannot support Wellington on 18th June, 195.
Treaty of 25th March against, 10.
Nassau troops, 26.
    At Waterloo, 216, 217.
Ney—
    Fails Napoleon, 131.
    Joined Napoleon three o'clock, 15th June, 73.
    Napoleon's first letter to, 16th June, 107.
    Reports to Napoleon, 15th June, 76.
    Reports to Napoleon, 16th June, 171.
    Soult's first letter to, 16th June, 107.
    Soult's second letter to, 16th June, 107.
    Soult's third letter to, 16th June, 109, 154.
    Soult's fourth letter to, 16th June, 112.
    Soult's fifth letter to, 16th June, 124, 140.
    Soult's sixth letter to, 16th June, 125.

    Soult's letter to, 17th June, 160.

Old Guard at Ligny, 133.
    At Waterloo, 259-265.
Ompteda, 17, 251.
    Death of, 251.
Orange, Prince of, 17.
    His contributions to campaign, 17, 148.
    His first contribution to campaign, 82.
    His second contribution to campaign, 145.
    His third contribution to campaign, 251.
    Position of his troops, 16th June, 136, 137.
    Position of his troops, 18th June, 216, 217, 221.

Pack, 17.
    At Quatre Bras, 139, 142, 144.
    At Waterloo, 217, 234, 236.
Pajol, 71, 81, 171, 181.
Paris, fall of, 308.
Pecheux, 128.
People, the dreads of the, 6.
Perponcher, 99, 117.
Pfuel, Colonel, 118.
Picton, 17.
    At Waterloo, 233.
Pirch II., 71, 112.
Piré, 81.
    At Quatre Bras, 126, 146.
Plancenoit, 257.
    Attack on, 257, 270.
    Description of, 222.
Position of Napoleon's troops, June 17th, 190, 191.
Position of Wellington's troops, June 17th, 185-187, 189, 190.
Prussian Army—
    At Ligny, distribution of, 122.
    At Waterloo, 257, 268-271.
    Composition of, Appendix, 324-327.
    Corps, composition of, 39.
    Likely to be attacked first, 44.
Pyrenees, 7th Corps watching, 15.

Qualities of the three commanders, Blucher, Napoleon, and Wellington, 36, 37.

INDEX

Quatre Bras, 17, 73, 112, 116.
    Attack commences, 138.
    Battle of, 17th June, 137.
    Comments on, 146-148.
    Dutch - Belgians driven back, 140.
    First Anglo-Allied reinforcements, 139.
    Second Anglo-Allied reinforcements, 144.
    Third Anglo-Allied reinforcements, 146.
    Jamin's brigade, 139.
    Kellermann joins Ney, 143.
    Napoleon's orders to Reille, 138.
    Ney's orders to d'Erlon, 138.
    Ney orders general advance, 141-143.
    Position of Dutch - Belgian troops, 137.
    Position at nightfall, 16th June, 146.
    Reille's hesitation, 138.
Quiot at Waterloo, 228 fn., 229, 235, 247.

Rapp, 51.
Reille, 71, 72, 112, 146.
    At Waterloo, 222, 225, 240.
Religious rancour, 4.
Reports—
    Behr's, from Mons, Merlen's, Steinmetz's, 83, 84.
    Berkeley's, 15th June, 86.
    Bernhard's, Prince, to Constant de Rebecque, 102.
    Blucher's, to Wellington, 89.
    Dörnberg's, 15th June, 85.
    Gagern's, to Constant de Rebecque, 99.
    Grouchy's, to Napoleon, 183, 194, 195.
    Zieten's, to Blucher, 87, 89.
        " to Wellington, 88.

Schwartzenberg, 40, 51, 113.
Skirmishers, English formation of, 221.
Soignes, forest of, position in front of, criticised, 284.
Soult—
    Chief of Staff, 14, 30, 112.
    His uncertainty with regard to Ney's troops, 106.

Second letter to Ney, 17th June, 107.
Third letter to Ney, 17th June, 109.
Fourth letter to Ney, to destroy forces of enemy, 112.
Fifth letter to Ney, 124.
Sixth letter to Ney, 125.
Reports to, from Ney and Lefebvre-Desnoëttes, 76.
Staff duties, criticism of, 298-300.
Steinmetz, 72, 81.
Suchet, 15.

Teste, 174.
Thielmann, 48.
    Orders to, 14th June, 64, 65.
Tippelskirchen, 127, 130.
Trois Bras, 155.

Uhlans, 6th, 134.

Valazé, General, opinions on march to Waterloo, 198.
Vandamme, 71, 72, 81.
Vandeleur, 17.
    At Waterloo, 237, 259, 267.
Vienna—
    Congress at, 1, 7, 8, 30, 32.
    " chooses Wellington, 32.
    Congress quarrels at, 7.
Vitoria, 30.
Vivian, 17.
    At Waterloo, 259, 267.

Waterloo—
    Adam's brigade, 252.
    Allix's division, 253.
    Anglo - Allied Army bivouac on the field, 271.
    Bachelu's division, 235.
    Battle divisible into five phases, 224.
    Bijlandt's brigade, 231-233.
    Bourgeois' brigade, 231.
    Comments on—
        Could Grouchy have saved Napoleon, 198, 296.
        Final cause of defeat, 281.
        French, Prussian, and English guns, 285.
        Hal and Tubize, troops at, 283.
        Hougomont, 277.

INDEX 339

Infantry four deep, formation of, 298.
La Haye Sainte, 278.
Line *v.* column, 278, 279.
Napoleon's plan of attack, 278.
Napoleon's errors in execution, 278.
Napoleon's reasons for delay in beginning battle, 276.
Napoleon's use of artillery, 284.
Position in front of Forest of Soignes, 284.
Prussian part in the battle, 282, 283.
Pursuit, the, by Prussians after Waterloo, 285.
Right exposed to enfilade, 276.
Suggested action for Napoleon, 289, 296.
The cavalry charges, 279.
The English cavalry, 285.
Wellington's position suitable, 276.
D'Erlon's corps, formation of, 228.
Dispositions of Anglo-Allied forces, 216.
Dispositions of French at, 222.
Donzelot's division, 234, 236, 258.
Dutch-Belgian cavalry, 237, 247-250.
Durutte's division, 284.
Formation of the 3rd Division at, 219.
Foy's division, 226, 227, 258.
French cavalry attacks, 240-242.
Cover infantry advance against Anglo-Allies, 245, 246.
Jerome's division, 225-227, 258.
Marcognet's division, 234, 258.
Napoleon attacks Anglo-Allied left centre, 228.
Napoleon concentrates 78 guns, 228.
Napoleon's force at, 215.
Napoleon observes Prussian advance, 238.
Napoleon's order for the attack, 223 and fn.
Position of, 208-214.
Position of Anglo-Allies at commencement of, 242-244.

Prussians at—
Advance-guard IV. Corps reaches St Lambert, 254.
Arrival at Paris Wood, 254.
IV. Corps attacks Paris Wood, 256.
IV. Corps carries Plancenoit, 270.
IV. Corps halts at St Lambert, 255.
IV. Corps sent on by Grolmann, 255, 256.
Cause final disaster, 273.
Orders for march of IV. Corps, 200.
Orders for march of III. Corps, 201.
Orders for march of II. Corps, 201.
Orders for march of I. Corps, 201.
IV. Corps march delayed, 239, 254.
IV. Corps order of march, 254.
1st Brigade arrives on Wellington's left wing, 269.
1st Brigade drives back French right, 269.
1st Brigade reaches Ohain, 268.
5th Brigade supports IV. Corps, 270.
Prince Bernhard's troops fall back, 269.
Prince Bernhard's troops, position of, 216.
Quiot's brigade, 228, 235.
Somerset's brigade, charge of, 230.
Travers' cuirassiers, 229.
Union Brigade, charge of, 234.
Vandeleur's brigade, 237, 259, 267.
Vivian's brigade, 259, 267.
Wellington's force at, 215.
Webster, Lieut., aide-de-camp to Wellington, 99.
Wellington, 15, 44.
After-orders of 15th June, 98, 99.
And Gneisenau, 203-205 fn.
Attack against, advantages of, 115.
Communications of, 30.

INDEX

Complains of Dutch-Belgian conduct, 22.
Chosen at Vienna to command troops in Belgium, 30, 32.
Despatch after Waterloo, Appendix, 311-318.
Determines to issue first series of orders, 87.
Disposition of, 162 (facing).
First orders on 15th June, 96-98.
Letter to Blucher, 16th June, 120.
Met Gneisenau, desire arrangement, assemble Anglo-Belgian armies, 114.
Object of, to support Blucher, 44, 45.
Orders of June 15th, 6 P.M., 162.
Orders of June 15th, 10 P.M., 98.
Orders for retreat, June 17th, 186.
Reports to Blucher, 60-63.

Secret memorandum, 57, 58.
Statement of, 95.
Subordinate leaders of, 16.
Thinks danger of attack almost disappeared, 59.
Undecided if attack on Prussians real or otherwise, 116.
Views of Napoleon's plans, 45.

Zieten—
Gosselies, fight at, 72.
Ligny, at, 113.
Initial position criticised, 49, 50.
Orders for holding outpost line, 49.
Orders for 18th June, 201.
Orders for 18th June criticised, 206, 208.
Marches on Waterloo, 268, 269.
Reports to Blucher, 15th June, 87, 88.
Reports to Wellington, 15th June, 88.
Waterloo, at, 268, 269.

THE END.

PRINTED BY WILLIAM BLACKWOOD AND SONS.

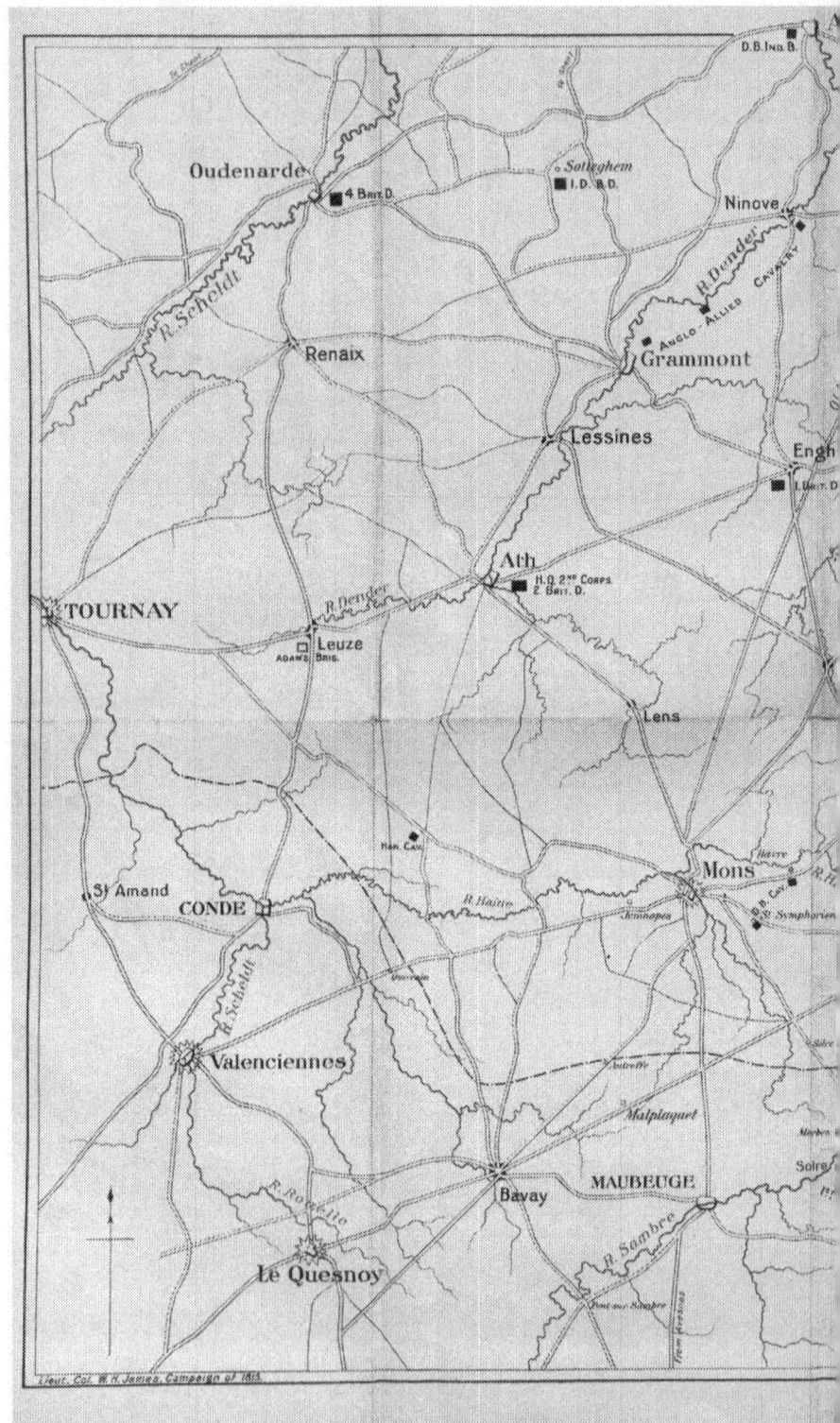

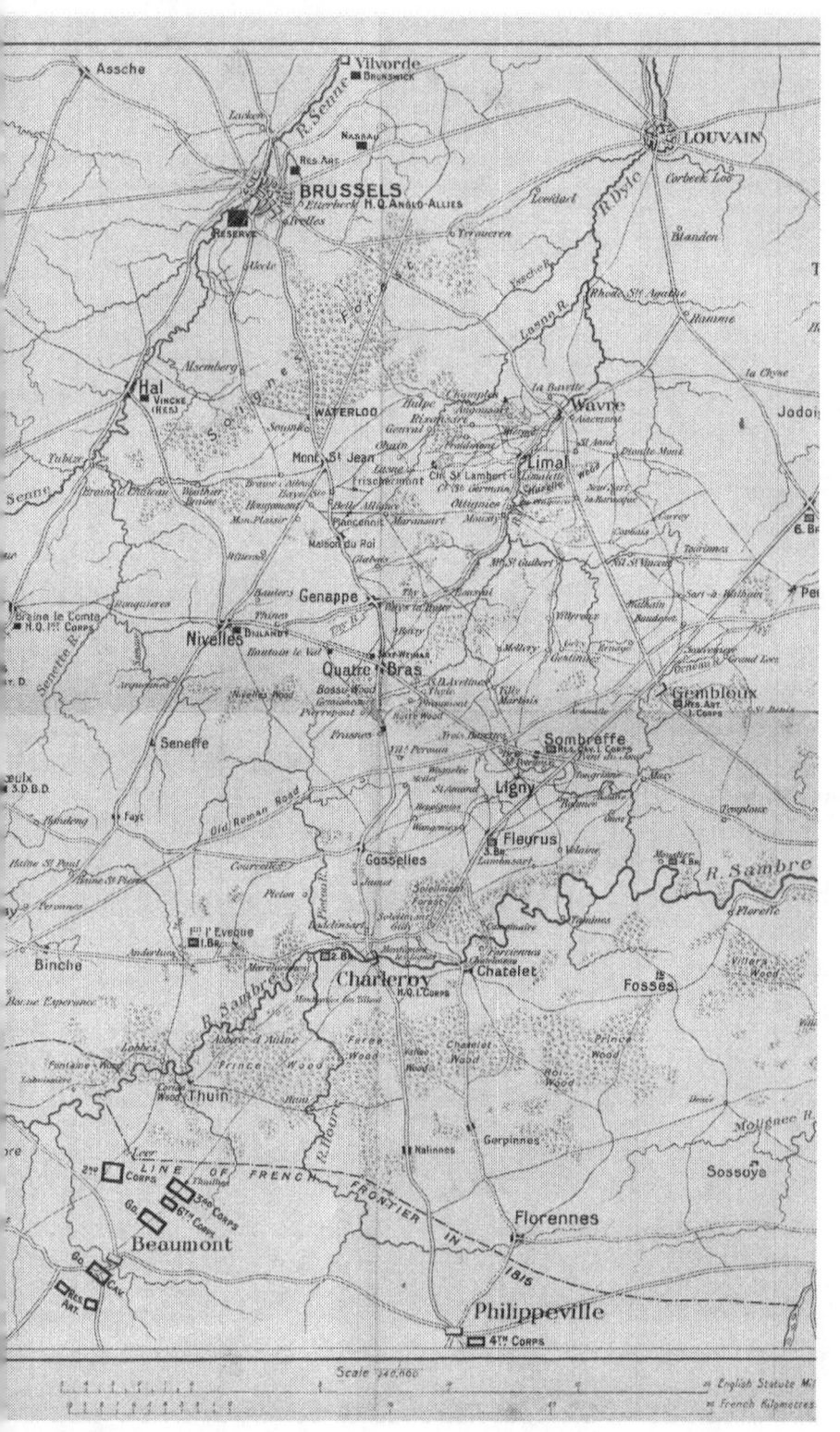

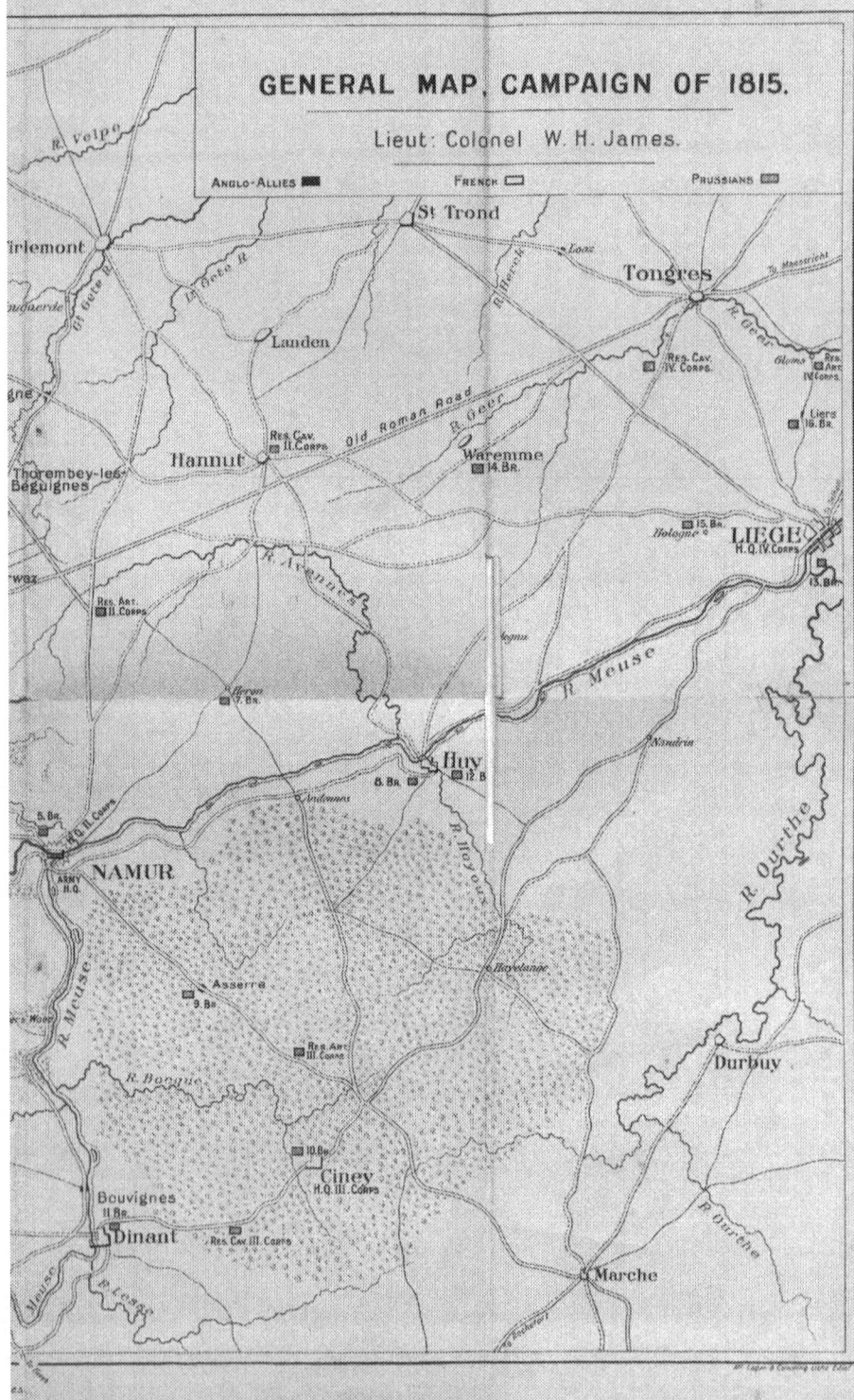

www.ingramcontent.com/pod-product-compliance
Lightning Source LLC
Chambersburg PA
CBHW031249230426
43670CB00005B/104